Developments in Telecommunications

Gerhard Rufa

Developments in Telecommunications

With a Focus on SS7 Network Reliability

Professor Dr. Gerhard Rufa
Department of Applied Physics and Mathematics
University of Applied Sciences Mannheim
Paul-Wittsack-Straße 10
68163 Mannheim, Germany
g.rufa@hs-mannheim.de

ISBN 978-3-540-74985-1   e-ISBN 978-3-540-74986-8

DOI 10.1007/978-3-540-74986-8

Library of Congress Control Number: 2008925373

ACM Computing Classification (1998): C.2.2

© 2008 Springer-Verlag Berlin Heidelberg

This work is subject to copyright. All rights are reserved, whether the whole or part of the material is concerned, specifically the rights of translation, reprinting, reuse of illustrations, recitation, broadcasting, reproduction on microfilm or in any other way, and storage in data banks. Duplication of this publication or parts thereof is permitted only under the provisions of the German Copyright Law of September 9, 1965, in its current version, and permission for use must always be obtained from Springer. Violations are liable to prosecution under the German Copyright Law.

The use of general descriptive names, registered names, trademarks, etc. in this publication does not imply, even in the absence of a specific statement, that such names are exempt from the relevant protective laws and regulations and therefore free for general use.

Cover design: KünkelLopka GmbH, Heidelberg

Printed on acid-free paper

9 8 7 6 5 4 3 2 1

springer.com

ALL is an endless fleeting abstraction,
THE WHOLE is reality!

Samuel Taylor Coleridge

Preface

In this book we summarize important developments in telecommunications with a focus on Signalling System No. 7 (SS 7) network reliability. But why is SS 7 network security and reliability so important?

According to the Open Systems Interconnection (OSI) model the term "network" refers to the Layer 3 network service, which is offered by the Message Transfer Part (MTP) and Signalling Connection Control Part (SCCP) to higher layers. An SS 7 network outage results in a breakdown of signalling between the individual nodes of the network, so that telecommunication network services are no longer available to customers. Apart from the tremendous financial damage to the network operator, the social consequences of such a network breakdown cannot be underestimated.

Since the MTP is the central part of the SS 7 network, it is of crucial importance for network security and reliability. The MTP is published in different versions and should now be what we call "stable". Is it really stable? Does it work properly in real networks? Does it fit new requirements so that no further changes within the MTP are needed?

Various different implementations have existed for a long time and are used in national as well as the international network. Due to this, an objective is not to perform any further changes within the MTP in order to avoid compatibility problems with existing and running systems. Experience shows that compatibility problems are always related to further development of the MTP. As a consequence, the overall opinion is that changes within the MTP should only be considered if problems occur which cannot be solved within other layers. Are there problems such that further changes within the MTP are really necessary? Could those be solved within the SS 7 over IP development?

This question has been studied intensively during the White Book study period and detailed discussions are going on now. The objective of this book is to provide a thorough discussion of SS 7 network security and reliability including SS 7 over IP applications. What is the subject of the work performed and how is it related to developments in telecommunications?

The foundations of new applications were laid in the ITU study periods 1984–1996. On the one hand studies on operations, administration, and maintenance were

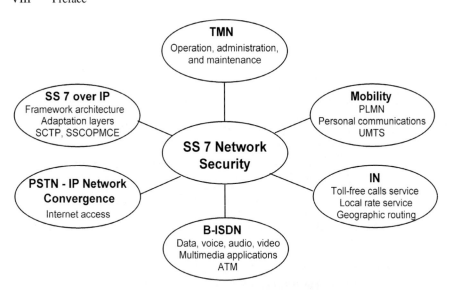

Fig. 0.1. Developments in telecommunications

embedded within the overall framework of the telecommunications management network concept (TMN) (see Fig. 0.1). On the other hand mobility in telecommunications, as first introduced by mobile communications in public land mobile networks (PLMN), was enhanced by the universal mobile communications system (UMTS) and personal communications which, as with other new services such as toll-free calls service, the local rate service, or geographic routing, were realized within the intelligent network concept. The intelligent network (IN) is an architectural concept for the operation and provision of new services, which is intended to be applicable to all telecommunication networks.

The broadband ISDN (B-ISDN) concept was developed to support a wide range of data, voice, audio, video, and multimedia applications in the same network. The realization of the B-ISDN concept required changes in the physical and data link layers. The asynchronous transfer mode (ATM) was foreseen to be the chosen transfer mode for implementing B-ISDN. ATM is a specific packet-oriented transfer mode using the asynchronous time-division multiplexing technique where the multiplexed information flow is organized in fixed-size blocks, called ATM cells. However, as a result of the discussion on new network convergence of PSTN/PLMN and IP-based networks the B-ISDN concept is currently being reconsidered, especially regarding the question of whether Internet protocol (IP) should be the preferred packet technology.

Recently the public telecommunication networks and the Internet have developed and grown nearly independently and now offer worldwide communication services. The question is raised as to whether two different networks which offer similar services are really needed? For the envisaged PSTN and IP network convergence the SS 7 message exchange between IP network elements and PSTN signalling points

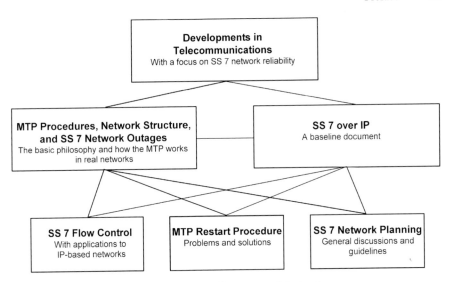

Fig. 0.2. The overall structure of the book

must be assured. With this objective, SS 7 over IP is designed to provide the signalling system for the interconnection of PSTN and IP networks. However, SS 7 network security and reliability is not considered as it is not within the scope of the procedures.

The interest in SS 7 network security and reliability goes back to the early 1990s when serious SS 7 network outages occurred, e.g., in Bell Atlantic and Pacific Bell networks[1]. An SS 7 network reliability group was established in the ITU-T study period 1992–1996 with the objective of investigating whether those SS 7 network outages were caused by faulty specified MTP procedures and, if so, to remove the problems. However, due to the complexity of the problems, the results of these studies were not very satisfactory. Nevertheless, it shows that network security and reliability, which is related to all the other areas of interest, is important.

This book is structured into five parts as shown in Fig. 0.2. The first basic part MTP Procedures, Network Structure and SS 7 Network Outages treats the problem of SS 7 network outages. In order to understand the problems we describe the development and fundamental conception of SS 7 as well as how problems with the MTP procedures were solved. We then discuss potential problems in real SS 7 networks, i.e., we discuss how the MTP works in real networks. Since the function of the SS 7 flow control and the MTP restart procedure play the central part with respect to correlated and uncorrelated network outages, we discuss in some detail the function of both procedures and problems with these procedures in real SS 7 networks.

We see that the existing problems in real networks cannot be solved. However, they may be avoided by going back to the original philosophy of SS 7 by using the

---

[1] CCS Network Outages in Bell Atlantic and Pacific Bell, June 10 through July 2, 1991, Bellcore, Special Report SR-NWT-002149, Issue 1, November 1991

MTP in the original sense and by assuring bidirectionality, loop-freeness, and sufficient nodes disjoint routes, i.e., by suitable network planning. Another approach to avoid the problems would be to introduce new transmission and switching technologies based on ATM and IP networks.

SS 7 over IP is the second major part and may be considered as a baseline document where we summarize basic knowledge regarding PSTN and IP network convergence. In more detail, we describe the framework architecture for signalling transport, signalling transport protocol, and signalling network architectures. We provide the detailed protocol description as well as a discussion of the migration to an overall IP-based network.

The book is written for non-SS 7 experts and tries to provide more detailed background knowledge about the problems and their solution during the specification work. Using the words of Richard Feynman *"We should always know how to solve every problem that has been solved"*. I was therefore asked to summarize all the discussions we had during the various ITU study periods and to treat the problem of SS 7 network security. The results are summarized in this book. It does not replace the fundamental specifications but tries to explain them in more detail for those who did not participate in the different study periods and thus complement the ITU and IETF specifications. It is intended to be a *network operators and implementers guide*, trying to help those working in these areas. As such it is also useful for students who would like to learn more about telecommunication protocols.

The specification work was ongoing throughout the time this book was written. Thus, especially the SS 7 over IP part should be regarded as work in progress. Nevertheless, I have tried to include all the changes made during that time and hope that the major parts are now mature.

I would like to thank Bosch Telecom, Deutsche Telekom, Arcor, DSC Communications, and British Telecom for supporting that work. Special thanks go to Joachim Zepf and Gert Willmann from the University of Stuttgart for the simulations regarding the SS 7 flow control as well as Lutz Krauss from the University of Karlsruhe for his work on the SS 7 network planning algorithms. I would like to thank Alfred Hofmann and Dr. Stefan Göller from Springer Verlag for their kind support and their help during the realization of this book. Last but not least I would like to thank all my collegues worldwide, especially Klaus Gradischnig, Bernd Muehldorfer, Walter Hlavac, Beate Letzas, Wilfried Lange, Jens Kuhfuß, Werner Poguntke, Kurt Losert, Dietmar Daum, Stefan Krämer, Matthias Reitz, David Espenlaub, Karen King, Dave Lane, Rob Spindley, and Doug Turner for useful discussions over the years and encouraging this work.

Mainz, September 24, 2007

Gerhard Rufa

Contents

1

Introduction and Overview

1.1 On the Interest in SS 7 Network Security and Reliability

Our modern industrial society requires high-performance communication systems which may be adapted very quickly and at low cost to individual customer's needs. With this objective network operators are introducing modern communication systems. These are open systems that need their own internal communication system to realize their different distributed tasks. This internal communication system for the interconnection of digital exchanges in public telecommunication networks is called Signalling System No. 7 (SS 7), the functions of which are based on the SS 7 network. According to the Open Systems Interconnection (OSI) model the term *"network"* refers to the Layer 3 *network service*, which is offered by the Message Transfer Part (MTP) and Signalling Connection Control Part (SCCP) to higher layers. An SS 7 network outage results in a breakdown of signalling between the individual nodes of the network, so that telecommunication network services are no longer available to customers. Apart from the tremendous financial damage to the network operator, the social consequences of such a network breakdown cannot be underestimated.

Since the MTP is the central part of the SS 7 network, it is of crucial importance for network security and reliability. The MTP is published in different versions within the *"Yellow Book"*, the *"Red Book"*, the *"Blue Book"* and the *"White Book"*. This means that the MTP has been developed and specified for about 16 years and should now be what we call *"stable"*. Is it really stable? Does it work properly in real networks? Does it fit new requirements so that no further changes within the MTP are needed?

Various different implementations have existed for a long time and are used in national as well as the international network. Due to this, an objective is not to perform any further changes within the MTP in order to avoid compatibility problems with existing and running systems. Experience shows that compatibility problems are *always* related to further development of the MTP. As a consequence, the overall opinion is that changes within the MTP should only be considered if problems occur which cannot be solved within other layers. Are there problems such that further changes within the MTP are really necessary?

This question has been studied intensively during the White Book study period and detailed discussions are going on now. In particular, the following items were raised:

- There are some indications that existing MTP procedures do not work properly during normal operation. What are the reasons?
- New applications like mobile or intelligent network (IN) applications, the realization of high-speed links by using the MTP-3 over the Internet protocol (IP) or the use of the MTP-3 above the signalling ATM adaptation layer (SAAL) in a broadband ISDN (B-ISDN) environment could cause a change or an adaptation of the MTP to new requirements.
- Several SS 7 network outages have occurred. Are modifications of the MTP procedures necessary in order to assure SS 7 network security and reliability?
- The sending of preventive transfer prohibited messages (TFP) via routes with highest priority and other items for further study are still not clarified.

After 20 years of development, specification, and implementation, we should now expect the MTP procedures to work well. However, serious SS 7 network outages have occurred in real networks. The great interest in the question of SS 7 network outages is shown by the fact that, during the study period 1992–1996, an SS 7 network reliability group was established within the ITU-T with the objective to investigate whether those SS 7 network outages were caused by faulty specified MTP procedures and, if so, to remove those problems. However, due to the complexity of the problems, the results of these studies were not very satisfactory.

First of all, the question of SS 7 network outages might be rather curious because, in the case of local outages of single signalling links and/or exchanges, and thus signalling routes, the specified changeover and rerouting procedures within the MTP specification cater for a proper diversion of the signalling traffic towards alternative links and routes. In addition, the SS 7 flow control caters for a reduction of the signalling traffic in the case of a congestion situation as long as it exists. How do SS 7 network outages actually occur?

In fact, especially with respect to further development of the SS 7 network to meet new requirements, there are many more problems and questions at least some of which we will summarize in the following:

- Does the level of signalling traffic influence network security?
- Are faulty implementations responsible for SS 7 network outages?
- Are the MTP procedures working correctly, or are there faulty MTP procedures which could cause SS 7 network outages?
- Are the MTP procedures based on fundamental assumptions and have they to be taken into consideration in network planning?
- Could problems result from network management activities?
- Is compatibility between different color book versions necessary and assured?

- Is the function of the MTP procedures influenced by network planning or affected by failure situations within the network?
- Does the network size influence SS 7 network security?
- Could awkward network planning cause SS 7 network outages?
- Is a transfer of problems from foreign networks to the home network via gateway nodes possible?
- Is bidirectionality within the SS 7 network important and, if so, how can it be assured also in the case of outages?
- How can routing loops be avoided, also in the case of failure situations?
- Can bidirectionality, loop-freeness, and node-disjoint routes between *any* two nodes in the network be realized?
- Is the chosen network structure important with respect to SS 7 network security and which structures are suitable?
- How can continuous network development be performed without causing problems?
- Could different applications (B-ISDN, IN, mobile communications, TMN, etc.) have an influence on network security?
- Are there problems with PSTN and IP network convergence?
- Are there problems arising from fixed and mobile network integration?
- Is it possible to achieve network security and reliability, and how can this be performed?

For a network operator, it is important to be aware of the problems and to know how they may be avoided. It would be wrong to change any MTP procedure in order to solve a specific problem without detailed investigations, since solving one problem might cause other and more serious problems. Thus, the objective of the presented investigations is to provide a clear understanding of how SS 7 network outages can occur, and it is discussed how network reliability and security of an SS 7 network can be reached and maintained while the network is further developed with respect to the introduction of new services and applications.

First of all, the fundamental development and conception of SS 7 is considered in the second chapter, so far as it is relevant to network reliability and security. In the third chapter, the development of the MTP procedures is discussed in describing the problems that were identified during the specification of the MTP procedures and how they were solved. Especially, it is shown that the fundamental philosophy has been changed over the years.

1.2 Basic Developments in Telecommunications

Recently the public telecommunication networks and the Internet have developed and grown nearly independently and now offer worldwide communication services. In parallel to the ITU specification work, the Internet Engineering Task Force (IETF) has been developing the *distributed IP telephony model* which provides the framework for the convergence of the *voice world* of the public switched telephone networks (PSTN) and the *data world* of the Internet. What is the reason for these efforts and why is there interest in this network convergence?

The first services offered by the public switched telephone networks (PSTN) were the telephone, telefax, and data transfer services which were extended during the realization of the integrated services digital network (ISDN) concept by the various ISDN services as well as the new intelligent network (IN) services. Due to the emerging demand for broadband services, the need to integrate both interactive and distributed services, and the need for high-speed transmission and switching technologies the broadband ISDN (B-ISDN) concept has been foreseen to integrate the various data, voice, audio, video, and multimedia services within the same network. The public land mobile networks (PLMN) offer a mobility service which allows a roaming subscriber to be reached by a calling party, who need not know where the mobile subscriber is actually located. Besides the ISDN and telefax services, there is a short message service (SMS) offered via mobile phones, which is used extensively. The interconnection of PSTN and PLMN is improved within the framework of fixed-mobile network integration. To summarize, in telecommunication, convergence of the various services and the integration of circuit and packet transfer modes into one universal network has been foreseen for a long time.

The Internet was optimized for data exchange between computer systems. Today, nearly any information is available via the Internet without major time delays and worldwide. We can do our banking activities or shopping via the Internet and can use the email service, one of the most popular services offered by the Internet. Also video and multimedia services are foreseen to be offered via the Internet. Are two different networks which offer similar services really needed?

In fact, we are now at the stage that both networks are growing together. This is due to the following reasons. First, since Internet services are currently accessed via the subscriber lines of the PSTNs, the growing Internet traffic requires an improvement of the network transition. Furthermore, the services offered via both networks are increasingly mixing:

- It is possible to send an email message to a called party which is, for example, converted to a short message and transferred to a mobile subscriber or transferred as a voice message to a mail box system, and vice versa.
- Considering that fixed network and mobile phones are increaslingly becoming multi functional terminals, shouldn't it be possible to access special Internet web sites via mobile phones?
- Shouldn't it be possible to enhance a PC with a telecommunication system that supports a wide range of data, voice, audio, video, and multimedia applications?
- Could IN services, available in telecommunication networks, be used for the realization of Internet services?

The increasing Intelligent Network Application Part (INAP) traffic to service control points (SCPs) and Mobile Application Part (MAP) traffic to home location registers (HLRs) can cause congestion problems and problems with the flow control. In order to avoid these problems it is recommendable to use high-speed links between SCPs/HLRs and the intermediate transfer nodes. Those high-speed links can be realized as IP links. Finally, considering that the MTP Level 2 protocol

- Has been based on and adapted to unreliable transmission systems,
- Has been based on ancient processor technology,
- Was specified in order to save "expensive" memory and
- That it is optimized for 64 kbit/s transfer rate and, thus, limited to a low bandwidth,

there is a need for a new and cost effective transport protocol for switched circuit network (SCN) messages. Due to the cost benefits of the Internet protocol (IP) some network operators would like to migrate completely to an IP-based network, where every type of information is just viewed as packets of information, called datagrams, with IP being the predominantly preferred packet technology. The realization of these ideas necessarily leads to the convergence of both networks. However, how can this network convergence be performed?

In order to realize the above objectives, the IETF signalling transport (SIG-TRAN) group is currently defining SS 7 over IP to enable SS 7 message exchange between IP network elements and with PSTN signalling points. In this respect the following fundamental questions arise:

- Is there a need for MTP-2 and MTP-3 functionality within the overall signalling system?
- Do we need MTP-3 network management functions within the overall signalling system?
- How can SS 7 signalling messages be transported over IP?
- How can the signalling performance requirements for voice and data services over IP be realized?
- How can PSTN and IP network convergence be performed?
- What is the detailed protocol structure for IP links or voice over IP (VoIP)?
- Is there a transfer of problems from one network to the other via signalling gateway nodes and how can they be avoided?

SS 7 over IP is designed to provide the signalling system for the interconnection of PSTN and IP networks. However, basic SS 7 knowledge and a discussion of SS 7 network security and reliability is not covered. Thus, regarding the SS 7 over IP developments, this book intends to provide more detailed background knowledge and, in this way, complement the IETF specifications.

In the fourth chapter we first describe how the SS 7 and IP network convergence can be realized, i.e., we describe the overall distributed IP telephony model, the basic signalling requirements, and the framework architecture for signalling transport. In the fifth chapter we summarize the different signalling transport protocol architectures based on the various adaptation modules. The SCTP as the underlying common transport protocol cannot by itself provide the availability and performance of MTP-3. Thus, redundant signalling network architectures are needed and are discussed in the sixth chapter. In the seventh chapter we describe in more detail the underlying protocols.

1.3 MTP Procedures, Network Structure, and SS 7 Network Outages

Behind the isolation and outage of wide network areas or an outage of the whole network, there exist a lot of more or less likely reasons. In the presented investigations, however, only protocol relevant network outages and those caused by network planning are considered. The cause of an SS 7 network outage is not faulty MTP procedures, but the causes may be searched for within implementations, the network structure, and network planning as well as the application of the MTP, especially in large SS 7 networks. With this objective we describe in Chap. 11 real SS 7 networks and discuss routing and topology aspects as well as network interconnection.

In order to judge the risk of a real SS 7 network outage, we describe in Chap. 8 how SS 7 network outages occur where we distinguish between correlated and uncorrelated network outages. In the twelfth chapter we summarize potential problems related to the application of the MTP in real networks. In particular, we describe the occurrence and consequences of a loss of bidirectionality within the network. Because of the fact that the SS 7 flow control plays the central part with respect to SS 7 network outages, we describe in some detail the function of the SS 7 flow control in Chap. 9 as well as potential problems with the flow control in real networks. Given that an unprotected node may be the source of correlated and uncorrelated network outages a functioning restart procedure is of crucial importance. Thus, we describe in Chap. 10 problems with the restart procedure and their solutions that eventually led to the White Book restart procedure.

Unfortunately, the described problems, especially in the case of a growing signalling network, cannot be solved after all. However, the problems can be avoided by going back to the original philosophy of SS 7. This may be done by using the MTP in the original sense and by assuring bidirectionality and loop-freeness of the routing data within the network as well as the function of the flow control, or by the introduction of new high-performance transmission and switching technologies, as would become possible in ATM- or IP-based networks. In particular, we show in Chap. 13 how SS 7 network security and reliability can be increased by changing the network structure, by the introduction of IP-based high-speed links as well as the separation of different traffic streams in the new SS 7 over IP environment, and how problems with the network convergence can be avoided. Finally, we end with a short discussion of the migration to an IP-based network in Chap. 14.

2

Development and Fundamental Conception of SS 7

The overall development of SS 7 caused a lot of changes within the MTP. Thus, we briefly summarize in this section the fundamental conception as well as the development of SS 7, which is still going on, as far as it is important with respect to network security and reliability.

2.1 Basic Concepts

2.1.1 The Fundamental Philosophy of SS 7

The Signalling System No. 7 (SS 7) [1] is an internationally standardized general-purpose common channel signalling system that is optimized for operation in digital telecommunications networks in conjunction with stored program controlled exchanges. It provides a *reliable* means for transfer of information within telecommunications networks and was designed to meet present and future requirements of information transfer for inter processor transactions for call control, remote control and management, and maintenance signalling. The system was originally optimized for operation over 64 kbit/sec digital channels. The fundamental idea of common channel signalling is that a single channel is used to convey, by means of labeled messages, signalling information relating to, for example, a multiplicity of circuits or other information such as that used for network management.

With respect to the realization of a large number of applications that, in fact, were not all foreseen when SS 7 was born in the mid 1970s, a modular functional architecture was chosen, separating the SS 7 functions into two independent functional blocks (see Fig. 2.1)

- The application-independent network service part (NSP)[1] and
- The application-dependent part that comprises the users of the NSP

---

[1] According to OSI the term *network* refers to the Layer 3 entity, which has responsibilities including routing and relaying of messages on behalf of *users* of the network towards indicated destinations.

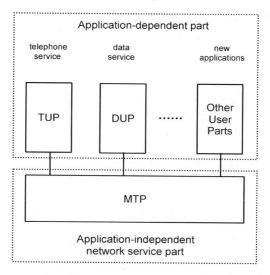

Fig. 2.1. The modular concept of SS 7

According to the early requirements the only users of the NSP were the Telephone User Part (TUP) [2] and the Data User Part (DUP) [3]. The TUP was specified to provide the telephone call control signalling functions whilst the DUP comprises the functions to control interchange circuits used on data calls.

2.1.2 Fundamental Requirements

At that time the NSP consisted merely of the Message Transfer Part (MTP) [4] that is responsible for reliable transport and delivery of signalling information, exchanged as message signal units (MSU) between peer User Parts. More precise

The fundamental objective of the MTP is to provide a transfer of signalling messages in correct sequence without message loss or message duplication.

Thus, User Parts were specified *assuming* that the MTP fulfils these requirements with a high probability. Furthermore, the fundamental idea was that new applications were introduced within SS 7 by adding new application-specific User Parts. The important progress of SS 7 was that all these different User Parts exchange their user-specific messages via a *common* transport system, the MTP. The requirements for the MTP have been determined primarily by the requirements of call control signalling for the telephone and circuit-switched data transmission.

Thus, when the MTP procedures were specified, one of the fundamental assumptions was that a signalling point only needs a local view of the SS 7 network, i.e., it only needs routing data for its adjacent nodes to which circuits are established.

Since the MTP forms the interface at a node with the rest of the SS 7 network the signalling network will have a significant impact on the MTP (see Chap. 12). In this respect the following requirement was formulated as a basis for the specification of the MTP procedures.

"The MTP must be independent of the signalling network in that it has to be capable of performing its set functions and attaining its objective no matter what network structure or status prevails."[2]

Therefore, the MTP has to contain the necessary functions to ensure that any impact the network has does not impair MTP performance.

2.1.3 The Functional Levels of the MTP

The functions of the MTP are separated into three functional levels (see Fig. 2.2).

Signalling Data Link Functions

Level 1 (MTP-1) defines the physical, electrical, and functional characteristics of a signalling data link and the means to access it. A signalling data link is a bidirectional

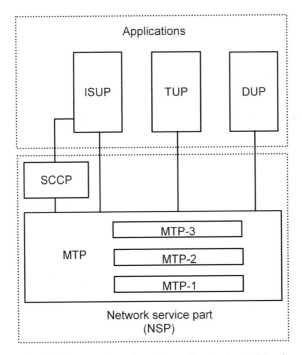

Fig. 2.2. The structure of SS 7 according to the Red Book

---

[2] Q.701, section 3: Message Transfer Part and signalling network.

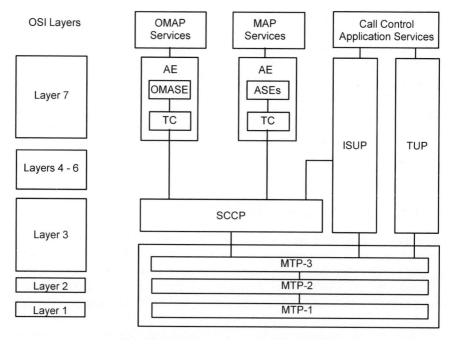

Fig. 2.3. The White Book architecture of SS 7

transmission path for signalling consisting of two data channels operating together in opposite directions. It fully complies with the Open Systems Interconnection definition of the physical layer (Layer 1) (see Fig. 2.3). In a digital environment, 64 kbit/sec digital paths are normally used. A signalling data link provides a bearer for a signalling link.

Signalling Link Functions

Level 2 (MTP-2) defines the functions and procedures for and relating to the transfer of signalling messages over one individual signalling data link. The Level 2 functions, together with a signalling data link as the bearer, provide a signalling link for reliable transfer of signalling messages between two adjacent nodes. The signalling functions include:

- Message delimitation
- Error detection
- Error correction by retransmission
- Message sequence control
- Flow control

The signalling link functions correspond to the OSI data link layer (Layer 2) (see Fig. 2.3).

Signalling Network Functions

Level 3 (MTP-3) defines those transport functions and procedures that are common to and independent of the operation of individual signalling links. These functions are structured into *signalling message handling functions*, which ensure that an MSU originated by a particular User Part at the originating node of that message is delivered to the same User Part at the destination node (which need not be an adjacent node) and *signalling network management functions* which provide a reconfiguration of the signalling network in the case of failures and to control signalling traffic in the case of congestion.

2.2 The Realization of the ISDN Concept

The realization of the integrated services digital network (ISDN) concept to provide switched services and user facilities for voice and nonvoice applications, e.g., data, required enhancements to the SS 7 that were worked out in the study period 1980–1984 and included in the Red Book version of SS 7. On the one hand, a new User Part related to the ISDN application, the ISDN User Part (ISUP) [5], was introduced to provide the signalling functions of the basic bearer service and call control as well as supplementary services, e.g., call forwarding, calling line identification, connected line identification, user-to-user signalling, etc. (see Fig. 2.2).

On the other hand those supplementary services required connection-oriented end-to-end signalling. Since:

- The MTP was not designed to provide end-to-end signalling between any two nodes in the network, and
- The MTP does not provide global addressing capability, which means that only destination nodes within the home SS 7 network may be addressed, so that ISDN supplementary services via interconnect nodes using the MTP routing are not possible

new approaches were needed. Some network operators decided to use the TUP enhanced by some supplementary services together with *the pass along method* to exchange signalling information between end users section by section over the same signalling path as that used to set up the call and establish the physical connection. However, the ISUP is more flexible in providing new services and features.

If the MTP is used to provide the required end-to-end signalling between any two nodes in the network, problems arise in large SS 7 networks, which require specific actions to avoid them (see Chap. 12). Another approach, connection-oriented end-to-end signalling, was realized by enhancing the NSP by the Signalling Connection Control Part (SCCP) [6]. The SCCP provides additional functions to the MTP. It offers connectionless and connection-oriented network services to transfer circuit-related and non-circuit-related signalling information between *any two* nodes of the network or *between different networks*. In addition, it enhances the addressing capabilities of the MTP by using global titles (GT), e.g., dialled digits, the destination point code (DPC) and the subsystem number (SSN) that identifies subsystems, the users of the SCCP, which are accessed via the SCCP. The ISUP can invoke the services of either the MTP or SCCP depending on the function being performed (see Fig. 2.2). Both the MTP and SCCP provide the functions of the OSI network layer (Layer 3).

With the described enhancements, the Red Book version of SS 7 yields the basis for the realization of the ISDN concept at the national and international level.

2.3 Further Development of the SS 7 Structure

2.3.1 OSI Layering

The evolution of the SS 7 architecture, since the Red Book, has increasingly been based on the Open Systems Interconnection model (OSI) [7]. The purpose of the OSI model is to provide a well-defined structure of modeling the interconnection and exchange of information between users in a communications system. It provides not only a communication between users in the same network but also interworking between networks, i.e., communication between users over several networks in tandem.

According to the OSI model the overall functions of a communication system are partitioned into seven layers. The relationship between the OSI model and SS 7 is shown in Fig. 2.3. Currently, there are no protocols used in the SS 7 architecture that map into Layers 4–6. All new applications are defined based on the OSI model.

2.3.2 OAM, Mobile, and IN Applications

The foundations of new applications were laid in the study periods 1984–1996. On the one hand the studies on operations, administration, and maintenance (OAM) were embedded within the overall framework of the telecommunications management network (TMN) concept. On the other hand mobility in telecommunications, as first introduced by mobile communications in public land mobile networks (PLMN), was enhanced by personal communications which, as with other new services such as the *toll-free calls service*, the *local rate service* or *geographic routing*, were realized within the intelligent network (IN) concept. Related with these new applications were new application parts.

The Operations, Maintenance, and Administration Part (OMAP) [8] comprises functions including measurement initiation and collection as well as initiation of tests within the SS 7 network like, for example, the MTP routing verification test (MRVT). The Mobile Application Part (MAP) [9] provides for mobile facilities the necessary signalling functions for voice and nonvoice applications in a mobile network and provides information exchange related to a roaming mobile station.

The intelligent Network is an architectural concept for the operation and provision of new services, which is intended to be applicable to all telecommunications networks. Those services are realized by creating service logic programs (SLP), which combine service independent building blocks (SIB) and service-specific data to build up the specific services. Various service providing capabilities are grouped together in functional entities, i.e., the service switching function (SSF), service control function (SCF), the service data function (SDF) and the specialized resource function (SRF). These functional entities are implemented in physical entities called service switching points (SSP), service control points (SCP) and intelligent peripherals, which are normal nodes in the SS 7 network. Within the distributed IN architecture the various functional entities are linked via SS 7 using the Intelligent Network Application Part (INAP) [10].

For all these new applications a new non-circuit-related protocol was required, called transaction capabilities (TC) [11]. TC provides a transfer of signalling information in form of *components* between TC users located within interactive applications distributed over exchanges, databases or specialized network centres within the network. It consists of two sublayers. The component sublayer is responsible for the exchange of components between TC users, called a dialogue or transaction, and provides dialogue facilities, allowing several dialogues to run currently between two TC users. The transaction sublayer deals with the exchange of messages that contain such components, which involves the establishment and management of a transaction between TC users in different nodes of the SS 7 network. The TC directly accesses the connectionless SCCP services (see Fig. 2.3).

The TC users are application service elements (ASE). An ASE is the basic component of an application entity (AE). TC is a special ASE common to the various application entities. Such an application entity is the function that an application process (AP) uses to communicate with its peers. The SS 7 architecture according to the White Book including the new applications is shown in Fig. 2.3.

2.3.3 Broadband ISDN

Considering

- The emerging demand for broadband services
- The need for high-speed transmission, switching, and signal processing technologies
- The need to integrate both interactive and distributed services
- The need to integrate both circuit and packet transfer mode into one universal network

the broadband ISDN (B-ISDN) [12] concept has been developed to support a wide range of data, voice, audio, video, and multimedia applications in the same network. The realization of the B-ISDN concept required changes at the physical and data link layers (see Fig. 2.4).

The asynchronous transfer mode (ATM) has been foreseen to be the chosen transfer mode for implementing B-ISDN. ATM is a specific packet-oriented transfer mode using the asynchronous time-division multiplexing technique where the multiplexed information flow is organized in fixed-size blocks, called ATM cells.

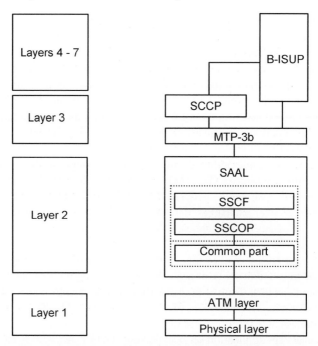

Fig. 2.4. B-ISDN layer structure according to capability set 1

ATM provides a dynamic bandwidth allocation on demand with a fine degree of granularity and is independent of the means of transport at the physical layer. The ATM layer provides the functions to transfer ATM cells via ATM virtual channel connections (VCC). Since ATM offers a flexible transfer capability it is also used to transfer signalling information, which is carried on specific VCCs that correspond to signalling data links.

The signalling ATM adaptation layer (SAAL) [13] is a protocol which operates at the data link layer of the OSI model and which provides the MTP-2 services to the MTP-3. Thus, the SAAL comprises functions to transfer signalling messages via ATM links that are based on an ATM VCC as the bearer. The SAAL functions are divided in two sublayers, the common part (CP) and the service specific convergence sublayer (SSCS). At the common part signalling messages are mapped into ATM cells. At the transmitting end, messages are segmented and inserted into ATM cells and at the receiving end the messages are reassembled from the ATM cells.

The convergence sublayer is functionally divided into the service-specific connection-oriented protocol (SSCOP), which is a common connection-oriented protocol with error recovery and flow control to provide a generic reliable transfer service, and the service-specific coordination function (SSCF) which maps the services provided by the SSCOP to the needs of the MTP-3. For ATM-based signalling networks the SAAL provides the same service with a similar quality as the MTP-2. Therefore, the MTP-3 is supposed to be reused *without modifications*. However, since messages with up to 4096 byte may be transferred, the 272 byte length restriction of the MTP is removed. The broadband MTP is generally denoted by MTP-3b [14].

Finally, the B-ISDN User Part (B-ISUP) was introduced to provide the signalling functions required to support the basic bearer services, call control, and supplementary services for B-ISDN applications. The B-ISUP protocol has evolved from the ISUP protocol and, like the ISUP, interfaces with the SCCP and MTP-3b.

Existing narrow-band network signalling focus on call control, bearer control, and network management and maintenance. With B-ISDN there will be additional capabilities, e.g., the capability for point-to-multipoint calls, multimedia calls, and calls with asymmetric traffic as well as capabilities for interworking with other networks or network elements such as narrowband ISDN (N-ISDN), PLMNs, and IN entities. Those added capabilities for signalling in B-ISDN require significantly more sophisticated methods for connection control than in N-ISDN. In order to allow a graceful and less expensive evolution from today's network to B-ISDN a series of releases or capability sets (CS) have been defined. CS1 is used to set up simple single-connection calls. CS2 is developed to support multipoint virtual paths, virtual channels, and multiconnection calls whilst CS3 adds multimedia and broadcast connections. The approach recommended in CS2 and beyond is to separate bearer control from call control functions. The signalling information could be carried on a *separate* overlay network or it could be carried directly on VCCs in the ATM network. The separation of call and bearer control functions allows more efficient call setup in a multipoint and mobile customer environment and more flexibility in directing information to destinations at all stages of the call. The separation may be realized using the TC protocol.

At this stage, it is important to note that all these new applications lead to different traffic streams and characteristics with MSU lengths in the range of up to 4096 bytes, which fundamentally differ from those of the early TUP and DUP era (about 15 byte).

Note: As a result of the discussion on the network convergence of PSTN/PLMN and IP-based networks (see Chap. 2) the B-ISDN concept is currently reconsidered, especially regarding the question of whether IP should be the preferred packet technology.

◇

2.3.4 PSTN and IP Network Convergence

The *voice world* of the public switched telephone network (PSTN) and the *data world* of the Internet have developed and grown nearly independently and today offer worldwide communication services. We are now at the stage that both coexisting networks are growing together. For the convergence of the networks and the realization of, for example, voice over IP (VoIP) [15] an overall signalling system for the call and bearer control is needed.

The signalling system for the interconnection of digital exchanges in public telecommunication networks is the Signalling System No. 7 (SS 7). Since SS 7 can control several thousand connections and thus a high bandwidth, and since SS 7 offers the gateway to a large number of existing telephony and ISDN supplementary services as well as the IN services, SS 7 is the core signalling system. However, in the current IP protocol suite no signalling system exists that may be mapped onto SS 7. The reason is that, for the function of the SS 7 application protocols, e.g., ISUP, MAP or INAP protocols, it is required that signalling messages are delivered in sequence, without errors, loss, duplication or excessive time delay. This requires that failures within the network are detected and measures to assure signalling are taken very quickly by an appropriate network management.

The framework architecture [16] that has been defined by SIGTRAN for switched circuit network (SCN) signalling message transport over IP uses multiple components which are the IP network layer [17], the stream control transmission protocol (SCTP) [18] and the switched circuit network (SCN) adaptation modules [19] (see Chap. 7). In parallel, ITU-T has provided a similar protocol structure (see Fig. 2.5).

The service-specific connection-oriented protocol in a multi-link and connectionless environment (SSCOPMCE) [20] is similar to the SCTP and provides assured data delivery between peer SSCOPMCE users. The SSCOPMCE is an extension of the service-specific connection-oriented protocol (SSCOP) defined for use in the service-specific convergence sublayer of the SAAL (see Fig. 2.4). In particular, the extensions enable SSCOPMCE to operate in environments other than SAAL. One of three modes of operation of the SSCOPMCE is called *connectionless environment*. In this mode, one or more links to the connectionless environment, e.g., IP or UDP, may be deployed and links may be added or removed during the operation of the SSCOPMCE protocol entity. Figure 2.5 shows the principle protocol stack for SS 7 over IP using SSCOPMCE.

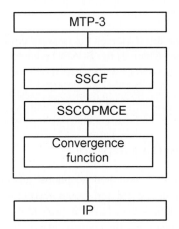

Fig. 2.5. SS 7 over IP protocol architecture using SSCOPMCE

Through the lower service access point, SSCOPMCE protocol data units (PDU) payload fragments of SSCOPMCE user information are exchanged via IP (or via UDP and IP) with peer users. Through a specific convergence function the SS-COPMCE PDUs are mapped onto IP datagrams and vice versa, and appropriate headers are created as is customarily done in the IP environment. As within the SAAL, the adaptation to MTP-3 can be performed by the service specific coordination function (SSCF).

3

On the Specification of the MTP

Besides the developments at the user level a further development of the MTP took place during the White Book study period. On the one hand, this was necessary due to new requirements at the user level. On the other hand, problems with the MTP procedures were identified and solved. Finally, we recognized important problems with the MTP, which were solved by the introduction of new procedures.

In the following we describe this development of the MTP not only with the objective of describing the philosophy and the function of the MTP procedures but also to show that the solution of most of the problems caused other and sometimes more difficult problems that had to be solved. This is why the stability of the MTP is one of the most important objectives. Finally, this knowledge about the problems and the corresponding solutions is important regarding the discussions on PSTN and IP network convergence and the question of whether in an overall IP-based network the MTP-3 functionality is needed or not.

3.1 Flow Control

The objective of the SS 7 flow control is to reduce signalling traffic at its source in the case that the signalling network is not capable of transferring all signalling traffic because of congestion situations. On the one hand, local congestion situations can occur within a digital exchange and the surrounding network due to bottlenecks towards a specific destination. These bottlenecks occur if the amount of signalling traffic towards the considered destination point cannot be transferred via the available route set due to outages of local links and/or exchanges, and thus signalling routes, as well as an awkward network planning. On the other hand, digital exchanges have a finite processor speed and capacity. Thus, if the amount of user signalling messages to be handled or the network management activities to be performed by the exchange are increasing, then the exchange can become congested. This means that the internal buffers fill up, leading to serious problems.

As a first problem a loss of messages may occur. A loss of message signal units (MSUs) may cause problems with the User Parts whilst a loss of network management messages means that the MTP procedures do not work properly, leading to outages and congestion situations within other network areas (see Chap. 8). In addition, the loss of important internal messages or other faulty internal processes caused, for example, by faulty software or hardware failures, leads to the fact that the internal processor communication does not work properly so that the exchange may run into an undefined state which may be ended merely by an out of service of the exchange followed by a restart. Furthermore, a congestion situation may cause a failure of single links. If a congestion situation at the receiving end of a signalling link does not terminate within 3–6 s, then the Level 2 timer T6 (see Appendix A) expires, which leads to an out of service of the concerned link.

Congestion situations are also of importance concerning an outage of an exchange. Due to the load sharing mechanism there is a high probability that, in a high signalling traffic load situation, not only one but many, if not all, links within a route set are congested. Due to the fact that both directions of a route are nearly equally loaded, a lot of links of an exchange may be involved. Note that a Level 3 congestion may lead to a congestion of *all* links of the exchange. Related link failures lead to the fact that, in a high signalling traffic load situation, the status of the exchange gets worse, so that more and more links are taken out of service. Thus, at some stage, the exchange is completely isolated or performs a restart because of too many failed links. Finally, due to the nature of SS 7, local congestion situations *will spread* throughout the whole SS 7 network if no specific actions are taken to remove the congestion situation. The consequences are a reduction of signalling performance, an outage or isolation of wide network areas, or an outage of the whole SS 7 network (see Chap. 8).

In order to avoid those problems the SS 7 flow control has been introduced within the Red Book specification with the objective to reduce temporarily the user traffic streams so that link or route set congestion and the congestion of exchanges are removed *before the congestion situations spread within the network.* In the case of a congestion situation MTP STATUS primitives with cause *CONGESTION* are created by the Message Transfer Part (MTP) for local User Parts and transfer controlled (TFC) messages are created by the MTP, addressed to the originating nodes of the concerned signalling traffic.

For the relevant User Parts, the congestion indication (CI) primitive rate contains the information about how much they should reduce their traffic towards the concerned destination point. Thus, the User Part congestion control is based on a stepwise reduction of the user traffic controlled by the received CI primitive rate (see Sects. 9.2 and 9.3).

In order to keep the SS 7 flow control as simple as possible it was based on the following fundamental assumptions:

• **All traffic streams are of about the same characteristics**
  The traffic streams created by the early telephone (TUP) and data (DUP) User Parts had nearly the same characteristics. *Thus, at that time, it was not considered necessary to distinguish between the different User Parts. As a consequence, all User Parts within an exchange are informed with the same congestion indica-*

tion primitive rate, independent from their actual contribution to the congestion situation.

- **The MSUs from different User Parts are of about the same length**
  The message signal units (MSU) created by the early User Parts are of nearly the same length, i.e., about 15 bytes. *Thus, the contribution of a User Part to the congestion situation is reflected by the number of messages sent by this User Part.*

- **The DPC uniquely identifies the traffic stream to be reduced**
  During the Red Book study period, when the fundamentals of the SS 7 flow control were developed, non-circuit-related applications that need the global title addressing mechanism were not foreseen. *Thus, the only information needed to specify the traffic stream to be reduced towards a given destination uniquely was the destination point code (DPC).*

During the further development of the Signalling System No. 7 these assumptions have been unconsciously violated, when the maximum MSU message length has been increased during the Blue Book study period from 62 to 272 bytes length, and as new applications, like the B-ISUP, create messages of up to 4096 byte length. However, traffic streams with different message length have an influence on the function of the flow control or may destroy it (see Sect. 12.3).

During the White Book study period these problems were recognized and some improvements were introduced. Besides the *route set method (RSM)*, the *congested link method (CLM)* as well as the *octet method (OM)* were introduced [21]. The CLM method is optimised to handle asymmetric load distributions caused, for example, by applications that create traffic streams with different message lengths, whilst the OM method allows to explicitly take into consideration the message length so that User Parts sending long messages receive a higher CI primitive rate.

Besides Level 2 any other Level may become congested. The early approach was that, whenever a congestion situation occurs within a higher Level, the messages are stored back to Level 2 causing a Level 2, i.e., a route set congestion, due to which the flow control measures are started. If, according to this philosophy, a User Part is congested the reception of MSUs from Level 3 is reduced or stopped. As a consequence, Level 3 becomes congested so that the reception of MSU from Level 2 is reduced or stopped causing a Level 2 or route set congestion, which leads to a load reduction at the originating signalling points.

During the Blue Book study period, however, it was recognized that this philosophy does not work. Problems within higher levels cannot be solved by creating problems within the lower levels. The problem with the original flow control philosophy consists in the fact that if, due to user congestion, Level 3 congestion is caused, then *all local links* of the considered node and, thus, *all neighbouring nodes* as well as *all signalling relations via this node* are affected.

As a consequence the flow control philosophy has been changed so that *any layer has its own responsibility to remove its layer congestion.* In this respect, measures to treat a Level 3 or signalling point congestion have been introduced into the MTP which consist of an information of relevant User Parts about the congestion situation, using congestion indication primitives or TFC messages, respectively, which are then forced to reduce the concerned traffic.

In addition, the MTP User Part availability control has been introduced, as described in the following section. According to this procedure, Level 3 has the possibility to stop very fast specific traffic streams towards one of its User Parts, in the case of problems with this User Part, so that an impact on Level 3 and other local User Parts may be avoided.

3.2 User Flow Control

If, within an exchange having user functions, a local User Part is unavailable for the MTP because the internal interconnection between the MTP and that User Part is not available or the User Part itself has failed or is even unequipped, Level 3 cannot distribute received user messages to that User Part. Level 3 either stores the received messages locally until the considered User Part is available again or it discards the received messages for that User Part. Nevertheless, both alternatives are problematic for the following reasons.

On the one hand, if the user messages are not discarded, Level 3 and/or signalling route set congestion is created for *all route sets* via the considered exchange. Because of the large amounts of TFC messages created the *local problem* may spread throughout the surrounding network. In addition, traffic streams will be reduced that are not destined for the unavailable User Part. On the other hand, if the relevant messages are discarded, in conflict with the MTP philosophy, then the MTP performance becomes worse and a loss of bidirectionality with related problems is caused at the user level, e.g., the specified emergency procedures are started and unnecessary information of the management is performed.

In order to avoid these problems the MTP user flow control procedure was introduced into the Blue Book. If a local User Part is unavailable for the MTP, User Part unavailability (UPU) messages are sent to the originating nodes of the concerned traffic streams on a response basis in order to stop them. The advantage of the UPU procedure is

- The traffic streams are stopped very fast and
- Traffic streams to other User Parts are not affected

However, within the Blue Book study period, it was not specified how to indicate the availability of the concerned User Part, so that *the Blue Book procedure does not work*.

This drawback was removed during the White Book study period and, in addition, the procedure has been renamed User Part availability control to reflect better the philosophy of the procedure. In particular, it has been agreed that *the detection of the availability of the concerned User Part is a subject of the peer User Parts*. It was emphasized that this availability must be detected very fast in order to avoid a loss of bidirectionality at the user level. According to the White Book we, in addition, distinguish whether a User Part is *inaccessible* or *unequipped*. The relevant information is contained in the UPU message. The reason for this distinction is that an availability test for an unequipped User Part does not make sense and, thus, should not be performed. Instead, management is informed about that situation.

3.3 Processor Outage

Another procedure that caused a lot of problems is the processor outage procedure. Processor outage refers to a situation when received signalling messages cannot be transferred by Level 2 to its local Level 3. This may be because of a failure of the node internal connection between Level 2 and Level 3. Furthermore, the case was foreseen that Level 3 does not accept messages from Level 2 because of local User Part unavailability (see Sect. 3.2) or congestion situations at Level 3 or Level 4. If the received messages are discarded by Level 2, this leads to a loss of bidirectionality as well as a reduction of the MTP performance. Instead, if Level 2 does not discard continuously received messages, a link and thus route set congestion is caused.

In order to avoid these problems it is necessary to stop the traffic streams via the concerned link. One possibility would have been to take the link out of service. However, this was not done since Level 2 is not the source of the problems and, thus, should not be affected. On the other side, the following link activation takes too much time, which could not be accepted. In order to solve the problems, the link was *blocked* in the sense that, at Level 3, it is considered to be unavailable for the transfer of user traffic whilst, at Level 2, the link is aligned. This link blocking is achieved by sending a link status signal unit (LSSU), indicating processor outage, which causes the remote end to transmit fill-in signal units (FISU) and to indicate remote processor outage to its local Level 3.

According to the Red Book, another use of the processor outage procedure is the management blocking of a link, by which a network operator is able to take off user traffic from the link without taking the link *out of service*. However, as an important drawback of management blocking, it was recognized during the Blue Book study period that due to the blocking of a link the Level 2 status of the link is changed and that the sending of test messages via the blocked link is not possible. Therefore, the management inhibiting procedure was introduced into the Blue Book (see Sect. 3.5) and, in addition, the management blocking of a link has been deleted from the White Book.

In the following, we describe further problems that were caused by the processor outage procedure and its application.

Problems with Unavailable User Parts

If processor outage is applied when Level 3 cannot deliver user messages to a particular User Part, because that User Part is unavailable or congested (see Sect. 3.2), there is a risk of an isolation of the whole node merely due to problems with *one*

User Part. As a consequence, not only is transfer traffic via the considered node diverted or stopped, but traffic to other local User Parts is interrupted and an outage of the node with a following restart provoked. Thus, in the considered case, processor outage should not be applied, although foreseen in the White Book. Instead, the described user flow control should be used to selectively stop the concerned traffic streams.

Message Duplication Due to Short-Term Processor Outage

Another problem results from applying processor outage at one side of the link for a very short time, i.e., if the link goes into the *in service* state after a short-term blocking. In the early days of SS 7, the Level 2 reception buffer space was kept small for cost reasons. Such a short-term processor outage could therefore be caused, if the internal connection between Level 2 and Level 3 is interrupted for a short time and, in order to stop the traffic streams, processor outage is applied during that time.

Although for those short-term failures, the Level 2 flow control would have been much more appropriate, there were implementations using short-term processor outage in those cases. The problem with a short-term processor outage is that, according to the Red Book specification, the remote end of the link starts normal changeover, so that a related changeover order (COO) is received at the former local processor outage side of the link, but which is now *in service* again. As a consequence, the link is taken *out of service*. However, after the finalization of the *local processor outage* state, the local side could have sent a FISU, which terminates the *remote processor outage* state, and further MSUs that might be accepted at the remote end of the link. Due to the fact that the local side receives an *old FSNC*, as contained in the COO, MSUs are retrieved that have already been sent. In this way, message duplication could occur, which was considered to be rather problematic.

The simplest way to avoid the problems with short-term processor outage would have been to explicitly exclude its usage and to apply in the considered case the Level 2 flow control. Instead, within the Blue Book study period, the introduction of time-controlled changeover at the remote processor outage side was choosen, since it is also applicable if no alternative links between both ends exist, so that no changeover messages can be exchanged to perform a proper retrieval of not yet sent messages. In addition, time-controlled changeover was used for the new introduced management inhibiting procedure (see Sect. 3.5).

According to time-controlled changeover, the remote end of the link does not send a COO but starts the Level 3 timer T1. If processor outage terminates *before* T1 expires, changeover is aborted and the sending of traffic via the concerned link is resumed normally, without causing an *out of service* of the link or message duplication. However, if T1 expires, i.e., if a long-term processor outage exists, then MSUs stored in the changeover buffer are sent to alternative links. In this way, the problem of message duplication has been solved by applying time-controlled changeover but, unfortunately, a new problem has been created.

Problems with the Sending of Old Messages in the Case of Long-Term Processor Outage

If, after a long-term processor outage, the link changes to the *in service* state, messages stored within the Level 2 buffers are sent. On the one hand, message missequencing occurs and, on the other hand, network management messages could be sent that refer to network situations that have long since passed and that could cause a lot of problems.

In addition, the remote end of the link could receive a COO that, according to the Blue Book specification, is not acknowledged, so that the local side initiates an *out of service* of the link. Especially, this can occur within the interworking between Red Book and Blue Book nodes, if the Red Book end of the link initiates a management blocking that has been removed from the Blue Book.

These problems were solved during the White Book study period. In particular, it was specified that a COO received at the remote processor outage side of a link is acknowledged, that a switch to the normal changeover procedure is possible, while T1 is running and that, after a long-term processor outage, the Level 2 buffers are flushed and the Level 2 sequence numbers are synchronized correctly, before the sending of traffic via the concerned link is restarted.

3.4 Restart Procedure

Due to faulty internal processes caused, for example, by faulty software, hardware failures or a loss of internal messages, an exchange may run into an undefined state which may be ended merely by an out of service followed by a restart. Such a restart of a digital exchange is a very complicated process. During the restart of an exchange there are two different sources of troubles: extensive Level 3 activities related to the network synchronization as well as early user traffic. When a signalling point is isolated from the network for some time, it cannot be sure that its routing data are still valid. As a consequence problems could be present, when the sending of user traffic is resumed, due to wrong routing data as well as due to many parallel Level 3 activities, which have to be performed within the node whose MTP is restarting.

Thus, if no specific actions are taken then problems can occur with

- The link activation
- A large number of parallel changeover, and changebacks
- The routing data update
- The sending, reception, and processing of signalling route management SRM messages
- Local link congestions
- Extensive message loss

which may result in a renewed failure of the restarting node as well as a spread of correlated and uncorrelated congestion situations within the SS 7 network (see

Chap. 8). Note, that an unprotected restarting node may be the source of correlated and uncorrelated network outages.

Within ITU-T these problems were recognized during the Blue Book study period. In order to assure a systematic restart of an STP, the Red Book specification was enhanced by the signalling point restart procedure with the objective of giving an STP time for the link activation and an update of the network status *before* the complete user traffic is restarted. However, two further problems are present with the Blue Book procedure:

- On the one hand, only stand-alone STPs are fully protected. The protection of a restarting STP having user functions, however, is incomplete. If the first link within the link set to an adjacent node is available again the restarting and adjacent signalling points are immediately allowed to restart local user traffic terminating at the adjacent node.
- On the other hand, a restarting signalling end point (SEP) is not protected, since the restart procedure is terminated if the first link to an adjacent node is available again so that, according to the Blue Book specification, no restart procedure is performed for an SEP.

The early user traffic causes the above-mentioned problems within the restarting node as well as the surrounding network.

Note: Congestion situations are not removed since *no flow control measures are taken* according to the Blue Book specification.

◊

During the White Book study period these problems were identified and solved [4]. The overall objective of the restart procedure is *to protect the node whose MTP is restarting and the network*. This is achieved by giving the restarting node time to activate sufficient links and to synchronize the network status with the surrounding network by an update of the routing data *before* user traffic is restarted. As a consequence, if the restart procedure lasts too long, the network status may change during the network synchronization. In this case, the restarting node and the surrounding network could resume the sending of user traffic with wrong routing data, which again would lead to the old problems. Thus, an overall restart time of about 60 s (see Appendix A) was introduced. In order to use the available time in an efficient way it was seen to be preferable to make all link sets available at nearly the same time by activating first one link per link set and by applying emergency alignment for at least the first link in each link set. Because of this measure the routing data update can be started for all routes at the very beginning of the restart procedure.

Finally, since the specified restart procedure can only solve the problems of the MTP, further problems are present at the user level. For example, an update of the network status is also necessary at the user level (SCCP, ISUP, etc.). Furthermore, the protection of a node requires that user traffic be increased smoothly so that, in addition to the activities within the MTP, some kind of user restart at the user level was seen to be necessary. Thus, the procedure specified within the MTP was renamed within the White Book study period to MTP restart.

3.5 Management Inhibiting

It may happen that hardware or software failures, leading to an *out of service* of the link, only occur when user traffic is sent via the concerned link. After a successful restoration of the link (user traffic is not sent during that phase) the same failure situation occurs, leading to an unwanted oscillation of the link status, which will cause a lot of short-term changeover and changeback processes and related problems. On the one hand, a network operator would like to keep user traffic off the link in order to avoid the problems and, on the other hand, he would like to send test messages via that link in order to prove the proper working of the link. How could this be achieved?

User traffic can be taken off the link by applying management blocking of the link (see Sect. 3.3). However, when blocking the link, the Level 2 status is changed to *aligned* so that the sending of test messages via this link is not possible. Therefore, the management inhibiting procedure was introduced into the Red Book with the objective that an inhibited link is *unavailable* for user traffic whilst the Level 2 state of the link remains *in service*, so that the sending of test messages via that link is possible.

With this objective the following problems were present. In order to divert user traffic from an inhibited link, this link must be *unavailable* at Level 3, so that a changeover is performed. However, an inhibited link should also be *in service* at Level 2, so that the reception of the COO at the other side of the link causes the link to fail, which is in conflict with the above objective. This is why in the Red Book specification an inhibited link is considered to be *available* at Level 3, leading to the question of how to divert user traffic from this link.

According to the Red Book this was achieved by applying short-term processor outage, which leads to a changeover of user traffic to alternative links. After that changeover of user traffic, processor outage was removed. Now, the link would have been *available* again at Level 3 that, however, was *explicitly excluded in the Red Book*.

Note: The inconsistency within the Red Book is that an available link at Level 3 is not always available.

◇

Another problem with the Red Book specification lies in the fact that it is not clearly specified which end of the link has to perform the blocking. It could happen that either side relies on the other to perform the blocking, so that no traffic diversion is performed. Finally, the possibility of the outage and restart of an adjacent node, while a link is inhibited, has not been considered. At the restarting end, the inhibiting status of the link is deleted and user traffic is sent via the concerned link when the restart is finalized. If the other end of the link is the remote inhibiting side, it can happen that the inhibiting status at that end of the link exists for a long time, since the inhibiting status is only removed by a forced uninhibiting request due to the unavailability of a destination point, detected by the routing control. As a consequence, loss of bidirectionality with related problems could occur (see Sect. 12.6).

These problems were solved during the Blue Book study period. On the one hand, an inhibited link is considered to be *unavailable* at Level 3 so that the described inconsistency of the Red Book version has been removed. On the other hand, normal changeover is not applied in the case of management inhibiting, which might lead to an *out of service* of the link. Instead, time-controlled changeover is used so that, while timer T1 (see Appendix A) is running, the Level 2 buffers are cleared. Therefore, no message missequencing occurs when user traffic is diverted to alternative links when T1 expires. Finally, the inhibiting test procedures were introduced into the Blue Book version to handle a restart at the far end of the inhibited link.

During the White Book study period, the remaining interworking problem between Red Book and Blue Book versions of the inhibiting procedure were clarified. In this respect, it has been specified that *either side of the link is responsible for the diversion of its own traffic*, which means that the Red Book side has to perform blocking of the link. In addition, the Red Book version has to detect by itself the restart of the other end and to delete the local inhibiting status.

3.6 Load Sharing

Every signalling message is transferred via a well-defined signalling link according to the assigned routing information. In order to avoid congestion problems with links or route sets, respectively, the objective has been to distribute the traffic load nearly equally over the available links. To this end, the load sharing function was introduced into the Yellow Book.

Assuming that the traffic streams, as created by the different User Parts, are of about the same characteristic, the destination point code (DPC) of the destination node and the signalling link selection (SLS) field were considered to be sufficient as routing information. This assumption implied a considerable simplification of the load sharing mechanism, because the load distribution need not be performed user-specific and the message length need not be taken into account.

According to the specified load sharing mechanism signalling traffic is normally sent via one link set, or two in the case of load sharing via a combined link set, based on the DPC of the destination node. In national networks a combined link set can consist of more than two link sets. Within a link set (combined link set) traffic is distributed via the available links nearly equally by using the SLS field. According to the specified load sharing mechanism it follows that an equal loading of the links can only be achieved if the link set contains 1, 2, 4, 8 or 16 links.

Now, if a link set (combined link set) fails, the concerned traffic is diverted to an alternative link set (combined link set), if available. All possible link sets (combined link sets) towards the considered destination point have a predetermined priority.

That link set (combined link set) is used for the transfer of traffic to the considered destination point, which has the highest priority at the considered time. The link set (combined link set) used when no failure situations are present is called the normal link set (combined link set). In analogy, all links within a link set (combined link set) are assigned a priority. The link used when no failure situation is present is called the normal link. Every traffic stream, uniquely identified by the DPC and SLS, has its own normal link and normal link set (combined link set). Note that, according to the Blue Book specification, this assignment is *fixed and not changed* under failure situations, when traffic is diverted to alternative links and link sets.

However, during the White Book study period, we recognized that this fixed assignment between traffic streams and normal links could cause problems with load sharing. This is due to the fact that, if a link becomes available again, then *only those traffic streams are diverted to the newly available link by the changeback procedure for which this link is the normal link*. In the case of multiple failures this could lead to an asymmetric load distribution within the link set (combined link set). In order to avoid this problem, the White Book specification was changed with the objective of *having the best possible load distribution between the available links at any time*. According to this philosophy, the assignment between traffic streams and normal links can be changed during the changeback procedure and traffic streams can be diverted to non-normal links within a link set (combined link set), if needed.

Finally, according to the Blue Book specification, *all* Level 3 messages are assigned the SLC 0000. Furthermore, they are routed by the normal routing function using this signalling link code (SLC) as the SLS value for load sharing. During the White Book study period we recognized that the sending of floods of network management messages, occurring in large SS 7 networks in the case of, for example, an outage of large network areas, can cause problems with the flow control that could then lead to network outages (see Chap. 8).

In order to avoid this problem it was specified within the White Book that non-link-related Level 3 messages can be assigned *any* SLC value in order to enable load sharing of Level 3 messages.

3.7 The Status of the MTP Procedures

At this stage, the question is raised of whether the White Book MTP procedures now work well? To summarize, apart from the missing alignment of the signalling point and route set congestion control, which in fact is network dependent, the White Book MTP procedures work well:

- If no serious interworking problems with older versions occur
- If the fundamental assumptions, summarized in the previous chapters, are not violated by network planning and the specific use of the MTP in real networks.

As is shown in the following chapters, those violations may have serious consequences, e.g., a considerable reduction of network performance, an isolation or outage of large network areas, or an outage of the whole SS 7 network.

4

SS 7 over IP Networks

As has been mentioned in the introduction further work has been done in the IETF by developing the distributed IP telephony model which provides the framework for the convergence of the *voice world* of the PSTN and the *data world* of the Internet. In the following we describe this distributed IP telephony model, the signalling requirements for the transport of SCN protocols as well as the framework architecture for signalling transport.

4.1 The Distributed IP Telephony Model

For the convergence of the PSTN and IP-based networks and the realization of, for example, voice over IP (VoIP) [15] an overall signalling system for the call and bearer control is needed. The signalling system for the interconnection of digital exchanges in public telecommunication networks is the Signalling System No. 7 (SS 7). Since SS 7 can control several thousand connections and thus a high bandwidth, and since SS 7 offers the gateway to a large number of existing telephony and ISDN supplementary services as well as the IN services, SS 7 is the core signalling system. However, in the current IP protocol suite no signalling system exists that may be mapped onto SS 7. The reason is that, for the function of the SS 7 application protocols, e.g., ISUP, MAP or INAP protocols, it is required that signalling messages are delivered in sequence, without errors, loss, duplication or excessive time delay. This requires that failures within the network are detected and measures to assure signalling are taken very fast by an appropriate network management. Due to some limitations, these requirements are not completely fulfilled by the IP standard protocols like the transmission control protocol (TCP) [22].

The distributed IP telephony model [23] provides the framework for the convergence of PSTN and IP networks based on three network elements (see Fig. 4.1). The media gateway (MG) is the first element, which forms an interface between the IP network and circuit-switched networks that allows the flow of data between the different networks. Data, voice, audio or video information flows from circuit-switched networks have to be packetized in a media gateway before they can be transported to

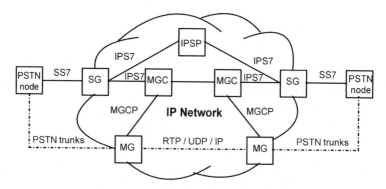

Fig. 4.1. The distributed IP telephony model

their final IP network destination, and vice versa. The second element is the media gateway controller (MGC) that controls the different media gateways and which is responsible for the information exchange between the different IP network elements. Finally, a third network element needed is the signalling gateway (SG) that transfers the signalling information between a PSTN node and a media gateway controller or an IP signalling point (IPSP), which may be an IP-resident database, or to another signalling gateway.

In order to carry SCN signalling messages transparently between the signalling gateway and the media gateway controller or IP signalling points the SCN messages are encapsulated in IP datagrams and transferred via an IP-based network. This SCN signalling transport (SIG) is called SS 7 over IP (IPS7) where the different protocol stacks are described in Chap. 5. In addition, signalling transport may also be applied to the MGC to MGC or MG to MGC interfaces, depending on the requirements for transport of the associated signaling protocol.

The media gateway controller performs the call control. In order to perform the connection control the media gateway controller and the media gateway are linked by the media gateway control protocol (MGCP) [24], which allows the transfer of commands to create, modify, and delete a connection. In Fig. 4.1 the functional model that separates the functions of the SG, MG, and MGC is shown. These functions may be implemented in separate physical units or may be combined within a physical unit, e.g., SG/MG functions or MG/MGC functions implemented in one unit.

4.2 Signalling Requirements

In order to assure the function of SS 7 application protocols, e.g., ISUP, MAP or INAP protocols, the transport of signalling messages across the IP network must fulfil the following signalling performance requirements:

- **Persistent associations**
  MTP routes are used by different applications to transport signalling messages that refer to many different calls. *Thus, like MTP routes, the IP-based transport associations should be persistent.*

- **Reliable transport of signalling messages**
  The SS 7 User Parts assume that the MTP provides a reliable transport of signalling messages in sequence, without errors, message loss, and duplication. In detail, it is expected that no more than 1 in 10^7 messages are lost, that no more than 1 in 10^{10} messages are delivered out of sequence, and that no more than 1 in 10^{10} messages contain an undetected error. *Thus, since no reliability actions are taken by the SS 7 User Parts, reliable transport of signalling messages is also subject to the underlying IP network transport functions.*

- **Time-dependent transport**
  Time-delayed SS 7 user messages are in most cases of no use, because the corresponding User Parts will time out and take alternative actions. The continuity test is one example of ISUP timer requirements. It requires that a tone generated at the sending end must be returned from the receiving end within 2 s of sending an IAM indicating continuity test. As a consequence one-way signalling message transport plus accompanying nodal functions must be accomplished within 2 s. In addition, MTP network management messages require a response time of 500–1200 ms, including round trip time and processing at the remote end. *Thus, there is a need to transport SCN signalling messages via IP networks without excessive time delay.*

- **Availability**
  The information exchange between SS 7 applications requires a high availability of the underlying SS 7 network. The availability of any signalling route set is expected to be at least 99.9998%, which means that the unavailability is 10 min per year or less. Within PSTNs, this is realized by alternative links and alternative MTP routes between the signalling points where the peer User Parts are located. Furthermore, failures within the network are detected and measures to assure signalling are taken very quickly by an appropriate network management. *In order to fulfil the SS 7 application requirements the same features are needed in IP-based networks.*

4.3 Framework Architecture for Signalling Transport

The framework architecture [16] that has been defined by SIGTRAN for switched circuit network (SCN) signalling message transport (SIG) over IP uses multiple components, as shown in Fig. 4.2. The three components are:

- The IP network layer
- The common signalling transport protocol
- The switched circuit network (SCN) adaptation modules

The SCN adaptation modules support the specific primitives required by a particular SCTP user. There are many SCN protocols which can be supported by the above-described modular structure. Since all SCN protocols have similar transport requirements, the protocol specific considerations are all treated in the adaptation modules.

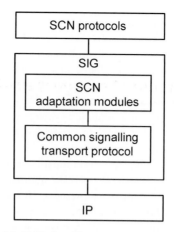

Fig. 4.2. IPS7 signalling transport components

Regarding the network convergence five adaptation modules are defined:

- The SS 7 MTP-2 user peer-to-peer adaptation layer (M2PA) that allows for full MTP-3 message handling and network management capabilities between any two SS 7 nodes, communicating over an IP network
- The SS 7 MTP-2 user adaptation layer (M2UA) that is suitable for the transport of MTP-3 messages over the IP network
- The SS 7 MTP-3 user adaptation layer (M3UA) that is suitable for the transport of MTP-3 user messages (ISUP, SCCP, TUP, etc.) over the IP network
- The SS 7 SCCP user adaptation layer (SUA) that is suitable for the transport of SCCP user messages (TCAP, RANAP, etc.) over the IP network
- The Q.921 user adaptation layer (IUA) that is suitable for the transport of ISDN Q.921 user messages (Q.931) over the IP network

They all use the services of the underlying reliable common signalling transport protocol, a realization of which is called stream control transmission protocol (SCTP) [18]. The SCTP is an application-level datagram transfer protocol that provides error control, sequence control and flow control functions required for the reliable transport of signalling messages over IP networks.

Note: The basic operation of SCTP is to run directly on top of IP. However, due to restrictions placed on implementers by operating systems, not all implementations may be able to run over IP directly. Instead, the SCTP messages are transported via the user datagram protocol (UDP) to the IP layer.

◇

5

SS 7 over IP Signalling Transport Protocol Architectures

The need has been identified for the transmission of SCN signalling messages from a signalling gateway (SG) to a media gateway controller (MGC) or an IP signalling point (IPSP), e.g., an IP-resident database, and between IPSPs. Within the SG, MTP-3, and SCCP functionality may be present or not. There are several applications foreseen for the use of SS 7 over IP: the realization of IP-based high-speed links, the migration of a PSTN network towards an IP-based network or the convergence of signalling and data networks, e.g., to improve the Internet access via PSTNs (see Chap. 14). For their realization, different protocol architectures are defined by SIG-TRAN using different SCN adaptation modules, which are described below.

5.1 Signalling Transport Using M2PA and IP-Based High-Speed Links

The increasing INAP traffic to SCPs, MAP traffic to HLRs or Internet traffic via SGs could cause congestion problems and problems with the flow control (see Sect. 12.3). In order to avoid these problems it is recommendable to use high-speed links between SCPs/HLRs/SGs and the intermediate SS 7 transfer nodes. In addition, these high-speed links are also important for the transfer of bulk data, e.g., operation, maintenance, and administration messages via the SS 7 network. Besides ATM-based high-speed links, with transmission rates of 150/600 Mbit/s, IP-based links could be used.

An IP link has to provide the complete MTP-2 functionality including a communication between layer management modules and to support the MTP-2/MTP-3 interface boundary. That protocol specified for the use between any two IP signalling points (IPSP), i.e., traditional SS 7 signalling points that communicate over an IP network, and which allows for full MTP-3 message handling and network management, is called SS 7 MTP-2 user peer-to-peer adaptation layer (M2PA) [25]. The M2PA uses the services of the SCTP. Figure 5.1 shows the protocol structure for IP-based links that transport MTP-3 messages between two IP signalling points. The MTP-3 is adapted to the SCTP using the M2PA. In this case, the SCTP association acts as

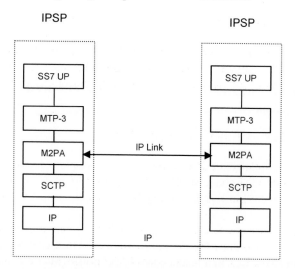

Fig. 5.1. IP-based SS 7 links using MTP-3

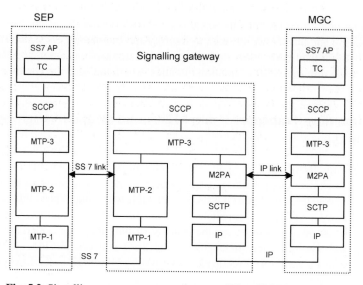

Fig. 5.2. Signalling message transport between SG and MGC using MTP-3

a normal SS 7 link between the IPSPs. In an IPSP, the SCCP or any SS7 User Part may be above the MTP-3.

According to the protocol structure shown in Fig. 5.2, a signalling gateway (SG) is an IPSP equipped with both traditional SS 7 links and IP-based links. When the M2PA is used, the transition between the SS 7 network and the IP network domain is performed via the MTP-3 at the SG, which acts as an STP. In order to provide the

SCCP functionality, e.g., global title translation (GTT), the SCCP can be present in the SG.

STPs may or may not be present in the SS 7 route between the SS 7 SEP and the SG. Since the IPSP contains the MTP-3 layer the IPSP must be represented by an SS 7 signalling point code, according to the MTP specification.

5.2 Signalling Transport Using M2UA

Another protocol architecture is specified for the transport of signalling messages over IP between the SG and a MGC, using the SS 7 MTP-2 user adaptation layer (M2UA) [26], as shown in Fig. 5.3. At the SG, no MTP-3 and SCCP functionality is available.

STPs may or may not be present in the SS 7 route between the SS 7 SEP and the SG. At the SG it is expected that the ISUP/SCCP messages are received from and transmitted to the PSTN over a standard SS 7 network interface including MTP-2, so that an SS 7 signalling link from an adjacent SS 7 SEP or STP terminates at the SG.

The M2UA uses the services of the SCTP. The SCTP allows a user-specified number of streams to be opened during the initialization of the SCTP association (see Sect. 7.2). For every SS 7 link terminating at the SG the M2UA as a user of the SCTP manages a uniquely identified SCTP stream. The nodal interworking function (NIF) within the SG provides the functional interworking of SS 7 transport functions with the IP signalling transport. Any incoming MTP-3 message received via a specific SS 7 link is mapped by M2UA on a uniquely identified stream within an association in order to transfer the signalling messages to an application server process (ASP) in the MGC where the peer MTP-3 is located, and vice versa (see Sect. 6.1.3). In this case, the SCTP association acts as a logical extension of the link set between

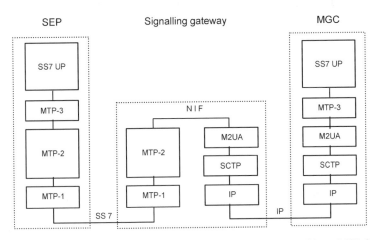

Fig. 5.3. Signalling message transport between SG and MGC without MTP-3

the SG and the adjacent SS 7 SEP or STP. In other words, the M2UA extends access to the MTP-2 layer services, available at the SG, to a remote IP-based application. The M2UA does not itself provide the full MTP-2 functions and services. In fact, the MTP-3 within the MGC is unaware that the expected MTP-2 services accessed via its lower layer interface at the MGC are offered remotely from the MTP-2 layer at the SG. In the same way, the MTP-2 at the SG is also unaware that its local MTP-3 is actually located in the MGC and accessed via M2UA. Using the terminology of traditional PSTN switches M2UA provides the node-internal interconnection between MTP-2 and MTP-3.

For the protocol architecture shown in Fig. 5.3 the SS 7 SEP and the MGC are adjacent nodes from the SS 7 point of view, connected via an extended direct link set. Furthermore, since the MGC contains the MTP-3 layer, the MGC functions as an IPSP, which must be represented by an SS 7 signalling point code, according to the MTP specification.

5.3 Signalling Transport Using M3UA

Transport of ISUP Messages

Figure 5.4 shows the transport of ISUP messages from an SS 7 SEP to an application server process (ASP) at the MGC via the SG using the MTP-3 and the SS 7 MTP-3 user adaptation layer (M3UA) [27]. In this example, the SG has no SCCP functionality.

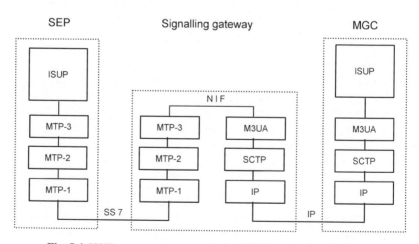

Fig. 5.4. ISUP message transport via the SG using MTP-3 and M3UA

At the SG, it is expected that the ISUP messages are received from and transmitted to the PSTN over a standard SS 7 network interface[1] including MTP-3, which is terminated at the SG. Thus, the SG is represented by an SS 7 signalling point code. The nodal interworking function (NIF) that sits above the MTP-3 in the SG serves to transport signalling messages within the SG between the MTP-3 and M3UA. The M3UA uses the services of the SCTP. The basic idea is that the M3UA extends access to the MTP-3 layer services, available at the SG, to a remote IP-based application, i.e., the M3UA does not itself provide the full MTP-3 functions and services.

Since the M3UA layer at the MGC provides the equivalent set of primitives as provided by the MTP-3 to its local User Parts the ISUP at the ASP is unaware that the MTP-3 services are offered remotely from the MTP-3 at the SG. In the same way, the MTP-3 at the SG may also be unaware that its local users are actually located at the MGC and accessed via M3UA. Using the terminology of traditional PSTN switches M3UA provides the node-internal interconnection between MTP-3 and its User Parts.

For internal SGP modelling, it is important whether the ASP at the MGC is addressed by its own SS 7 destination point code (DPC) or via the DPC of the SG. In the first case, the SG acts as an MTP transfer point for the ISUP messages from and to the ASP. The NIF transfers ISUP messages received at the SG from the MTP-3 routing function to the M3UA network address translation and mapping function (AMF) for ongoing routing to the ASP at the MGC, and vice versa. In the second case, the SG is considered from the SS 7 network as an SEP, where the ISUP peer at the MGC is logically located so that the SCTP association acts as an internal connection between the MTP-3 at the SG and the ISUP located at the MGC. The ISUP messages destined to the MGC are received by the NIF from the MTP-3 upper layer interface at the SG as MTP-TRANSFER indication primitives and are sent to the local M3UA message distribution function for the transfer to the final IP destination. In the same way, MTP-TRANSFER primitives received from the local M3UA network address translation and mapping function are sent by the NIF to the MTP-3 upper layer interface as MTP-TRANSFER request primitives for ongoing routing to the final SS 7 SEP.

Regarding the MTP-3 network management, it is required that the MTP-3 user located at the ASPs receive indications of SS 7 signalling point availability or unavailability, SS 7 network congestion, and User Part unavailability. To this end, the NIF delivers MTP-PAUSE, MTP-RESUME, and MTP-STATUS indication primitives, received at the local MTP-3 upper layer interface, to the local M3UA resident management function that is responsible for the transfer of the relevant network management information to the remote MTP-3 user lower layer interface at the ASP.

---

[1] The use of a traditional SS 7 signalling links is not the only possibility. Instead, ATM-based high-speed links or IP-based links could be used. Where ATM-based high-speed links are used, it is possible for the SG to use the services of the MTP-3b for reliable transport to and from an SS 7 SEP or STP. However, in this case it must be ensured that MTP-3b is used end-to-end between the SG and the SS 7 SEP.

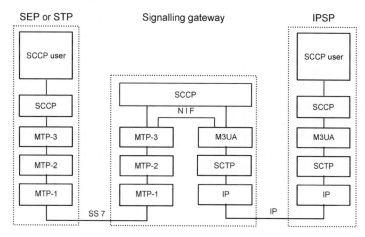

Fig. 5.5. Transport of SCCP messages between SG and MGC

Transport of SCCP Messages

The transport of SCCP messages via the SG using the SCCP functionality within the SG is shown in Fig. 5.5. The SCCP is adapted to the SCTP via the M3UA layer where all primitives between SCCP and MTP-3 are supported by this interface. At the SG, the SCCP may perform the global title translation (GTT) for messages received from the SS 7 network. If the result of the GTT yields an SS 7 DPC and possibly an SCCP subsystem number (SSN) for a peer SCCP located in the IP domain, a corresponding MTP-TRANSFER request primitive is sent to the local M3UA network address translation and mapping function (AMF) for ongoing routing to the final IP destination.

In a similar way, SCCP messages from peers in the IP network can be addressed to the SCCP within the SG for a GTT. These messages are forwarded from M3UA to the SCCP at the SG as an MTP-TRANSFER indication primitive. If the result of the GTT yields the destination address of a node in the SS7 network, then the corresponding MTP-TRANSFER request primitive is sent to the local MTP-3 at the SG for delivery to the final SS 7 destination. If, in the last case, the SCCP GTT yields the address of an SCCP peer in the IP domain, then the MTP-TRANSFER request primitive is sent back to the M3UA for transfer to the final IP destination.

Finally, the case is foreseen of exchange of SCCP user messages between two IPSPs using the SCCP as shown in Fig. 5.6. The SCTP is adapted to the SCCP layer via the M3UA, where all primitives between SCCP and MTP-3 are supported by this interface. Any MTP-PAUSE, MTP-RESUME, or MTP-STATUS indications given from M3UA to the SCCP are related to the status of the underlying SCTP association and IP network. In this case, the SCTP association acts as an MTP route set between the SEPs, where the SCCP peers are located.

However, in this case, the expected MTP-3 services are not offered remotely. The MTP-3 services are provided but, because of the simplified point-to-point relation-

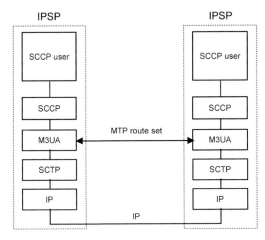

Fig. 5.6. Transport of SCCP messages between IPSPs using SCCP

ship, the full MTP-3 functionality is not needed so that the procedures offered are a subset of the MTP-3 procedures.

5.4 Signalling Transport Using SUA

Due to the ongoing integration of SCN networks and IP networks, the SCCP user adaptation layer (SUA) [28] has been defined to transport SCCP user messages (MAP, OMAP, INAP, etc.) over IP between the SG and an IPSP or between two IP-SPs. The difference from Figs. 5.5 and 5.6, where protocol architectures are shown for the transport of SCCP and SCCP user messages over IP using the SCCP and the services of M3UA, is that SUA does not need the SCCP layer.

SEP–IPSP Signalling Transport

In Fig. 5.7 the transport of SCCP user messages from an SS 7 SEP to an IPSP via the SG is shown.

At the SG, it is expected that the SCCP user messages are received from and transmitted to the PSTN over a standard SS 7 network interface including SCCP. The nodal interworking function (NIF) within the SG serves to transport signalling messages within the SG between the SCCP and SUA and provides seamless inter-working of SCCP management functions between the SG and the IPSP. The SUA uses the services of the SCTP and handles the SS 7 address to IP address mapping. At the IPSP the SUA layer provides the equivalent set of primitives as provided by the SCCP to its local users. Depending on the upper layer protocol supported, SUA will need to support SCCP connectionless and/or connection-oriented services.

In the case of connectionless transport of SCCP user messages destined for a peer in the IP domain there are two scenarios. On the one hand, the SG may act as an

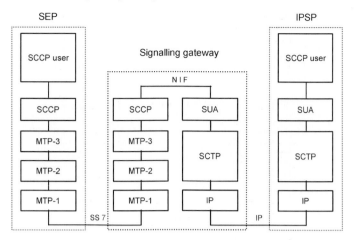

Fig. 5.7. SCCP user message transport via the SG using the SCCP and SUA

SCCP endpoint. In this case, the connectionless SCCP messages are routed on SPC and SSN. From the SS 7 network, the subsystem identified by the SSN and routing context is regarded to be local at the SG. In this case, the SCTP association acts as an internal connection between the SCCP at the SG and the SCCP user located at the IPSP. Based on the routing key the network address translation and mapping function (AMF) at the SGP transfers the SCCP message to the active ASP in the IP domain, which processes the SCCP message. On the other hand, the SG may act as an SCCP relay point so that a global title translation (GTT) must be executed at the SG. In this case, the actual location of the SCCP user is irrelevant to the SS 7 network. The GT translation yields an SCCP entity set, which now may contain one or more ASs. The selection of the AS is thus based on the SCCP called party address and possibly other SS 7 parameters depending on the implementation. Basically this means splitting the SS 7 traffic over different ASs based on GT information.

In the case of connection-oriented transport of SCCP user messages the SCCP and SUA layers interface in the SG to associate the two connection sections needed for the connection-oriented data transfer between an SEP and an ASP. The set up of both connection sections is performed when the CONNECT REQUEST message is routed from the SEP to an ASP or the other way round. Further messages for this connection are routed on DPC in the SS 7 section and on the IP address in the IP section. No other routing information is present in the SCCP or SUA messages themselves. The necessary information to forward messages from one section to another is kept within the SG.

All-IP Architecture

Finally, the transport of SCCP user messages between two IPSPs using SUA is foreseen, which is adapted to the simplified point-to-point relationship as shown in

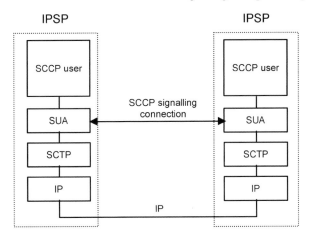

Fig. 5.8. Transport of SCCP user messages between IPSPs using SUA

Fig. 5.8. The SCTP is adapted to the SCCP user via the SUA where all primitives between the SCCP and SCCP user are supported by this interface. In this case, the SCTP association acts as an SCCP signalling connection between the IPSPs. This architecture allows extra flexibility in developing networks and removes the need for signalling gateway functionality.

6

SS7 over IP Signalling Network Architectures

In the last chapter it is described how SS 7 signalling messages may be transported over IP networks. In order to support the different applications, SCN adaptation modules are specified, which use the SCTP for their different purposes. In this chapter we discuss how the high availability and performance requirements for the SS 7 signalling message transport, described in Sect. 4.2, may be provided in the IP domain.

The SCTP cannot by itself provide the availability and performance of MTP-3, since the SCTP is an end-to-end protocol, which cannot guarantee the quality of service along the complete IP path taken by an SCTP message via a particular SCTP association. The SCTP can only try to increase the availability of the underlying IP network using multi-homing, which provides redundant communication between two SCTP endpoints in the event of failures along an IP path between the SCTP endpoints. In addition, the M2UA, M3UA, and SUA adaptation layer protocols are not designed to meet any performance and reliability requirements for the transport of SCN signalling messages.

Thus, in order to meet the stringent SS 7 signalling reliability and performance requirements, a network operator should ensure that no single point of failure is present in the end-to-end network architecture between an SS 7 node and an IP-based application. This can be achieved by distributed architectures and redundant network structures, e.g.,

- Through the use of redundant SGs
- By providing sufficient links in the link set from the SS 7 node to the SG
- By providing redundant IP network paths for SCTP associations
- By redundant hosts in the IP domain where the peer SS 7 application is located

Note, that when the M2PA is used the full MTP-3 functionality is also available in the IP domain to provide the required reliability and performance. Therefore, we concentrate in the following on physical network structures that may be used in the case of distributed ASPs, located in physically separated devices within the IP domain.

6.1 SS 7 User Part Representation and Addressing in the IP Domain

ISUP or SCCP messages received at the SG have to be transported to the peer User Part at a MGC or IPSP. To this end, this User Part must be uniquely addressable in the IP domain. Within the SS 7 network, any MTP-3 User Part is addressed by the destination point code (DPC) of the signalling point, where this User Part is located. The MTP-3 message distribution function at that destination node then uses the service indicator (SI) contained in the service information octet (SIO) to identify the considered local User Part.

In order to provide seamless interworking between MTP-3 User Parts within the SS 7 and the IP networks, the same addressing functionality must be provided in the IP domain. However, how are SS 7 User Parts represented in the IP domain, which addressing mechanism of MTP-3 User Parts are available in the IP-based network, and how can they be mapped onto the SS 7 addressing?

6.1.1 The Application Server and Application Server Process

In order to meet the stringent SS 7 reliability and performance requirements, the MTP-3 and its User Parts may be distributed in the IP domain over different hosts, where on every host normally many different applications are running. To this end, the MTP-3, ISUP or SCCP functionality provided by a signalling node may be partitioned, e.g., based on ISUP circuit identification code (CIC) values or database queries. This partial MTP-3 or user functionality is provided in the IP domain by an application server process (ASP), running on a host.

In order to avoid a single point of failure, at least two ASPs, resident on different hosts, should be available to handle the considered traffic. The logical collection of all ASPs that provide this partial MTP-3 or User Part functionality of a considered logical IP signalling point is called application server (AS). At the SG an application server is realized as a list that comprises all available ASPs that are capable of processing the relevant traffic. This range of traffic to be handled by a particular application server must be uniquely defined. For this, M3UA and SUA use a set of SS 7 parameters, e.g., SLS, SLC, DPC, SI, ISUP CIC value, SCCP SSN or TCAP transaction ID, which is called the routing key. Equally, M2UA uses the interface identifier that uniquely identifies the physical interface on the signalling gateway, i.e., an SS 7 link. Routing keys and the interface identifier should be unique in the sense that a received SS 7 message cannot be matched to more than one routing key/interface identifier, i.e., application server. A routing key or interface identifier may be configured using an implementation-dependent management interface or may be configured using dynamic registration and deregistration procedures, where ASPs may dynamically register or deregister at the SG as an ASP within an application server to handle a specific range of traffic.

Finally, an ASP may be configured to process signalling traffic related to more than one AS over a single SCTP association. At an ASP the routing context parameter is used to identify uniquely the range of signalling traffic associated with each AS.

6.1.2 The Signalling Point Management Cluster

Furthermore, many different MTP-3 User Parts can be present in a traditional SS 7 node (ISUP, SCCP, TUP, etc.), addressed by the same destination point code (DPC) and distinguished locally by the service indicator. Within the IP domain these local MTP-3 User Parts are represented by several application servers. Such a set or cluster of application servers, addressed by the same DPC, is called a signalling point management cluster (SPMC); for example, from the SS 7 point of view, a SPMC may provide the complete MTP-3 user services of a considered *distributed digital exchange* within the IP domain.

6.1.3 The Network Address Translation and Mapping Function

Finally, a SG has to direct SS 7 signalling messages received from an originating node in the SS7 domain to the peer layer within the IP domain. This is performed by the network address translation and mapping function (AMF) at the SG.

M3UA and SUA are comparing the SS7 address information contained in the MTP-3 user message (SLC, SLS, OPC, DPC, SIO, CIC, SSN, transaction ID, etc.) with routing keys available in the SG. The routing key then uniquely identifies the application server for a particular application and range of traffic. The application server list contains the active ASP(s) which finally identify the SCTP association for message transport that leads to the ASP where the peer User Part processes the message. Similarly, M2UA uses the interface identifier that uniquely identifies the application server as well as the specific stream within the association to the peer, on which the MTP-3 message should be sent. The list of ASPs in an AS is dynamic, i.e., may change during operation, taking into account availability, traffic-handling capability, and the congestion status of the individual ASPs as well as configuration changes. This mapping functionality is considered part of an adaptation layer but the way it is realized is considered to be implementation dependent.

For example, in order to transfer an ISUP message to the final IP destination, the DPC, service indicator, and the CIC value identify the AS, where the corresponding AS list at the SG contains the active ASP(s) where the peer ISUP is located, which is responsible for processing the ISUP message. Vice versa, an ASP must be able to send MTP-3 User Part messages via one or possibly more SGs to the SS 7 network destinations. To this end, the network address translation and mapping function at the MGC selects a proper SCTP association based on SS 7 routing information contained in the user message, the availability of signalling gateways, and signalling points in the SS 7 network, leading to a signalling gateway process (SGP) at a SG where the peer adaptation layer is running. This SGP is responsible for the ongoing transport of the considered ISUP message to the SS 7 domain using the nodal interworking function (NIF) at the SG (see Fig. 5.4). A signalling gateway may have more than one SGP which are, for example, responsible for the routing of signalling messages to different SS 7 networks, e.g., national or international networks, which are called network appearances.

As another example, the AMF is responsible for resolving the address presented in an incoming SCCP/SUA message to destinations within the IP network. The SUA AMF identifies the appropriate AS and selects an active ASP from the list of ASPs serving this AS and thus the appropriate SCTP association, which is determined based on the SS 7 routing information and the provided routing keys and routing contexts, local load sharing information, etc. The appropriate SUA message is then constructed and sent to the destination, which might be the end SUA node or a SUA relay node.

6.2 Application Server Redundancy

Application server redundancy requires maintenance of AS and ASPs as well as their states. In order to support high availability of call and transaction processing capabilities the network address translation and mapping function supports signalling process failover functions. In the following, we describe the AS and ASP states as well as the ASP failover model.

6.2.1 ASP States

All SS 7 signalling messages received at an SG from the SS 7 network are destined to an application server, which is uniquely identified by the provided routing keys and interface identifiers on the SG. The ASP in the IP domain, which is responsible for processing the received signalling messages, is then obtained from the AS list at the SG. The AS list contains all relevant ASPs, which may be in one of the following states:

- *ASP-ACTIVE*, i.e., the remote adaptation layer peer at the ASP is available and application traffic is processed;
- *ASP-INACTIVE*, i.e., the remote adaptation layer peer at the ASP is available and the SCTP association to the ASP is up but application traffic is stopped;
- *ASP-DOWN*, i.e., the remote adaptation layer peer at the ASP is unavailable and/or the related SCTP association is down.

The state of each remote ASP is maintained in the adaptation layer in the SGP. The state of an ASP in a particular AS can change due to the following specific events:

- Reception of messages from the peer adaptation layer at the ASP
- Reception of ASP state maintenance (ASPSM) and ASP traffic maintenance (ASPTM) messages
- Reception of indications from the SCTP layer, e.g., an SCTP communication down indication
- Local management interventions

6.2.2 AS States

Depending on the states of the ASPs the AS can be in one of the following states:

- *AS-ACTIVE*, i.e., at least one of its ASPs is in the *active* state, so that the AS is available and processes signalling messages;
- *AS-INACTIVE*, i.e., at least one of its ASPs is in the *inactive* state but none is *active,* so that the AS is available but no application traffic is processed;
- *AS-DOWN*, i.e., all of its ASPs are in the *down* state so that the AS is unavailable;
- *AS-PENDING*, i.e., the last remaining active ASP in the AS has transitioned to the *inactive* or *down* state. In this case, a recovery timer $T(r)$ is started and incoming messages are buffered. If another ASP becomes active before $T(r)$ expires, the AS enters the *active* state again, $T(r)$ is stopped and the buffered messages are sent to the new active ASP. If, however, $T(r)$ expires the SG discards all messages for the AS, which then moves to the *inactive* or *down* state, depending on its ASP states.

The state of the AS is maintained in the adaptation layer at the SGP. The AS state can change caused by the following events:

- ASP state transition
- Recovery timer triggers

6.2.3 Maintenance of ASP and AS States

The ASP/AS status is stored inside the adaptation layer on both the SG and MGC or IPSP sides. The layer management may use the M-ASP_STATUS and M-AS_STATUS primitives to request the status of an ASP or AS from the adaptation layer or the adaptation layer may use these primitives to indicate the status of an ASP or AS to the layer management. Furthermore, the layer management may change the status of an ASP using the M-ASP_UP, M-ASP_DOWN, M-ASP_ACTIVE and M-ASP_INACTIVE request primitives, so that the local ASP management (ASPM) of the adaptation layer can convey the ASP state change to the peer layer at the SG using the ASP state maintenance (ASPSM) and ASP traffic maintenance (ASPTM) messages. All ASP maintenance messages are sent on SCTP stream 0 whilst the ASP traffic maintenance messages can be sent on any stream. The peer layer at the SG will inform its local layer management of an ASP/AS state change by the corresponding layer management messages.

ASP State Maintenance

After an ASP has successfully established an SCTP association to an SGP it sends an ASP-UP (ASPUP) message to the SG, which indicates that the peer adaptation layer on the ASP is available, and starts the acknowledgement timer $T(ack)$ (for timer values see Appendix A).

When the SGP receives the ASPUP message it moves the remote ASP from the *down* to the *inactive* state and informs its layer management with an M-ASP_UP indication primitive. In addition, the SGP sends an ASPUP ACK message in response to the received ASPUP message. If for any local reason the SGP cannot respond with an ASPUP ACK the SGP responds with an ERROR message indicating the reason.

When the ASP receives the ASPUP ACK it informs its local layer management with an M-ASP_UP confirm primitive. If the ASP does not receive the ASPUP ACK within T(ack) the ASP may resend the ASPUP message and restart T(ack) until it receives an ASPUP ACK message.

When an ASP wishes to be removed from service in all AS of which it is a member it will send an ASP-DOWN (ASPDN) message to the SGP and starts timer T(ack). When the SGP receives the ASPDN message it marks the ASP as *down* and informs the local layer management with an M-ASP_DOWN indication primitive. Furthermore, the SGP sends an ASPDN ACK message in response to the received ASPDN message. If the ASP does not receive the ASPDN ACK within T(ack) it may resend the ASPDN message and restart T(ack) until it receives an ASPDN ACK message.

ASP Traffic Management

Any time after an ASP has received an ASPUP ACK message the ASP, which is ready to start processing traffic, sends an ASP-ACTIVE (ASPAC) message to the SGP and starts the acknowledgement timer T(ack). When an ASP wishes to register for more than one AS the ASPAC message contains a list of one or more routing context/interface identifier parameters to indicate for which AS the ASPAC message applies. Alternatively, the ASP may acitvate within an AS independently, by sending multiple ASP-ACTIVE messages. If the ASPAC message does not contain a routing context/interface identifier the ASP must know by configuration to which AS it belongs.

When the SGP receives the ASPAC message(s) it moves the ASP to the *active* state and takes further actions, depending on the AS traffic handling mode (see Sects. 7.4.2, 7.5.2, and 7.6.2). Furthermore, the SGP informs its layer management with an M-ASP_ACTIVE indication primitive that the peer ASP is *active*. Finally, the SGP sends an ASPAC ACK message in response to the received ASPAC message(s) for the application servers that the ASP can successfully activate. Data messages received by the SGP before an ASP ACTIVE message is received may be discarded.

When the ASP receives the ASPAC ACK message it informs its local layer management with an M-ASP_ACTIVE confirm primitive about the state change. If the ASP does not receive the ASPAC ACK within T(ack) the ASP may resend the ASPAC message and restart T(ack) until it receives an ASPAC ACK message. Note that an ASP must not send data messages before an ASPAC ACK is received.

When an ASP decides to stop processing traffic within an AS it sends an ASP-INACTIVE (ASPIA) message to the SGP and starts the acknowledgement timer T(ack). When the ASP is processing traffic for more than one AS one or more routing context/interface identifier parameters in the ASPIA message are used to indicate for which AS the ASP would like to deactivate. If the ASPIA message does not contain a routing context/interface identifier the ASP must know by configuration to which AS it belongs.

When, in the override mode, another ASP has already taken over the traffic within the AS, the ASP that sends the ASPIA message is already considered by the SGP to be *inactive*. In the case of a loadshare mode, the SG moves the ASP to the *inactive* state. Depending on the load sharing algorithm used the AS traffic is reallocated across the remaining *active* ASPs within the AS. When the broadcast mode applies the SGP moves the ASP to the *inactive* state and a broadcast of the AS traffic is only performed to the remaining active ASPs. After ensuring that all traffic to the ASP is stopped the SGP sends an ASPIA ACK message to the ASP and informs its layer management with an M-ASP_INACTIVE indication primitive.

When the ASP receives the ASPIA ACK message it informs its layer management with an M-ASP_INACTIVE confirm primitive. If the ASP does not receive the ASPIA ACK within T(ack) the ASP may resend the ASPIA message and restart T(ack) until it receives an ASPIA ACK message.

Note: An SG may be composed of one or more SGPs that are capable of routing SS 7 traffic. The M3UA or SUA layer at the MGC or IPSP maintains the availability status of each SGP at the SG, taking into account configuration changes or SGP failures. There is, however, no M3UA or SUA messaging to manage the status of an SGP. Whenever an SCTP association to a SGP exists the SGP is assumed to be available.

◇

As an example, Fig. 6.1 shows the message flow for an ASP activation between an SGP and two ASPs in the same AS where the active/standby traffic handling mode applies. To this end, ASP1 is configured to be active, processing the traffic received for the particular AS whilst ASP2 is the standby, taking over the traffic in the case of communication failure or withdrawal from service of ASP1.

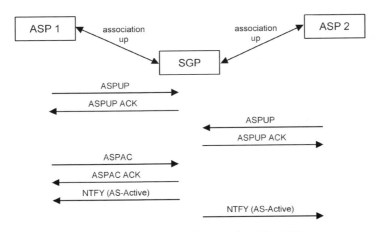

Fig. 6.1. ASP activation for active/standby ASPs

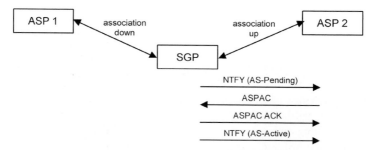

Fig. 6.2. ASP traffic failover through an SCTP failure

Figure 6.2 shows the message exchange for the failover to ASP2 in the case that the SCTP association to ASP1 fails. When the SGP detects an SCTP failure, and thus a loss of the peer adaptation layer, the exchange of ASPIA and ASPIA ACK messages between the SGP and ASP1 will not occur.

6.2.4 ASP Failover and Failback

The SCN adaptation layers support ASP failover to assure high availability of call and transaction processing capability. In more detail, they support an $n + k$ redundancy model, which means that n redundant ASPs are necessary to handle the signalling traffic and k ASPs are available to take over signalling traffic in the case of an active ASP failure. The $1 + 1$ model, for example, may be applied in two modes (see also Fig. 6.3):

Override Mode

In the override mode one ASP in the AS is *active* and processes application traffic. The AS list for the override or active/standby mode may be as shown below:

Routing Key ($DPC = Z$, $SI = 0101$) - Application Server #1 "ISUP"

ASP 1 / Host 1 : State = *active*
ASP 2 / Host 2 : State = *inactive*

In this case, all incoming ISUP messages with $DPC = Z$ would be sent to ASP 1 in host 1. If ASP 1 becomes *unavailable*, failover is performed, i.e., the ASP 2 in host 2 will be brought into the *active* state and following ISUP messages are sent to ASP 2. If ASP 1 becomes *available* again, failback may be performed, i.e., traffic is sent again to ASP 1 when it is *active* again and ASP 2 is brought into the *inactive* state again.

Loadshare Mode

In the loadshare mode application traffic is shared between two or more ASPs in the AS. The AS list for the loadshare mode is shown below:

SG

MGC

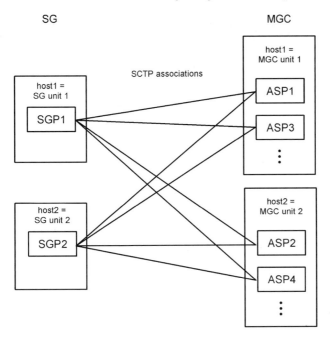

Fig. 6.3. Alternative SCTP associations for signalling transport between SG and MGC

Routing Key $(DPC = Z, SI = 0101)$ - Application Server #1 "ISUP"

ASP 1 / Host 1 : State $= active$
ASP 2 / Host 2 : State $= active$

In this case, both ASPs handle user traffic, which is shared between both *active* ASPs. In the case of a failure of ASP 1, ASP 2 takes over the whole user traffic. When ASP 1 becomes available again failback of user traffic is performed to loadshare the traffic again.

Note: In the case of call processing it should be assured that stable calls do not fail in the process of failover or failback. This requires communication between the involved ASPs.

◇

6.3 Signalling Point Code Representation

According to the MTP specification, every node that contains the MTP-3 layer must be assigned an SS 7 signalling point code (SPC). As a consequence, for the protocol structures shown in Figs. 5.1, 5.2, and 5.3 using M2PA and M2UA, ASPs within MGCs and IPSPs must be addressable via the SS 7 SPCs of the MGC or IPSP. For the protocol structures shown in Figs. 5.4, 5.5, and 5.7 the SG terminates the MTP-3 layer and is therefore a signalling point in the SS 7 network, identified by an SPC. This SPC is also used to address any local MTP-3 user at the SG, e.g., the SCCP. Furthermore, an SG is charged with representing a set of nodes in the IP domain to the SS 7 network for routing purposes. The question of how remote MTP-3 or SCCP users located at MGCs or IPSPs are addressed is related to the question of whether for the considered protocol structures ASs are assigned their own SPCs or not.

M3UA and SUA do not place any restrictions on the SS 7 point code representation of an AS. On the one hand, an AS can be addressed by the same SPC of the SG. In this case, the peer MTP-3 or SUA user in the SS 7 network considers the AS to be a user located at the SG and, from the SS 7 point of view, the SG acts as an SEP. On the other hand, an AS can be addressed by an individual SPC or grouped with other ASs to form an SPMC for point code preservation purposes. In this case, the SG acts as an STP or SCCP relay point for routing signalling messages to the considered ASs in the IP domain. Finally, a SG may be logically partitioned to operate in multiple SS 7 network appearances. In this case, the SG is assigned a separate SPC in each network appearance.

6.4 Physical Network Architectures

6.4.1 Alternative SCTP Associations

Application server redundancy is a key element to provide the SS 7 availability requirement. In order to avoid a single point of failure, at least two ASPs should be part of an AS. ASPs and SGPs are SCTP endpoints, i.e., an SGP has exactly one SCTP association to every ASP. In order to avoid AS unavailability due to the failure of a host, the ASPs of an AS should be resident in separate hosts, called media gateway control units (MGCU), and therefore available over different SCTP associations. Thus, in order to provide AS redundancy, a physical network structure is needed.

The SCN adaptation layers are designed to be flexible enough to allow their operation and management in a variety of physical configurations. This enables network operators to meet their performance and reliability requirements. In Fig. 6.3 a network structure is shown to support the $1 + 1$ redundancy model *active/standby* described in Sect. 6.2.4. In this example, the MGC is distributed over two hosts, which may be regarded as MGC units 1 and 2. In order to support ASP failover the SGP1/SGP2 of the SG have two SCTP associations leading to ASP 1 and ASP 2 of the considered AS in both MGC units.

6.4.2 Signalling Gateway Redundancy

In order to avoid the unavailability of an AS within the IP domain due to a failure of the SG, it may consist of more than one signalling gateway processes (SGP) distributed over several hosts (see Fig. 6.3), called signalling gateway units (SGU).

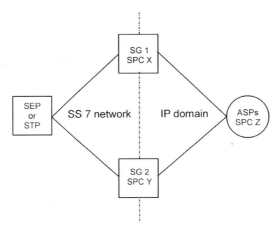

Fig. 6.4. Signalling gateway redundancy

Thus, a signalling gateway may be considered as a cluster of hosts acting as a single distributed signalling gateway. Furthermore, several independent SGs may be distributed over this cluster of signalling gateway units.

In the case that an SGP loses its SS 7 connectivity and if other SGPs exist to take over the traffic, the SGP may terminate the SCTP associations to the concerned ASPs. In this case, an ASP may reroute signalling traffic via an alternative SGP to the SS 7 network. A loadshare model is also possible in which signalling traffic to the SS 7 network is shared between multiple SGPs. When an ASP is configured to use multiple SGPs for the transmission of traffic to the SS7 network, the ASP must maintain the availability information and knowledge of the capability of the SGPs to handle traffic to specific destinations. This information may also be used to avoid congestion situations.

If the ASPs of an AS are available to the SS 7 network via more than one SG, each with its own SPC, the AS should be addressed by a different SPC (see Fig. 6.4). This requires that the MTP-3 layer is present at the SG, which means that the protocol structure shown in Fig. 5.3 using M2UA is excluded (see also Chap. 14).

In this case, both SGs would act as an STP or SCCP relay point for the transfer of signalling messages to the AS in the IP domain. Thus, if SG 1, for example, fails, a normal changeover or rerouting at the adjacent SS 7 node can be performed to transfer the relevant signalling messages via SG 2 to the considered ASP.

7

SS7 over IP Protocol Description

In the last section, different protocol architectures for signalling transport over IP as well as specific network structures to assure the stringent SS 7 signalling reliability and performance requirements are considered. We are now going to describe in more detail the different protocols used within these architectures, i.e., the Internet protocol (IP) as well as the new SIGTRAN signalling message transport protocols needed for the signalling transport, as far as this is needed in the following sections.

7.1 Internet Protocol

The Internet protocol (IP) [17] is the very cornerstone of the Internet protocol suite. IP is rich in freatures and provides the services and functions that all other protocols use. It is connectionless in nature and offers an unreliable, best efforts delivery system to higher layers. Given that IP itself has no error reporting mechanism, it is the responsibility of the upper layer protocols to provide reliability. Nevertheless, some low-level reporting is required which, however, is outside the scope of the protocol. This functionality is provided by the Internet control message protocol, which is considered to be integral to IP itself. It should be noted that the Internet protocol suite does not define any new network technologies. Instead, it is independent of the underlying local area network (LAN) technology, e.g. Ethernet (10 Mbit/sec), Token Ring (16 Mbit/sec), ATM etc. In order to map the IP addressing scheme to that used by the underlying network technology itself, the address resolution protocol is applied. In the following, we describe in more detail Internet addressing, IP routing principles, IP services and functions, the IP datagram structure, and the Internet control message protocol.

7.1.1 Internet Addressing

In order to allow the exchange of information, each station on a network must have a unique address. In order to make that address independent of the underlying LAN technology, the Internet protocol uses its own addressing scheme that is described in the following.

7.1.1.1 IP Addresses

An IP address consists of 32 bits[1]. In the case of decimal representation of the IP address, the four octets are separated by decimal points. An example of an IP address is 161.12.231.4 . In order to make the available address space as flexible as possible, the IP address is divided into a universally administered network ID and a locally administered host ID. We distinguish three types of IP addresses based on the most significant bits in the address.

Class A Address

When the most significant bit is '0', a class A address is present and the remaining 7 bits of the highest-order octet are used as a network ID, whilst the remaining 24 bits represent the host ID. With class A addresses a small number of networks may be created, each supporting a large number of hosts.

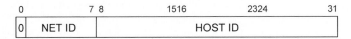

Fig. 7.1. Class A address

Since no network ID of all zeros is allowed and since the network address 127 is reserved for loop-back testing, class A addresses always have a leading octet in the range of 1 to 126. Generally, a host ID of all zeros must not be assigned to a host, since this is used to identify a network. For example, the IP address 12.0.0.0 identifies class A network 12. Finally, a host ID of all ones must not be assigned to a host since this means a broadcast to all stations of a network. To summarize, an example of a class A address is 12.250.120.16, meaning host 250.120.16 on network 12.0.0.0 .

Class B Address

Where the most significant bit pattern is '10', a class B address is implied. This means that the next 14 bits of the address are being used for the network ID and the remaining 16 bits for the host ID. With class B addresses a moderate number of networks may be created, each supporting a moderate number of hosts.

---

[1] IP addresses are now in extremely short supply. The next generation of IP, called IP version 6, increases the address length from 32 to 128 bits. However, while this solves the problem of address space, it creates other problems coming from the incompatibility. Hosts that need to talk to those running older implementations would need to either implement both versions of IP address or gateways would need to be implemented that could convert between the two.

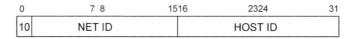

Fig. 7.2. Class B address

For class B addresses, the first octet will always be in the range 128 to 191. An example of a class B address is 129.16.12.8, meaning host 12.8 on network 129.16.0.0 .

Class C Address

Class C addresses are indicated by the most significant bits of the address being set to '110'. Then the next 21 bits are used to identify the network ID and the remaining 8 bits to identify the host ID. With class C addresses a large number of networks may be created, each supporting a small number of hosts.

Fig. 7.3. Class C address

Thus, the first octet of a class C address will always be in the range 192 to 223. An example of a class C address is 220.116.3.180, meaning host 180 on network 220.116.3.0 .

Remark: The remaining addresses are used for multicasting and experimentation.

◇

The classes and rules described so far show that certain constraints have been placed on the available address space. For instance, there are only 126 possible class A network addresses available or, when using class C addresses, each network can support only 254 hosts. Note, however, that if a network operator is setting up a private IP network that requires no communication with outside systems, then any IP addresses may be chosen and assigned to each device in a unique way.

7.1.1.2 Subnetting

The IP address described so far consists of two levels of hierarchy, namely the network ID and the host ID. However, there is the ability to define a further level of hierarchy, the subnet, allowing hosts to reside on subnets, which in turn may be grouped together to form a network. When is subnetting desirable? If, for example, a network operator wishes to interconnect LANs using point-to-point links that have only one station at each end or if a network operator would like to employ different LAN technologies, it would be of advantage to assign those logical groupings of stations their own subnet ID.

Subnetting is achieved by partitioning the host ID portion of the IP address using a programmable 32 bit subnet mask. This subnet mask identifies which bits in the address should be considered as host ID bits and which are used as subnet and network IDs. In particular, all bits of the subnet mask set to 1 indicate that the corresponding bits of the IP address are network or subnetwork ID bits whilst the bits of the subnet mask set to 0 indicate that the corresponding bits of the IP address belong to the host ID. For example, the class B address 158.152.30.248 with subnet mask 255.255.255.0 means host 248 on subnet 158.152.30.0 of network 158.152.0.0 .

7.1.1.3 MAC/IP Address Translation

On the one hand, every device is uniquely assigned an IP address whilst, on the other hand, every device is attached to a LAN, thus having in addition a six-octet physical or media access control (MAC) address. We therefore need to translate an IP address into the MAC address. However, because of incompatible address lengths, incompatible representations of LAN addresses, and the susceptibility to change this translation is not straightforward.

The Internet protocol uses the address resolution protocol (ARP) [29] that allows dynamic mapping of IP to MAC addresses over any broadcast LAN network. The ARP allows any station to determine the MAC address of any target host on the same network knowing only the target's IP address. To this end, the source station broadcasts an ARP request message on its network, which contains its own MAC and IP address as well as the IP address of the destination station whose MAC address is unknown. Since Ethernet, Token Ring, etc. are broadcast networks all stations will receive the ARP frame. Only the considered destination station will recognize its IP address in the destination address field of the ARP request and will then send an ARP response message back to the source station that now includes both the IP address and the requested MAC address of the destination station. Both stations now know the IP and MAC address pairs of the peer, which are stored in an ARP cache and may now be reused as required.

7.1.1.4 Multi-homing

So far, we have seen that an IP address is uniquely assigned to a particular network device, i.e., a host or a gateway. However, a device may have multiple network interfaces where the different parts should each connect to a different network. In this case, the device is said to be multi-homed. Multi-homing allows the use of different routes from an originating host to a destination host, thus increasing the availability of a connection. It requires, that our device be assigned several IP addresses, one for each network connection. Thus, although an IP address uniquely identifies a device, it would be more precise to say that it identifies one of the physical connections of that device.

7.1.2 Routing Principles

The motivation behind any addressing scheme is to allow the exchange of data between any communicating hosts. For such communication the IP addresses of the source and destination hosts are needed. Each device will know its own IP address since this is part of the device configuration. The destination IP address is normally provided by the application process with the message to be transferred.

Direct and Indirect Routing

Once the data is ready for transmission, it is passed together with the IP address of the destination host to the IP layer of the source host. The IP then identifies whether the destination host resides on the same network, or subnetwork when subnetting applies, as itself. This is done by examining the high-order bits of the source and destination IP address, which yield the class and therefore the network ID and host ID part. In the case of subnetting, the subnet mask yields the host ID and the subnet ID. If the result of the comparison indicates that both hosts reside on the same network/subnetwork, the message is delivered directly to the destination host via the local network port of the source host. This process is called direct routing. Where the result of the comparison indicates that the destination host resides on a different network/subnetwork, the message is sent from the source host to a router, which is responsible for the onward routing and eventual delivery to the destination host. This process is called indirect routing. Thus, stations need to be preconfigured not only with their own IP address but also with the IP address of a router.

Router

A router is a relay station which has more than one physical interface and is connected to multiple networks. When a router receives a message it determines whether it can deliver the message directly to a destination host on one of the networks to which it is connected. If not, it will pass the message to another router to onward route the message. To this end, routers maintain routing tables that list those networks that are reachable. Since routers are concerned with the interconnection of networks they are also called gateways. In this way, the message is passed from router to router until it eventually arrives at a router that is able to deliver it directly to the destination host. The set of routers and interconnecting networks a message takes from the source host to the destination host is called an IP route. Finally, the IP incorporates the concept of type of service, which allows applications to request that particular routes are chosen such to meet specific requirements on throughput, reliability or delay.

Static and Default Routes

For routing purposes each router uses its routing table of network IDs and how the networks may be reached. However, when a router is first powered on, it will not know much about the environment in which it is operating. It will have been pro-grammed with IP addresses for each of its ports and some preprogrammed static routes, which means that the router will know the route to some distant destina-tion networks. On the one hand, while this is sufficient for small static networks, no account can be made for changes that may occur. On the other hand, it would be impractible to hold reachability information about every network in the case of large backbone networks. Thus, if a router has no specific routing information for a target network, it directs messages via a programmed default route to a router that is able to onward route the message.

Routers use adaptive routing through the application of routing protocols to dynamically learn about reachable networks by exchanging information with their neighbors. A router tells its neighbors to which networks it has a direct connection and therefore to which networks it can directly route messages. Its neighbors update their routing tables correspondingly and in turn provide information about the net-works they can reach. These neighbors also inform their neighbors of the new routes and, in this way, information is propagated through the whole network.

7.1.3 IP Services and Functions

The Internet protocol (IP) is a connectionless datagram delivery system, which means that each message, called a datagram, is delivered in isolation, even with ref-erence to other related datagrams. IP does not offer connections or logical circuits. Furthermore, the datagram delivery service is unreliable in the sense that the IP pro-tocol does not guarantee that a datagram will ever arrive at its destination. Neverthe-less, the Internet protocol has become an extremely robust and versatile protocol. In the following, we describe in short the services and functions provided by IP.

Basic Datagram Delivery

The basic service IP offers to its users is the transfer of user data, which are encap-sulated in IP datagrams and transferred connectionless from the source host to the destination host. This datagram delivery service is unreliable because

- Datagrams may be duplicated or arrive out of sequence at the destination host,
- IP provides no acknowledgements, and
- Datagrams may be lost or legitimately discarded due to insufficient resources, without informing the source host.

Fragmentation

Fragmentation of a datagram applies where a datagram must travel across a network whose maximum transmission unit (MTU) size is smaller than the datagram length. Each fragment (except the last) must contain a multiple of eight octets and must be at least eight octets long. Reassembly will take place only at the destination host. Note, that fragments are treated as datagrams in their own right, they may arrive at the destination host out of order and may even be refragmented, if required. So, how can a datagram be reassembled at the destination host?

To overcome this problem, all fragments of a datagram are identified by the same datagram number, contained in the *IDENTIFICATION* field of the datagram header. In addition, every fragment is assigned the *FRAGMENT OFFSET* field, which identifies the octet number after which the considered fragment should be inserted into the overall datagram structure. Thus, the *FRAGMENT OFFSET* field of the first fragment is zero and the *MORE FRAGMENT FLAG* is set, indicating that one or more fragments follow. The last fragment is identified by the *MORE FRAGMENT FLAG* being not set.

If the first fragment of a multifragment datagram is received, the destination host will allocate buffer space, start the reassembly timer, and insert received fragments at their correct position. All fragments have to be received before this timer expires. If this timer expires because some of the fragments are lost or delayed all fragments received so far will be discarded and an ICMP message sent to the source host (see Sect. 7.1.5).

Type of Service

IP users may request a certain quality of service provided by the network between the source and destination host regarding delay, throughput, and reliability. In this respect, the *TYPE OF SERVICE* field of the datagram is used. It contains three precedence bits that allow a user to specify the importance of the considered datagram and may therefore be used to give priority to network control traffic over normal user data. Eight precedence levels are available that range from 0 for *routine datagram delivery* through to 7 for *network control*. The D (0 = normal delay, 1 = low delay), T (0 = normal throughput, 1 = high throughput) and R (0 = normal reliability path, 1 = high reliability path) bits are used to specify the requested delay, throughput, and reliability, respectively. If multiple routes exist to a given network and if the routing protocol supports the type of service concept, these bits would be used to determine the best path for providing the best overall performance.

Time-to-Live

Within an IP network, there is always the possibility that a routing loop exists or that a datagram may not be deliverable. In order to avoid problems the *TIME-TO-LIVE* field provides a self-destruct timer which indicates the maximum time a datagram is allowed to exist in the network. In fact, the *TIME-TO-LIVE* field is used as a hop counter where its value fixes the number of router hops that the datagram is allowed to take. If a router receives a datagram this value is decremented by one as the datagram is processed. If the value has been decremented to zero, the datagram is discarded and an ICMP message is sent to the source host (see Sect. 7.1.5).

Header Checksum

In order to ensure that the control information contained in the IP datagram header has arrived either at the destination or some intermediate router correctly, IP checks the information contained in the *HEADER CHECKSUM* field. Note, that since the *TIME-TO-LIVE* field is modified each time the datagram is processed by a router, the *HEADER CHECKSUM* must also be recomputed by each router enroute to the destination.

Options

IP provides a number of options like

- *Loose* or *strict source routing*, where the source host may define the route a datagram should take to its destination
- *Record route*, which allows the route taken by a datagram to be recorded
- The *Internet timestamp*, which allows a host to determine delay times between itself and intermediate hosts

Error Reporting

Although IP itself has no inherent error reporting mechanism there is, however, a further protocol called Internet control message protocol (ICMP) that conveys messages about errors and other conditions and that is considered to be an integral part of IP (see Sect. 7.1.5).

7.1.4 The IP Datagram Structure

An IP datagram consists of the IP header and the IP data field. The general format of an IP datagram is shown in Fig. 7.4.

Version Field

The four-bit *VERSION* field identifies the version of the IP protocol, e.g., IP version 4 or 6, and therefore the format of the IP header.

Internet Header Length

The length of the IP header in 32-bit words is specified by the four-bit *INTERNET HEADER LENGTH* field. In addition, it indicates where the IP data begin. In the absence of options, the header will be 20 octets long, so that the IP header length is 5.

Type of Service

The 8-bit *TYPE OF SERVICE* field allows hosts to define the desired quality of service.

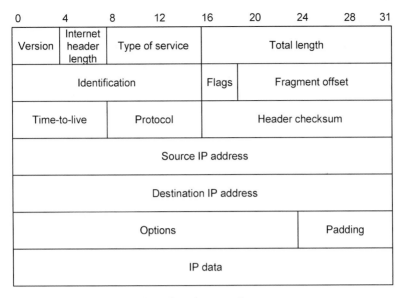

Fig. 7.4. IP datagram format

Total Length

The 16-bit *TOTAL LENGTH* field is measured in octets. It describes the total length of the datagram for both header and data. Since this field is 16 bits long the maximum datagram size is 2^{16} or 64 kbit. Although this upper bound is not used, all hosts must be able to accept datagrams of up to 576 octets. Equally, hosts must only send datagrams that exceed 576 octets if they are sure that the destination host can process the received larger datagrams.

Identification

The *IDENTIFICATION* field contains a 16-bit integer that uniquely identifies the datagram and each of its fragments in the case of datagram fragmentation.

Flags

The *FLAG* field provides three bits where

- The first bit is reserved and will currently be zero,
- The second *DO NOT FRAGMENT* bit indicates that under no circumstances must this datagram be fragmented and
- The third *MORE FRAGMENTS FOLLOW* bit is used when datagrams have to be fragmented (see Sect. 7.1.3).

Fragment Offset

The 13-bit *FRAGMENT OFFSET* field informs destination hosts of the relative position of the received datagram fragment within the overall datagram structure.

Time-to-Live

The 8-bit *TIME-TO-lIVE* field indicates the number of routing hops the datagram is allowed to take.

Protocol

The 8-bit *PROTOCOL* field indicates the IP user protocol to which the data field should be delivered.

Header Checksum

The 16-bit *HEADER CHECKSUM* field is used to provide an integrity check on the IP datagram header.

Source and Destination Address

The 32-bit *SOURCE ADDRESS* and *DESTINATION ADDRESS* fields identify the source and destination hosts of the datagram.

Options

Using the variable-length *OPTIONS* field multiple options may be specified in the IP datagram header (see Sect. 7.1.3).

Padding

The length of the *PADDING* field may be between one and three octets. It is used to ensure that the datagram header ends on a four octet boundary.

7.1.5 The Internet Control Message Protocol

The Internet protocol does not have any inherent error reporting mechanism. Instead, for sending control messages to transmitting hosts the Internet control message protocol (ICMP) [30] is used. The ICMP is a user of IP, identified by the IP protocol type code '01' and thus a totally separated protocol. Nevertheless, ICMP is considered to be an integral part of IP and must be implemented in all IP modules. ICMP messages are always carried in the data field of an IP datagram with a *TYPE OF SERVICE* set to *NORMAL* or '0'. They are typically sent to report errors that have occurred in the processing of datagrams. As a rule, however, *ICMP messages are not sent for lost or corrupted ICMP messages*. We distinguish two different classes of ICMP messages, called error messages and querry messages. In the following, we describe the basic ICMP message format and the function of these messages.

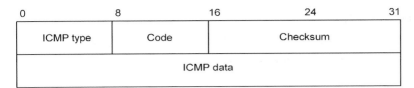

Fig. 7.5. Basic ICMP message format

7.1.5.1 The Basic ICMP Message Format

The basic ICMP message format is shown in Fig. 7.5.

ICMP Type

The 8-bit *ICMP TYPE* field is used to distinguish the different ICMP messages described in Sects. 7.1.5.2 and 7.1.5.3.

Code

The 8-bit *CODE* field, if not zero, is used to further specify the reason for sending the ICMP message.

Checksum

The 16-bit *CHECKSUM* field provides an integrity check on the entire ICMP message, including header and data field.

ICMP Data

The variable-length *ICMP DATA* field is used to convey specific information for the destination host. For example, certain messages need to transfer the IP header of the datagram that is being reported, together with the first 64 bits of IP data.

7.1.5.2 ICMP Error Messages

Destination Unreachable

A router will send an *ICMP destination unreachable* message to the corresponding source host when it receives a datagram

- For an unknown or unreachable network
- For a local network but the destination host is unavailable
- That needs to be fragmented to onward route it but the *DO NOT FRAGMENT* flag is set

Furthermore, a host will send an *ICMP destination unreachable* message where an IP user protocol or the specified user port is not available.

Time Exceeded

Every time a datagram passes from one router to the next enroute to its destination host, the *TIME-TO-LIVE* field is decremented by one. Any router that finds this field to be zero must discard the datagram. In this case, an *ICMP time exceeded* message with code *TIME-TO-LIVE EXCEEDED* is sent to the source host. Similarly, when a destination host receives the first fragment of a multifragment datagram, it starts a reassembly timer. In the event, that this timer expires, e.g., due to lost fragments, the fragments received so far are discarded and an *ICMP time exceeded* message with code *FRAGMENT REASSEMBLY TIMER EXPIRED* is sent to the source host.

Note: Errors are not reported for all fragments but only for the first fragment. If that fragment is lost, no error message will be sent for the lost datagram.

◇

Parameter Problem

When a router finds a problem with an IP header parameter, the IP datagram is discarded and an *ICMP parameter problem* message is sent to the source host, which contains a pointer to identify the octet of the original IP datagram header where the error was detected.

Source Quench

In the case of a router or host congestion the internal buffers fill up. When these are exhausted further received datagrams are discarded. In this case, *ICMP source quench* messages are sent to the corresponding source hosts informing them that the datagrams must be resent. Upon reception of a source quench message, a source host will also slow down the transmission rate of datagrams until no source quench messages are received. Hosts will then begin to increase the sending rate again. In this way, equilibrium will be achieved between the rate at which a host sends datagrams and the rate at which a router or destination host can process the datagrams, thus providing some kind of flow control.

Note: Implementations may send source quench messages when the buffer capacity is approached, which could result in duplicated datagrams.

◇

Redirect

A router sends an *ICMP redirect* message to source hosts in order to inform them that a better route exists to a destination host, and that they should use another router, identified by its IP address, as default router for that destination host.

7.1.5.3 ICMP Query Messages

Echo Request/Reply

In order to determine the reachability of a remote network or host, a router or host may send an *ICMP echo request* message to the considered destination. On receipt of this request the destination returns an *ICMP echo reply* message.

Timestamp Request/Reply

An originating host may send an *ICMP timestamp request* message to a considered destination host in order to determine round trip delays or delays within congested hosts. The originating host places the time that it sends the request in the 32-bit *ORIGINATE TIME STAMP* field. On reception of a timestamp request message the destination host enters the time when it receives the request in the 32-bit *RECEIVE TIMESTAMP* field, changes the type of the message to reply, and immediately prior to transmission of the reply message, it enters the time in the 32-bit *TRANSMIT TIMESTAMP* field. All times are specified in milliseconds since midnight GMT.

Address Mask Request/Reply

A host may broadcast an *ICMP address mask request* message to an authoritative host, typically a router, to determine its subnet mask. Upon receipt, the authoritative host enters the subnet mask for the network on which the request was received into the *SUBNET MASK* field of the received request, changes the type to reply, and sends the *ICMP address mask reply* message back to the originating host.

7.2 Stream Control Transmission Protocol

The stream control transmission protocol (SCTP) [18] is a connection-oriented end-to-end protocol that provides a reliable transfer of user messages between peer SCTP users. It is designed to allow PSTN signalling message transport over IP networks and operates on top of the Internet protocol. It performs this service based on multiple streams within an SCTP association, established between two SCTP endpoints. An SCTP endpoint may be multi-homed, which means that this endpoint can be reached via different IP routes.

User data and SCTP control information are transferred in SCTP packets via the SCTP association between peer SCTP layers. The SCTP offers a sequenced delivery of user messages within multiple streams with an option to bypass the sequenced delivery for individual messages. The advantage of using multiple streams within an association is that, while one stream may be blocked waiting for the next in-sequence user message, the delivery from other streams may proceed. When needed, SCTP message fragmentation and reassembly is provided to ensure that the SCTP packet conforms to the underlying network path MTU. The SCTP is built upon the principle of making the best use of the available network resources. One way of achieving this is the bundling of DATA and CONTROL chunks into one SCTP packet. Another way is to allow cumulative TSN acknowledgement of multiple DATA chunks, i.e., allowing multiple unacknowledged DATA chunks to be on the network. Finally, SCTP includes resistance to flooding and masquerade attacks and congestion avoidance measures.

In the following, we describe the basic SCTP packet format, the association initialization and termination, user data transfer, congestion control, path management, and fault management.

7.2.1 Basic SCTP Packet Format

Information is exchanged between two peer SCTPs using SCTP packets. An SCTP packet is composed of a common message header and chunks, as shown in Fig. 7.6. We distinguish between data chunks and SCTP control information chunks.

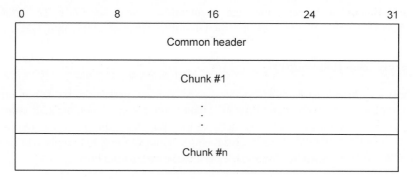

Fig. 7.6. Basic SCTP packet format

In order to make the best use of the available bandwidth multiple chunks can be bundled into one SCTP packet up to the MTU size of the underlying network technology. SCTP allows bundling DATA chunks and control information chunks into one packet, except the INIT, INITACK, and SHUTDOWN COMPLETE chunks (see Sect. 7.2.2), which must not be bundled with any other chunk in a packet.

SCTP Packet Common Header Format

The SCTP packet common header format is shown in Fig. 7.7.

The *SOURCE PORT NUMBER* and the *DESTINATION PORT NUMBER* fields contain the port numbers or application addresses of the communicating SCTP user. An SCTP port number combined with the IP address of a host is called transport address that uniquely identifies an SCTP endpoint application anywhere within an IP network. The *VARIFICATION TAG* is a 32-bit unsigned integer in the range from 1 to 4294967295 that is randomly generated by each end of the association and exchanged during the initialization of the association (see Sect. 7.2.2). It is used to

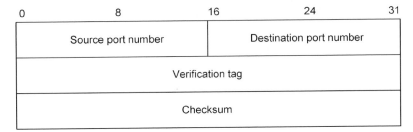

Fig. 7.7. SCTP packet common header format

validate SCTP packets, i.e., packets received without the expected verification tag value are discarded as a protection against blind masquerade attacks and against stale SCTP packets from a previous association. Finally, the *CHECKSUM* provides additional protection against data corruption in the network.

Chunk Format

The general chunk format is shown in Fig. 7.8.

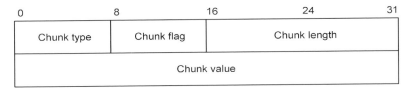

Fig. 7.8. SCTP chunk format

The different chunks are distinguished by the *CHUNK TYPE* value. The usage of the *CHUNK FLAG* value depends on the chunk type. Unless otherwise specified they are set to zero on transmit and are ignored on receipt. The *CHUNK LENGTH* value represents the size of the chunk in bytes including the chunk type, chunk flags, chunk length, and chunk value fields. The total length of a chunk must be a multiple of four bytes. If the total chunk length is not a multiple of four bytes, the sender must pad the chunk with all zero bytes, which the receiver must ignore. Note that the chunk length value does not count any padding.

The *CHUNK VALUE* field contains the actual information to be transferred in the chunk, i.e., data or control information. For SCTP control chunks this chunk value field starts with a chunk-type-specific header followed by zero, one or more parameters. The optional and variable length parameters contained in a chunk are defined in a type–length–value format (see Fig. 7.9).

The individual parameters are distinguished by the *PARAMETER TYPE* field. The *PARAMETER LENGTH* field contains the size of the parameter in bytes, which includes the parameter type, parameter length, and parameter value fields. The *PA-RAMETER VALUE* field contains the actual information to be transferred in the parameter. If necessary the sender pads the parameter with all zero bytes.

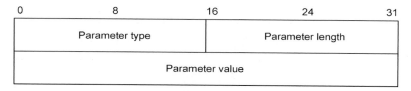

Fig. 7.9. Chunk parameter format

Compatibility

A further development of the SCTP protocol could result in new chunk or parameter types. For compatibility reasons it must be specified how to handle an unrecognized chunk or parameter type received by a processing endpoint. With this objective the chunk and parameter types are encoded such that the two highest-order bits indicate the specific action to be taken:

- '00' means to stop processing of the considered SCTP packet and to discard it.
- '01' means to stop processing of the considered SCTP packet and to discard it, but in addition to report that an unrecognized chunk or parameter type has been received.
- '10' means to skip the considered chunk or parameter and to continue processing.
- '11' means to skip the considered chunk or parameter and to continue processing, but in addition to report that an unrecognized chunk or parameter type has been received.

7.2.2 Association Initialization and Termination

7.2.2.1 Association Establishment

INIT and INIT ACK Chunks

Before an SCTP user can exchange any information, an SCTP association must be established between the peer SCTP layers in the corresponding nodes. Note that two SCTP endpoints must not have more than one SCTP association between them with the same IP address and port number at any given time. An SCTP user located at node A initiates the establishment of an SCTP association to a peer SCTP destination node Z using the ASSOCIATE primitive, which contains the destination transport address of the peer endpoint and the number of outbound streams the user would like to open towards its peer. For every association, an SCTP endpoint creates an internal data structure, called transmission control block (TCB), which contains all the status and operational information for the endpoint to create, maintain, and manage the association. On receipt of the ASSOCIATE primitive, SCTP A creates such a TCB for the considered association and sends an SCTP packet with an initiation chunk (INIT) to SCTP Z with the chunk type value of 1.

The *VERIFICATION TAG* field of this packet must be set to zero whilst the selected verification tag (Tag_A) of SCTP A is contained in the *INITIATE TAG* field of

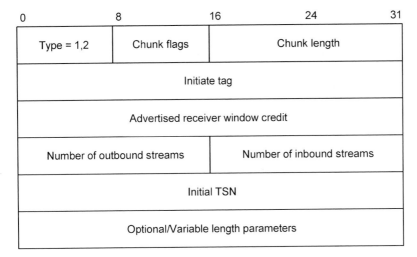

Fig. 7.10. INIT/INIT ACK chunks

the INIT chunk. The *ADVERTISED RECEIVER WINDOW CREDIT* field indicates the reception buffer space in number of bytes that A has reserved for buffering and processing received chunks. Since the SCTP must be able to receive a minimum of 1500 bytes in one packet, this means that an SCTP endpoint must not indicate less than 1500 bytes in this parameter. Finally, the *INITIAL TSN* field contains the initial transmission sequence number (TSN) that the sender will use (see Sect. 7.2.3). After sending the INIT, SCTP A starts the T1-init timer.

When SCTP Z receives the INIT chunk it shall respond immediately with an initiation acknowledgement chunk (INIT ACK), identified by the chunk type value of 2. The destination IP address of the INIT ACK must be set to the source IP address of the INIT to which the INIT ACK is responding. The *VERIFICATION TAG* field of this SCTP packet is set to *TAG_A* and the selected verification tag (Tag_Z) of SCTP Z is contained in the *INITIATE TAG* field of the INIT ACK chunk. Furthermore, Z indicates its allocated reception buffer space in the *ADVERTISED RECEIVER WINDOW CREDIT* parameter (a_rwnd) and adds its initial TSN. In addition, Z creates a temporary TCB for the considered association. In order to prevent resource attacks, the *state cookie mechanism* is employed during the initialization of the association.

State Cookie Mechanism

To this end, SCTP Z generates and includes the mandatory variable length *STATE COOKIE* parameter into the INIT ACK which contains all the necessary state and parameter information required by Z to reconstruct the TCB and to create the considered association, along with a message authentication code (MAC), a time stamp on when the state cookie is created and the lifespan of the state cookie (60 s).

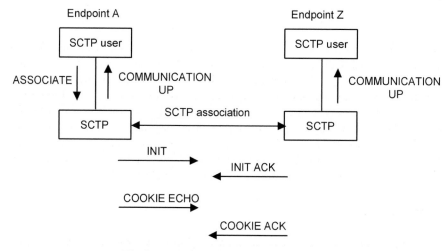

Fig. 7.11. Normal association establishment

After sending the INIT ACK chunk SCTP Z deletes the temporary TCB and any other local resources related to the new association in order to prevent resource attacks.

Upon reception of the INIT ACK chunk, SCTP A stops the T1-init timer, returns the *STATE COOKIE* received using a cookie echo chunk (COOKIE ECHO) and starts timer T1-cookie. When the endpoint Z receives a COOKIE ECHO chunk it first authenticates the state cookie by computing the MAC, based on the TCB data carried in the state cookie and a secret key, and comparing this MAC with the one contained in the *STATE COOKIE*. If the state cookie is identified as one it previously generated, it compares the elapsed time with the lifespan carried in the state cookie in order to check whether it is a stale cookie or not.

If the state cookie is valid, Z will reply with a cookie acknowledgement chunk (COOKIE ACK) after creating the association to SCTP A based on the rebuilt TCB with the information contained in the *STATE COOKIE* for the considered association. In addition, SCTP Z sends to its local user the COMMUNICATION UP notification primitive to indicate the establishment of an association to peer SCTP A. Upon reception of the COOKIE ACK, endpoint A stops the T1-cookie timer and notifies its local user about the successful establishment of the association to peer SCTP Z using the COMMUNICATION UP notification primitive.

If the T1-init or T1-cookie timer expire at A after the INIT or COOKIE ECHO chunks are sent the same INIT or COOKIE ECHO chunks with the same initiate tag or state cookie are retransmitted and the corresponding timer is restarted. After a suggested number of eight unsuccessful attempts, A considers Z to be unreachable and reports the failure to its upper layer.

Initialization Collision

When an INIT chunk is received in the *cookie-wait* or *cookie-echoed* state, this usually indicates that both endpoints are trying to establish the association at about the same. In this case, an endpoint must respond with an INIT ACK using the same parameters it sent in its original INIT chunk. These original parameters and those from the newly received INIT chunk are combined. The endpoint also generates a *STATE COOKIE* with the INIT ACK, using the parameters sent in its INIT chunk to calculate the *STATE COOKIE*. Note that the endpoint does not change its state, i.e., the TCB must not be destroyed. The normal procedure for handling state cookies when a TCB exists will resolve the duplicated INITs to a single association.

SCTP Streams

The term stream is used to refer to a sequence of user messages that have to be delivered to the SCTP user in order, with respect to other messages within the same stream. The number of streams to be supported by the association is specified by the SCTP user at association startup time. To this end, both ends of the SCTP association include in the INIT and INIT ACK chunks the parameters *NUMBER OF OUTBOUND STREAMS (OS)*, which defines the number of streams the sender wishes to create in the association, and *NUMBER OF INBOUND STREAMS (MIS)*, which is the maximum number of streams the sender allows the peer to create in this association. After receiving the stream configuration information from the other side, each SCTP endpoint checks whether the peers MIS is less than the endpoint's OS. This means that the peer is incapable of supporting all the outbound streams the endpoint wants to create. In this case, the SCTP endpoint may abort the association. If the association is not aborted, the endpoint will realize a number of outbound streams, which in any way corresponds to the minimum of the local OS and remote MIS values. Note that the number of streams established in both directions of the association can be different.

7.2.2.2 Association Restart

During the lifetime of an association it may happen that, for example, endpoint A has crashed without being detected by the other endpoint Z. When SCTP A has restarted it will sent out a new INIT chunk to restore the association, which includes a new verification *TAG_A* value. For SCTP Z this INIT is unexpected since there already exists a TCB for that association. In this case, Z establishes a temporary TCB and creates a new verification *TAG_Z* and a *STATE COOKIE*, which are included in the INIT ACK with other parameters from the existing association. Z must copy its old verification *TAG_Z* and the old peer verification *TAG_A* into a reserved place within the *STATE COOKIE*, referred to as *LOCAL-TIE-TAG* and *PEERS-TIE-TAG*. After sending out the INIT ACK, Z destroys the temporary TCB but leaves the original TCB in place for the association.

On reception of the INIT ACK, A will return the COOKIE ECHO with Z's *STATE COOKIE*. Again, this COOKIE ECHO is unexpected for Z. After proving the *STATE COOKIE* to be valid, Z will unpack the TCB into a temporary TCB for the considered association. SCTP Z finds that the tags as contained in the *STATE COOKIE* do not match the tags it has stored for the association, but finds that the tie-tags match the old tags. This indicates to Z that A has restarted, so that it will use the new tag values in the following and sends a RESTART notification primitive to its local user regarding the considered association.

7.2.2.3 Association Termination

The SCTP provides for two ways to close an active association: a graceful termination through a shutdown or an ungraceful termination through an abort.

Abort of an Association

An abort may be requested from an SCTP user using the ABORT primitive or may be initiated by either end of the association as a result of an error condition, detected within the SCTP layer (see Sect. 7.2.6). When an endpoint decides to abort an active association, it discards any data in queue and sends an abort chunk (ABORT) to its peer endpoint, which must be the only chunk in the SCTP packet. When the peer endpoint receives the abort chunk, it checks the verification tag and, if valid, discards any pending messages for that association and removes the association from operation. Note that this endpoint must not respond to the abort chunk. Finally, at both endpoints, the SCTP informs the local user with a COMMUNICATION LOST notification primitive. If a peer SCTP aborts the association for any reason and the ABORT chunk is lost, the local SCTP will only discover this lost ABORT chunk by sending a DATA or a HEARTBEAT chunk (see Sect. 7.2.5) thus causing the peer to send another ABORT chunk.

Shutdown of an Association

With a SHUTDOWN primitive, a user may request a graceful termination of an active association. When the SCTP at endpoint A receives this primitive from its upper layer, it stops accepting any new messages from its local user, sends and, if necessary, retransmits all outstanding data to the far end. Once all of the outstanding DATA chunks have been acknowledged by the peer, A sends a shutdown chunk (SHUTDOWN) to its peer endpoint Z and starts the T2-shutdown timer. If this timer expires, A must resend the SHUTDOWN chunk. After ten unsuccessful retransmission attempts, A should destroy the TCB for the considered association, which closes the association, and must report the peer endpoints unreachability to its upper layer.

When the peer endpoint Z receives the SHUTDOWN chunk, it stops accepting new data from its user. Note, that when Z has received a SHUTDOWN chunk, it must

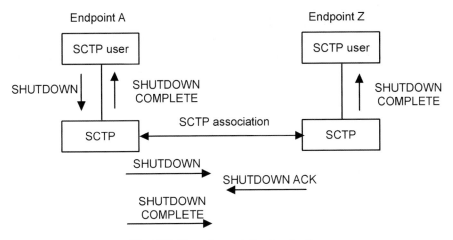

Fig. 7.12. Normal association termination

not send a SHUTDOWN chunk in response to a local user request and should discard subsequent SHUTDOWN chunks received. All outstanding DATA chunks are sent until all are acknowledged by the peer. If Z has no more outstanding DATA chunks it sends a shutdown acknowledgement chunk (SHUTDOWN ACK) and starts a T2-shutdown timer of its own. If this timer expires, Z must resend the SHUTDOWN ACK. After ten unsuccessful retransmission attempts, the endpoint Z should destroy the TCB for the considered association, which closes the association, and may report the peer endpoints unreachability to the upper layer.

Upon receipt of the SHUTDOWN ACK, A stops the T2-shutdown timer, deletes the TCB for the association, which closes the association, and sends a shutdown complete chunk (SHUTDOWN COMPLETE) to Z. When Z receives the SHUTDOWN COMPLETE chunk in response to a SHUTDOWN ACK previously sent, it stops its T2-shutdown timer and deletes the TCB for the association, which closes the association. When both SCTP endpoints have completed the shutdown procedure, they pass a SHUTDOWN COMPLETE notification primitive to their upper layer.

7.2.3 User Data Transfer

When the association is established a given number of unidirectional streams are available in both directions to carry SCTP packets to the peer endpoint. The SCTP provides a reliable transfer of user messages without message duplication, message loss or message missequencing through an acknowledged sequenced delivery of user messages within multiple streams. In addition, it offers the option for order-of-arrival delivery of user messages. In the following we describe in more detail how these functions are realized.

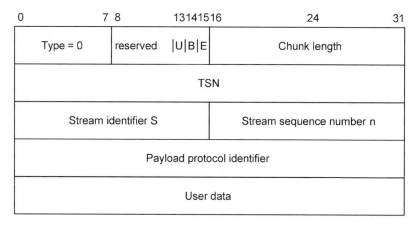

Fig. 7.13. DATA chunk

7.2.3.1 Assembly of SCTP Packets

Data Chunks

User messages are transferred to the local SCTP for transmission using the SEND primitive, along with the destination transport address and the stream identifier S, which indicates the stream to send the data on. If not specified, stream 0 will be used. Before user data can be send to the peer SCTP they are converted into DATA chunks.

Every DATA chunk is uniquely identified by the transmission sequence number (TSN) which varies in the range from 0 to 4294967295 ($2^{32} - 1$), where the first DATA chunk is assigned the initial TSN as transferred to the peer SCTP in the INIT or INIT ACK chunk. The *PAYLOAD PROTOCOL IDENTIFIER* is an application-specified protocol identifier. It is passed to the SCTP by its upper layer and may be used by the peer SCTP user to identify the type of information being carried in the DATA chunk. The value 0 indicates that no application identifier is specified for the considered DATA chunk.

Ordered and Unordered Delivery of User Data

Within stream S, the sequence of DATA chunks is fixed by the stream sequence number (SSN) n within a range from 0 to 65535. For an ordered delivery of user data within stream S the U bit in the *CHUNK FLAG* field is set to '0'. Within a stream an endpoint must deliver received DATA chunks with the U flag set to '0' to the upper layer based on the order of their SSN. This means, if data chunks arrive out of order the endpoint must store and reorder the received DATA chunks based on the SSN before they are delivered to the upper layer protocol.

In addition, the SCTP user may request in the SEND primitive to bypass the sequenced delivery of an individual user message. In this case, the U bit is set to

'1' and no SSN is assigned to the DATA chunk and the receiver must ignore the stream sequence number field. An unordered DATA chunk must bypass the ordering mechanism so that the endpoint delivers the data immediately to the upper layer.

Note that a stream can be used as an *unordered stream* by simply setting the U bit to '1' in all DATA chunks sent via that stream.

Message Fragmentation and Reassembly

When converting user messages into DATA chunks an endpoint will fragment user messages larger than the current association path MTU, which is the smallest path MTU of all destination addresses to the peer endpoint, into multiple DATA chunks. In addition it must provide the peer SCTP endpoint with all the information to correctly reassemble the user message.

To this end, the beginning fragment bit B is set to '1' and the ending fragment bit E to '0', indicating the first fragment of a multifragment user message. Setting both B and E to '0' indicates that the received DATA chunk contains a middle fragment of the user message. These middle fragments are distinguished by their TSNs, which in addition are used to identify the correct position within the overall user message. Thus, it is required that the TSNs for each fragment of the fragmented user message must be strictly sequential. The last fragment is uniquely identified by 'B = 0' and 'E = 1'. All fragments must be assigned the same stream identifier and stream sequence number. Once the user message is reassembled by the peer SCTP, it shall pass the reassembled user message to the specific stream for possible reordering and final delivery to its SCTP user.

Each fragment of an unordered user message must have the U bit set to '1'. When reassembled it is immediately dispatched to the SCTP user, bypassing the ordering mechanism.

Finally, an unfragmented user message will have both B and E bits set to '1'.

Chunk Bundling

The chunk bundling function of the SCTP is responsible for the assembly of the complete SCTP packet and its disassembly at the receiving endpoint. Multiple DATA and CONTROL chunks may be bundled by the sending SCTP into a single SCTP packet for transmission as long as the final size of the resultant IP datagram, including the SCTP packet and IP headers, does not exceed the current path MTU size. However, CONTROL chunks must come before DATA chunks in the packet. Within an SCTP packet DATA chunks are transmitted in increasing order of TSN. An SCTP user may request that no bundling is performed, e.g., in the case of congestion situations, but this will only turn off any delays that SCTP implementations may be using to increase bundling efficiency. It does not in itself stop all bundling from occurring.

7.2.3.2 Disassembly of SCTP Packets

Packet Validation

When an SCTP endpoint receives an SCTP packet a check is performed whether data corruption occurred in the network layer. To this end, the sending SCTP calculates the CRC-32c checksum [31] of the whole SCTP packet, with the checksum field bits all set to '0', and puts the relevant value into the *CHECKSUM* field of the SCTP common header (see Fig. 7.7). The receiving endpoint stores the received checksum value aside and calculates the CRC-32c checksum of the whole packet by itself with the checksum field bits all set to '0'. If both checksums are not the same, the packet is considered to be invalid and is silently discarded.

If the packet is not corrupt the SCTP then validates that packet. For this the *VARIFICATION TAG* field in the SCTP common header (see Sects. 7.2.1 and 7.2.2) is used to determine whether the concerned packet is received from the peer endpoint and is related to the current SCTP association. Packets received without the expected verification tag are discarded (see also Sects. 7.2.2.2 and 7.2.6).

Acknowledgement of Data Chunks

When disassembling a valid SCTP packet the receiving endpoint must process the received chunks according to their order in the packet. It uses the *CHUNK LENGTH* field (see Fig 7.13) to determine the end of a chunk and the beginning of the next chunk, taking account of the fact that all chunks end on a four-byte boundary. Detected partial chunks must be dropped.

All data chunks are acknowledged even if there are gaps in the sequence. In this way, reliable delivery is functionally separated from sequenced delivery of user data chunks in streams. Thus, while one stream may be blocked, waiting for the next in-sequence user message, delivery from other streams may proceed.

Upon the reception of a new DATA chunk an endpoint shall examine the continuity of the TSNs received. An acknowledgement should be generated for at least every second SCTP packet received but not more than one for every incoming packet. This acknowledgement should be generated within 200 ms of the arrival of any unacknowledged DATA chunk.

Note: The maximum delay for generating an acknowledgement may be configured by the SCTP administrator. This offers the possibility to meet the specific timing requirements of the upper layer protocol.

◇

Selective Acknowledgement Chunk

Selective acknowledgement (SACK) chunks (see Fig. 7.14) are used to acknowledge data chunks unless shutdown was requested by the SCTP user, in which case the SCTP may send a cumulative TSN acknowledgement in the SHUTDOWN chunk.

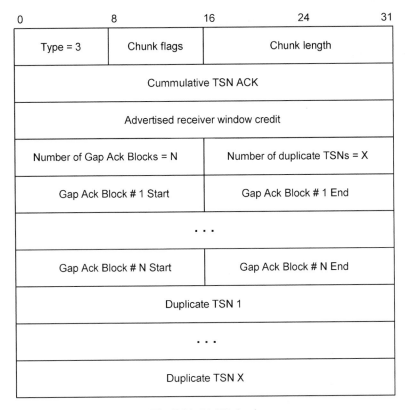

Fig. 7.14. SACK chunk

SACK chunks are also used to indicate gaps in the received subsequences of DATA chunks. In the absence of data loss an SCTP endpoint performs delayed acknowledgement. However, whenever it detects a gap in the arriving DATA chunks, and thus TSN sequence, it should start sending a SACK chunk to its peer every time a packet arrives carrying data, until the gap is filled.

The *CUMULATIVE TSN ACK* parameter contains the last TSN received correctly before a break in the sequence of received TSNs occurs, i.e., the next TSN value following this one has not yet been received correctly at the SACK sending endpoint. Thus, the *CUMULATIVE TSN ACK* parameter is used to acknowledge the receipt of all TSNs less than or equal to the cumulative TSN contained.

The SACK chunk also contains zero, one or more gap acknowledgement blocks (Gap Ack Blocks) the number N of which is contained in the *NUMBER OF GAP ACK BLOCKS* parameter. Each Gap Ack Block acknowledges all TSNs received in sequence following a gap of one or more TSNs. The first TSN acknowledged by Gap Block i is calculated by adding the value of the *GAP ACK BLOCK # i START* parameter to the *CUMULATIVE TSN ACK* value whilst the last acknowledged TSN

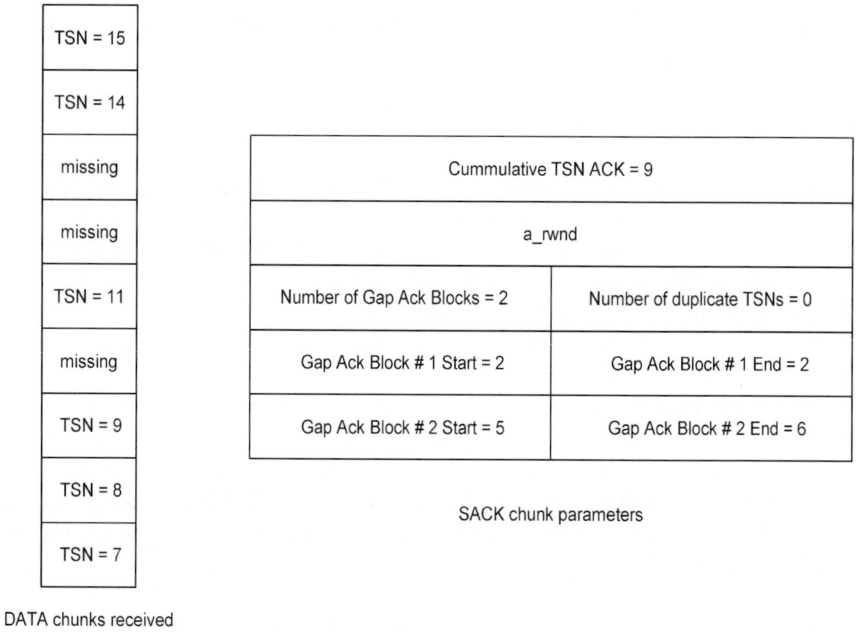

| TSN = 15 |
| TSN = 14 |
| missing |
| missing |
| TSN = 11 |
| missing |
| TSN = 9 |
| TSN = 8 |
| TSN = 7 |

DATA chunks received

Cummulative TSN ACK = 9	
a_rwnd	
Number of Gap Ack Blocks = 2	Number of duplicate TSNs = 0
Gap Ack Block # 1 Start = 2	Gap Ack Block # 1 End = 2
Gap Ack Block # 2 Start = 5	Gap Ack Block # 2 End = 6

SACK chunk parameters

Fig. 7.15. Selective acknowledgement of DATA chunks

of this block is calculated by adding the value of the *GAP ACK BLOCK # i END* parameter to the *CUMULATIVE TSN ACK* value.

For example let us assume that, at the receiving SCTP endpoint, the data chunks as shown in Fig. 7.15 are newly arrived since the last in sequence acknowledged TSN = 6. Given that TSN 7, 8, and 9 are received in sequence but TSN 10 is missing, the cumulated TSN acknowledgement parameter is 9. In addition, TSN 12 and TSN 13 are missing so that we have two gap acknowledgement blocks, i.e., $N = 2$. The first gap acknowledgement block consists of TSN 11 so that both the Gap Ack Block #1 Start and Gap Ack Block #1 End parameters are 2. Furthermore, Gap Ack Block #2 Start is set to 5, indicating that the second gap acknowledgement block starts with TSN 14 whilst the value 6 for the Gap Ack Block #2 End indicates that TSN 15 is the last acknowledged TSN of the second block. The relevant parameters of the SACK chunk to be sent are summarized in Fig. 7.15.

Duplicated DATA Chunks

The receipt of duplicated DATA chunks indicates that a SACK has been lost and the corresponding retransmission timer T3-rtx expired at the peer SCTP (see Sect. 7.2.3.3). When a SCTP packet arrives with duplicated DATA chunks and, thus, duplicated TSNs the endpoint must send a SACK chunk. In this SACK chunk the number of duplicated DATA chunks is contained in the *NUMBER OF DUPLICATE TSNs* parameter whilst each duplicated TSN is listed in the *DUPLICATE TSN* parameters following the Gap Ack Block list.

Receive Buffer Management

Both SCTP endpoints are responsible for maintaining their receive buffers. At initialization of the association an SCTP endpoint allocates receive buffer space to the association and stores the buffer size (in bytes) in the receiver window "a_rwnd" variable. As DATA chunks are received and buffered, a_rwnd is decremented by the number of bytes buffered. As DATA chunks are delivered to the upper layer protocol and released from the receive buffer, a_rwnd is incremented by the number of bytes delivered to the SCTP user.

An SCTP endpoint should inform its peer in a timely manner of changes in its ability to receive and process data. With this objective an SCTP endpoint notifies the peer about the available space in its receive buffer by inserting the current value of a_rwnd into the *ADVERTISED RECEIVER WINDOW CREDIT* parameter of the INIT or INIT ACK at initialization of the association (see Sect. 7.2.1) or every SACK chunk during operation (see Fig. 7.14).

Upon reception of a SACK chunk the SCTP endpoint removes all DATA chunks which have been acknowledged by the cumulative TSN from its transmit queue and sets the cumulative TSN acknowledgement pointer to the last acknowledged cumulative TSN, contained in the *CUMULATIVE TSN ACK* parameter, and which we call the cumulative TSN acknowledgement point. Furthermore, it records all missing DATA chunks with TSNs not acknowledged by the SACK for retransmission. Finally, the SCTP uses the information provided by a_rwnd, the cumulative TSN, and the Gap Ack Blocks to develop a representation of the peer's receive buffer space. This information is used during transmission and retransmission of DATA chunks and to detect congestion at the peer SCTP as described in the following sections.

Discard of Acknowledged DATA Chunks

It may happen that a receiving SCTP may need to drop DATA chunks that have been received but not yet delivered to its user and, thus, not yet released from its receive buffer. Such a situation may occur if the SCTP may be holding data in its receive buffer for sequencing reasons, while reassembling a fragmented user message from its peer, when it runs out of buffer space. It may drop these DATA chunks even though it has acknowledged them in Gap Ack Blocks. In this case, the SCTP must not include their TSNs in Gap Ack Blocks in subsequent SACK chunks until they are received again via retransmission. Note, however, that an SCTP will not retransmit DATA chunks that have been acknowledged by the cumulative TSN. When the peer SCTP receives the SACK chunk missing a TSN that was previously acknowledged via a Gap Ack Block, it marks the corresponding DATA chunk as available for fast retransmit (see Sect. 7.2.3.3). In addition, the retransmission timer for the destination address to which the missing DATA chunk was originally transmitted is started if not already running.

7.2.3.3 Transmission and Retransmission of DATA Chunks

Before the SCTP transmits new DATA chunks it must first transmit any outstanding DATA chunks marked for retransmission. Thus, in the case of bundling, DATA chunks being retransmitted must come before new DATA chunks. Furthermore, if any received DATA chunks have not yet been acknowledged by that SCTP it should create a SACK chunk and bundle it with the outbound DATA chunks. Note that, at any given time, the SCTP must not transmit new data to any destination transport address if the peer SCTP has insufficient buffer space indicated by the receiver window variable a_rwnd.

Retransmission Timer

There may be the case that SACK chunks are lost or delayed. In order to ensure data delivery in the absence of any feedback from its peer an SCTP endpoint uses the retransmission timer T3-rtx. The time interval defined by this timer is called retransmission time-out (RTO). In the following, we assume a single retransmission timer per destination transport address, but implementations may have a retransmission timer for each DATA chunk.

The retransmission time-out is computed for each destination transport address of the peer endpoint, based on round-trip time (RTT) measurements. Until the first RTT measurement has been made, the timer value is set to the initial value of 3 s, whilst the calculated values may vary from 1–60 s, depending on the results of the measurements.

Every time a DATA chunk is sent to any transport address, including retransmission of a DATA chunk, the T3-rtx timer of that address is started, if it is not yet running. When a SACK chunk, that acknowledges the DATA chunk with the earliest outstanding TSN for that address is received, the T3-rtx timer for that address is restarted. Equally, when a SACK chunk missing a TSN that was previously acknowledged via a Gap Ack Block is received (see Sect. 7.2.3.2), the T3-rtx timer is started for that destination address, if not already running. The retransmission timer is stopped when all outstanding data sent to the address concerned have been acknowledged.

Retransmission Timer Expiration

If the retransmission timer for a given destination address expires the SCTP doubles the retransmission timer value for that destination address. Furthermore, the SCTP performs a fast retransmit of outstanding DATA chunks, i.e., it determines how many of the earliest DATA chunks with lowest TSN for the address for which the T3-rtx timer has expired will fit into a single packet and retransmits these DATA chunks in a single packet to the destination endpoint. Those DATA chunks that were sent to the address for which the T3-rtx timer expired but that did not fit in one packet should be marked for retransmission and sent as soon as possible. Once a new RTT measurement is available for the considered destination address the RTO is recalculated, which may result in collapsing RTO back down after it has been subject to doubling.

Fast Retransmit on Gap Reports

When an SCTP endpoint receives information about missing TSNs in the fourth consecutive SACK chunk, it starts a fast retransmit of the reported TSNs. To this end, it marks the missing DATA chunk(s) for retransmission. Furthermore, it determines how many of the earliest DATA chunks with lowest TSN marked for retransmission will fit into a single packet and retransmits these DATA chunks in a single packet. Finally, the retransmission timer is restarted if the last SACK chunk acknowledged the lowest outstanding TSN to that address or the SCTP endpoint is retransmitting the first outstanding DATA chunk sent to that address.

7.2.4 Congestion Control

One of the basic functions provided by SCTP is congestion control. For some applications it may be unlikely that during normal operation severe congestion situations will occur. However, under adverse operational conditions, congestion situations which can lead to (partial) network outages or unexpected traffic surges might occur. For example, problems will occur if a local SCTP user is not able to accept the user data rate as provided by its local SCTP, because of internal difficulties, or imagine that the receiving SCTP is running slower than the sending SCTP or that the underlying transport network is not able to transfer the data rate as received from the sending SCTP. In those situations the receive and send buffers fill up, leading to congestion situations. Since the SCTP must also operate under those conditions, SCTP congestion control, which aims to avoid message loss and a spread of congestion situations into the network, is needed. *Note that SCTP congestion control is applied to the SCTP association and not to individual streams.*

Since the SCTP is not the source of the user data traffic, the basic idea of congestion control is to avoid message loss during congestion situations by regulating the SCTP transmission rate. Regarding the flow control actions taken, the SCTP distinguishes three phases: *slow start, congestion avoidance*, and *congestion*. Furthermore, in order to govern the amount of data the transmitting SCTP may send, the SCTP congestion control makes use of four control variables, the advertised receiver window (a_rwnd) size, the congestion control window (cwnd), the slow-start threshold (ssthresh), and the partial_bytes_acked variable. Since the variables cwnd, ssthresh, and partial_bytes_acked are maintained on a per-destination address basis, the SCTP must keep a set of these control variables for each destination address of its peer if it is multi-homed. Only the a_rwnd variable is kept for the whole association, no matter if the peer is multi-homed or not.

7.2.4.1 The Congestion Window Mechanism

If we would wait for a DATA chunk to be acknowledged before we are allowed to send the next, this would not make best use of the available bandwidth. So, instead of acknowledging each DATA chunk and waiting for the acknowledgement, the SCTP employs the congestion window mechanism, which allows the SCTP to have multiple DATA chunks unacknowledged. However, under adverse conditions, this could lead to filling of the receive buffer at the peer SCTP endpoint. In this case, the transmitting SCTP is not allowed to transmit further DATA chunks (see Sect. 7.2.3.3). Since the transmitting SCTP is allowed to accept further DATA messages from its local user this may lead, in addition, to filling of its transmit buffer and, if no messages are discarded, to the fact that the traffic is stored back to its upper layer. In order to avoid these problems with receive and send buffer overflow the SCTP uses special variables.

On the one hand, the SCTP flow control makes use of the receiver window (a_rwnd) variable (see Sect. 7.2.3.2), which is transmitted by the receiving endpoint during initialization of the association and in every SACK chunk, so that it can communicate the state of its receive buffer. The transmitting SCTP then has all necessary information to develop a representation of the peer's receive buffer and can control its DATA chunk transmission. On the other hand, the transmitting SCTP uses the congestion control window (cwnd) variable that limits the data, in number of bytes, the sending SCTP can transmit to a particular destination transport address *before receiving an acknowledgement*. At any time, the sending SCTP must not transmit new DATA chunks to a given transport address if it has cwnd or more bytes of data unacknowledged to that transport address. The principle of the congestion window mechanism is shown in Fig. 7.16.

A window with size cwnd (in bytes) is placed over the data such that any DATA chunk to the left of the window has been transmitted and acknowledged by a cumulative TSN, data chunks under the window have been transmitted but an acknowledgement has not yet been received for all of them, and all DATA chunks to the right outside the window are untransmitted. In Fig. 7.16, for example, DATA chunks 3 and 4 have been transmitted and are acknowledged by the cumulative TSN of the last SACK whilst DATA chunks 5–8 have been sent but 5, 7, and 8 are still unacknowledged. Finally, DATA chunks from 9 on have not yet been transmitted. Whenever an acknowledgement for an outstanding DATA chunk is received, e.g., TSN 5, the window moves and new DATA chunks on the right can be transmitted, as long as the total number of bytes of the outstanding DATA chunks is less than cwnd.

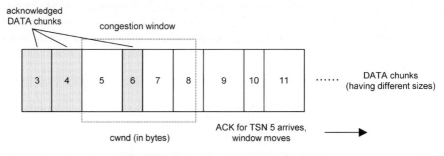

Fig. 7.16. Congestion window mechanism

By adjusting the congestion control window, i.e., by changing the cwnd variable based on observed network conditions, the transmitting SCTP can control its data flow such that filling of the receive buffer of its peer and, thus, receive congestion at the peer endpoint can be avoided and that it can react appropriately to IP network congestion. Transmit congestion at its local side is avoided by adapting the rate it accepts data from its local user to the transmission rate to the peer SCTP. The adjustment of the cwnd depends on the different phases as described below.

7.2.4.2 Slow Start

When an SCTP starts to send traffic into a network with unknown conditions or after a sufficiently long idle period, it is required that the SCTP probes the network to determine the available capacity. To this end, the SCTP uses slow start at the beginning of the message transfer as well as after repairing message loss detected by the retransmission timer.

Before DATA chunk transmission begins, the cwnd value is set to at most double of the path MTU of the destination address. The initial cwnd value after a retransmission timeout must not be more than one MTU length. If an incoming SACK advances the cumulative TSN ACK point, cwnd must be increased by at most the lesser of

1. The total size of the previously outstanding DATA chunk(s) acknowledged
2. The destination's path MTU

If the received SACK does not advance the cumulative TSN ACK point, the cwnd variable must not be adjusted.

Finally, when the SCTP endpoint does not transmit data on a given transport address cwnd of the transport address should be adjusted to $max(\frac{cwnd}{2}, 2 \cdot MTU)$ per retransmission timeout. Basically, a retransmission timeout causes cwnd to be cut in half.

7.2.4.3 Congestion Avoidance

The slow-start threshold (ssthresh) variable (in bytes) is used to distinguish between the slow start and congestion avoidance phases. The initial value of ssthresh may be arbitrarily high, e.g., implementations may use the size of the advertised receiver window. An SCTP endpoint enters the congestion avoidance phase if cwnd is greater than ssthresh. In this case, cwnd should be increased as follows:

The partial_bytes_acked variable (in bytes) is initiated to 0. Upon each SACK arrival that advances the cumulative acknowledgement point partial_bytes_acked is increased by the number of bytes of all new DATA chunks acknowledged in that SACK, i.e., the DATA chunks acknowledged by the new cumulative TSN ACK and by the Gap Ack Blocks. When the value of partial_bytes_acked is equal to or greater than the value of cwnd and before the arrival of the SACK the sender had cwnd or more bytes of data outstanding, the value of the partial_bytes_acked variable is reduced by the cwnd value and cwnd is increased by one MTU size.

When all of the data transmitted has been acknowledged by the receiver the par-
tial_bytes_acked variable is initialized to 0.

When the sender does not transmit DATA chunks on a given transport address
cwnd of the transport address should be adjusted to $max(\frac{cwnd}{2}, 2 \cdot MTU)$ per retransmission timeout, i.e., a retransmission timeout causes cwnd to be cut in half.

7.2.4.4 Congestion

The congestion phase is entered upon detection of packet losses from SACK chunks.
In this case, an endpoint should change the variables as follows:

$$ssthresh = max(\tfrac{cwnd}{2}, 2 \cdot MTU)$$
$$cwnd = ssthresh$$

Basically, a packet loss causes cwnd to be cut in half. When the retransmission
timer expires on an address the SCTP should enter the slow-start phase with variables

$$ssthresh = max(\tfrac{cwnd}{2}, 2 \cdot MTU)$$
$$cwnd = 1 \; MTU$$

It has to be assured that no more than one SCTP packet will be in flight for that
address until an acknowledgement for successful delivery of data to that address is
received.

7.2.5 Path Management

Multi-Homed SCTP Endpoints

An SCTP endpoint may be multi-homed, which means that it has multiple network
interfaces with related IP addresses (see Sect. 7.1.1.4). In this case, there are more
than one IP routes and related transport addresses available to reach that endpoint.
The path management function is responsible for reporting the eligible set of local
transport addresses to the far end during association startup and for reporting the
transport addresses returned from the far end to the SCTP user. To this end, an SCTP
endpoint collects the destination transport address(es) of its peer during the initialization of the association as described in the following:

- If there are no *ADDRESS* parameters present in the received INIT or INIT ACK
  chunk, the endpoint records the source IP address from which the chunk arrives in
  combination with the SCTP source port number as the only destination transport
  address for the peer.
- If the *ADDRESS* parameter represents a host name, the endpoint shall resolve
  that host name to a list of IP addresses and derive the transport addresses of the
  peer by combining the resolved IP addresses with the SCTP source port.
- If there are only IPv4 and/or IPv6 addresses present, the receiver shall derive
  and record all the transport addresses from the received chunk and the source IP
  address that sent the INIT or INIT ACK chunk.

The SCTP user can manipulate the set of transport addresses used as destination addresses for SCTP packets. At association startup, a primary path is defined by the SCTP user at each endpoint. It may be changed by the SCTP user during the operation of the association with the SET PRIMARY primitive. The SCTP path management function chooses the destination transport address for each outgoing SCTP packet based on the SCTP user instructions and the currently perceived reachability status of the eligible destination set. By default, the SCTP transmits packets to the primary path unless the SCTP user explicitly specifies the destination transport address to be used.

Path Heartbeat

In addition, the path management function monitors reachability of transport addresses by using HEARTBEAT chunks when other packet traffic is inadequate to provide this information and informs the SCTP user when reachability of any far-end transport address changes. In this respect, a transport address is considered to be:

- *Active*, if the peer SCTP can be reached via this address
- *Inactive*, if the peer SCTP cannot be reached via this address
- *Idle*, if no new chunk (DATA, INIT, COOKIE ECHO, etc.), which can be used for updating the path RTT (see Sect. 7.2.3.3), and no HEARTBEAT chunk has been sent to the transport address within the current heartbeat period of that address, which is normally the RTO period, but that may be changed by the SCTP user

Some of the transport addresses of a multi-homed SCTP endpoint may become inactive due to either the occurrence of certain error conditions (see Sect. 7.2.6) or adjustment from SCTP user. When the primary path becomes inactive and if there are outband data chunks to be sent the SCTP should try to send the data to an alternative active destination transport address, if one exists.

By default, an SCTP endpoint monitors the reachability of an inactive or idle transport address by sending a HEARTBEAT chunk periodically to this address. The receiver of a HEARTBEAT chunk should immediately respond with a HEARTBEAT ACK chunk. Upon the receipt of a HEARTBEAT ACK chunk the SCTP marks the destination transport address as active, if it is not so marked.

7.2.6 Fault Management

7.2.6.1 Endpoint Failure Detection

For an SCTP endpoint it is important to detect a failure of its peer so that appropriate actions can be taken. With this objective, the SCTP keeps a counter of the total number of consecutive retransmissions to its peer, including retransmissions to all the destination transport addresses of the peer if it is multi-homed. If that counter exceeds the limit of ten consecutive retransmissions the SCTP considers the peer endpoint to be unreachable and stops transmitting further data to it. Note that the association is automatically closed when the peer endpoint becomes unreachable. Finally, the SCTP reports the endpoint failure to its local user and optionally report back all outstanding user data remaining in its outbound queue.

Whenever a DATA chunk sent to the peer SCTP endpoint is acknowledged by the reception of a SACK or a HEARTBEAT ACK is received from the peer endpoint, the error counter is reset.

7.2.6.2 Path Failure Detection

In order to perform a failover from an inactive destination transport address to an alternative active transport address to its multi-homed peer, an SCTP endpoint must detect a path failure. To this end, the SCTP should keep an error counter for each of the destination transport addresses of the peer endpoint. An SCTP endpoint should increment this counter each time the retransmission timer T3-rtx expires on any address or when a HEARTBEAT chunk, sent in the case of an idle address, is not acknowledged within a retransmission timeout. When the error counter of the considered destination address exceeds 5, the SCTP marks the corresponding destination address as inactive and reports the change of reachability of the considered transport address to its user. After this, the endpoint should continue to check the reachability using HEARTBEAT chunks but should stop increasing the counter.

When an outstanding TSN is acknowledged or a HEARTBEAT chunk sent to that address is acknowledged with a HEARTBEAT ACK chunk the SCTP shall reset the error counter of the destination transport address to which the DATA or HEART-BEAT chunk was sent.

7.2.6.3 Operation Errors

In order to inform a peer SCTP endpoint of certain error conditions, the OPERA-TION ERROR chunk is used. An operation error is not considered to be fatal in itself but may be used with an ABORT chunk to report a fatal condition. It may contain one or more parameters specifying the error causes. Those error causes are:

- *Invalid stream identifier*, which indicates that the SCTP endpoint received a DATA chunk which has been sent to a nonexistent stream.
- *Missing mandatory parameter*, which indicates that one or more mandatory parameters are missing in a received INIT or INIT ACK chunk.
- *Stale cookie error*, which indicates the receipt of a valid state cookie that has expired.
- *Out of resource*, which indicates that the sender is out of resource and which is usually sent in combination with an ABORT chunk.
- *Unresolvable address*, which indicates that the sender is not able to resolve the specified address parameter, e.g., because the type of address is not supported by the sender, and which is usually sent in combination with an ABORT chunk.

- *Unrecognized chunk type*, which indicates to the originator of the considered chunk that the receiver does not understand that chunk.
- *Invalid mandatory parameter*, which indicates to the originator of an INIT or INIT ACK chunk that one of the mandatory parameters is set to an invalid value.
- *Unrecognized parameters*, which indicates to the originator of an INIT ACK chunk that the receiver does not recognize one or more optional parameters in the INIT ACK chunk and which is normally send to the peer bundled with the COOKIE ECHO chunk when responding to the INIT ACK chunk.
- *No user data*, which indicates that the received DATA chunk has no user data.
- *Cookie received while shutting down*, which indicates that a COOKIE ECHO chunk was received while the endpoint has sent a SHUTDOWN ACK chunk waiting for a SHUTDOWN COMPLETE, and which is usually sent with a re-transmitted SHUTDOWN ACK.

7.3 MTP-2 User Peer-to-Peer Adaptation Layer

The MTP-2 user peer-to-peer adaptation layer (M2PA) protocol is designed to transport MTP-3 message signal units (MSUs) over IP using the services of SCTP. This protocol applies between SS 7 signalling points employing the MTP-3, where both IP-based links and standard SS 7 links may be present. The M2PA allows for full MTP-3 functionality between any two SS 7 nodes communicating over an IP network. An SS 7 node equipped with IP-based links is called an IP signalling point (IPSP), which functions as a traditional SS 7 node. The protocol structure for an IP-based link is shown in Fig. 5.1 whilst the SS 7 and IP network interconnection via a SG using the M2PA is shown in Fig. 5.2. In the following we describe in some detail the functions and services provided by the M2PA.

7.3.1 M2PA Messages

The peer-to-peer communication is performed by M2PA using two types of messages called user data messages, which are used to transfer the MSUs as received from MTP-3, and link status messages, which are used by M2PA to exchange link status information with its peer and, thus, are similar to MTP-2 link status signal units (LSSU). In Fig. 7.17 the basic M2PA message format, which consists of a common message header, the M2PA message header, and the message data that contains either user data or a link status is shown.

Common Message Header

The common message header, which is common to all adaptation layer protocols, is shown in Fig. 7.18.

The version of the M2PA adaptation layer is contained in the *VERSION* field. For the current release 1.0 of M2PA the value is '01'. The only message class defined by

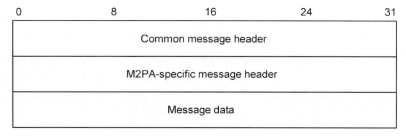

Fig. 7.17. M2PA message format

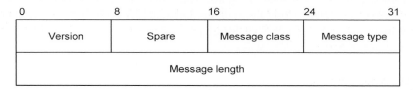

Fig. 7.18. Common message header

the *MESSAGE CLASS* field refers to the M2PA messages with value '11' whilst the *MESSAGE TYPE* field identifies the M2PA message, i.e., User data '01'and link status '02' messages. Finally, the *MESSAGE LENGTH* field defines the length of the message in octets including the common header.

M2PA Message Header

The M2PA-specific part starts with an M2PA header followed by the message data. The M2PA-specific header, as shown in Fig. 7.19, contains the forward sequence number (FSN), which is as within MTP-2 the sequence number of the user data message being sent, and the backward sequence number (BSN), which is the sequence number of the user data message being acknowledged. Both FSN and BSN range from 0 to 16,777,215.

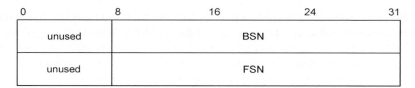

Fig. 7.19. M2PA-specific message header

User Data Messages

For user data messages the message data part corresponds to the *Data* field, which contains the MSU as received from MTP-3 including the message priority field (PRI), which may be used in national networks as an MTP-3 message priority field, the service information octet (SIO), and the service information field (SIF). For the detailed MSU format we refer to ITU Q.703, Sect. 2.2 *Signal unit format* [4].

Note: All other components of the MTP-2 message format, like flags, backward sequence number (BSN), backward indicator bit (BIB), forward sequence number (FSN), forward indicator bit (FIB), length indicator (LI), and check bits (CK), are not used by M2PA and, thus, are not present.

◇

The *Data* field is optional. If, for example, M2PA needs to acknowledge a received message, and it has no new MSU of its own to send, an empty user data message, not containing the *Data* field, can be sent which functions like a fill-in signal unit (FISU) of MTP-2.

Link Status Message

The M2PA uses the link status message to indicate the local link status to the peer, wherein the message data part contains the *STATE* field with the following values:

- 01   Alignment
- 02   Proving normal
- 03   Proving emergency
- 04   Ready
- 05   Processor outage
- 06   Processor recovered
- 07   Busy
- 07   Busy ended
- 07   Out of service

7.3.2 Management of SCTP Associations

Establishment and Termination of an SCTP Association

M2PA uses one SCTP association for one IP-based link. However, an SCTP endpoint application is uniquely identified by its transport address, i.e., IP address and port number (see Sect. 7.2.1). Given that SCTP does not allow one to establish more than one association between two endpoints with the same IP address and port number, how can multiple IP-based links between two endpoints be established?

In this respect, two different associations (IP-based links) between the M2PA peers must be distinguished by either the IP addresses, if they are multi-homed, or the port numbers, or both. At least one of the port numbers should be the M2PA-registered port number. If, for example, only one network interface is available and if only one association should be established between the two IP addresses, then both endpoints should use the registered M2PA port number. If both endpoints have two network interfaces with two IP addresses each, then the registered M2PA port number should be used to establish both associations. However, if multiple IP links should be created between two endpoints with only one network interface, i.e., if multiple associations should be created between two IP addresses, different port numbers can be used for each association, where the registered M2PA port number should be used for one of these associations. Finally, each combination of IP address/port number, i.e., transport address, must be mapped to the same signalling link code (SLC) at each endpoint, which uniquely identifies the IP link.

In order to avoid the duplicated establishment of associations each endpoint should know the IP address (or IP addresses in the case of multi-homing) and port numbers of both endpoints. The establishment and termination of an association is described in Sect. 7.2.2.

Association State Control

At the M2PA level an SCTP association can be in one of three states. It is in the IDLE state during power-up initialization. The state changes to ASSOCIATING when M2PA is attempting to establish an SCTP association with its peer, which then moves to the ESTABLISHED state when the association is established. An SCTP SEND FAILURE, COMMUNICATION ERROR, or COMMUNICATION LOST notification primitive leads to a corresponding SCTP state change.

If the SCTP association for a link is lost M2PA reports to MTP-3 that the corresponding link is *out of service*.

Number of Streams

A user-specified number of streams can be opened during the initialization of an SCTP association. M2PA uses two streams, with stream identifiers 0 and 1, in each association. Stream '0' is designated for the link status messages *Alignment*, *Proving normal*, *Proving emergency*, *Ready*, *Busy*, *Busy ended*, and *Out of service*, whilst user data messages and link status messages that must remain in sequence with the user data, i.e. *Processor Outage*, *Processor Recovered*, and *Ready* (when sent at the end of processor outage), are sent via stream '1'. M2PA sends all user data messages using the sequenced delivery service of SCTP.

Note that the changeover procedure makes it impossible for M2PA to use multiple user data streams. This is because buffer updating would have to be done for each user data stream separately to avoid message loss, duplication, and missequencing. However, MTP-3 provides for only one changeover message for sending the BSNT to indicate the last MSU accepted from the unavailable link.

According to the MTP-2 recommendation LSSUs have a higher priority than MSUs. This is realized by giving M2PA a higher priority to sending and reading the link status stream '0' over the user data stream '1'. Finally, notifications received from SCTP have a higher priority than reading either the link status stream or the user data stream.

It is the responsibility of M2PA to ensure proper management of the streams allowed with each association.

7.3.3 Interface Boundaries

M2PA–MTP-3

All services and primitives between MTP-2 and MTP-3 are provided by M2PA. This allows for seamless operation of MTP-3 peers over an IP link, which means that the MTP-3 peers will operate over IP links in the same way as over SS 7 links. To this end, M2PA processes primitives received from its MTP-3 or maps them to appropriate SCTP primitives. Note that, due to the larger sequence numbers used by M2PA, the MTP-3 changeover procedure must use the extended changeover order and extended changeover acknowledgement messages [14]. The same holds for the MTP-3 primitives BSNT INDICATION and RETRIEVAL REQUEST AND FSNC.

M2PA–SCTP

Finally, M2PA uses the SCTP services by passing primitives to SCTP and receiving notifications from SCTP as described in Sect. 7.2.

7.3.4 M2PA-Specific Functions

The M2PA provides the complete MTP-2 functionality to the MTP-3 layer. Since the SCTP provides reliable and in-sequence delivery of user messages, there is no need for M2PA to perform signal unit delimitation, error correction through retransmission, error rate monitoring, and the acceptance procedure of MTP-2. Therefore, M2PA only provides by itself the MTP-2 functionality that is not offered by SCTP, i.e., data retrieval to support the MTP-3 changeover procedure, link state control and status change report to MTP-3, link alignment, MTP Level 2 flow control, and processor outage.

Link Alignment

When an SCTP association is established and no START request is received from MTP-3 for the corresponding link M2PA sends the link status *Out of service*. However, unlike the MTP-2 status indication out of service (SIOS) signal unit, the link status *Out of service* should not be sent continuously but may be repeated before alignment begins.

The link alignment provides a handshaking procedure between the M2PA peers to verify that the association is ready to be used as an SS 7 link and to prevent messages from being sent before the peer is ready. Link alignment is started after the corresponding SCTP association is established and an MTP START request primitive is received for the link. The beginning of alignment is indicated by sending the link status *Alignment* to the peer. Although, M2PA should not send the link status *Alignment* continuously it may send additional alignment status messages until it receives the link status *Alignment* from its peer, which stops the link alignment.

After link alignment the proving period begins. During the proving period M2PA sends link status *Proving normal* or *Proving emergency* messages, as requested by MTP-3. At the end of the proving period the link status *Ready* message is sent, which terminates the proving period. When the link status *Ready* is received by both endpoints the link enters the *in service* state. The M2PA sends a corresponding primitive to its local MTP-3 and the link is now ready to send data messages.

Link State Control

An IP link moves from one state to another in response to various events, which are MTP-3 primitive requests, SCTP notifications, receipt of status messages from the peer M2PA, and the expiration of certain timers. These events affect the M2PA link state in a similar manner to the SS 7 link, and M2PA indicates the link status change to its local MTP-3 in the same way as MTP-2.

When a link changes to the *out of service* state M2PA sends a link status *Out of service* message to its peer, which should not be transmitted continuously. However, additional link status *Out of service* messages may be sent as long as the condition exists. Note that when M2PA changes to the *out of service* state the corresponding SCTP association should not be terminated.

Processor Outage

Processor outage refers to a situation when received signalling messages cannot be transferred by M2PA to its local MTP-3 (see Sect. 3.3). This may be because of a failure of the node internal connection between M2PA and MTP-3 or that MTP-3 does not accept messages from M2PA because of conditions at a higher layer. When M2PA detects a local processor outage condition it sends a link status *Processor outage* message to its peer. Unlike MTP-2 this status message should not be sent continuously but may be repeated as long as the processor outage condition persists. The link status *Processor outage* message must be sent via the user data stream (see Sect. 7.3.2). Any user data messages received from the peer M2PA must be buffered but not acknowledged. However, user data messages received and accepted by MTP-3 before the local processor outage situation occured are acknowledged. Furthermore, M2PA should continue to transmit MSUs received by the local MTP-3 before the local outage condition occured.

Upon receipt of the link status *Processor outage* the peer M2PA indicates the *remote processor outage* status change to its local MTP-3 and continues to acknowledge user data messages received and accepted by its MTP-3. However, if user messages are received from the peer in the *remote processor outage* state which cannot be delivered to the local MTP-3, then these messages are buffered but not acknowledged.

In the case that processor outage is long term, M2PA receives a FLUSH request primitive from its MTP-3. This causes any incoming messages that were queued and are unacknowledged during the processor outage condition and all messages in the transmit and retransmit queues to be discarded. However, if processor outage is short term M2PA receives a CONTINUE request primitive from MTP-3, which causes M2PA to process the incoming messages that were queued and unacknowledged during the short-term processor outage condition.

When the local processor outage condition ceases, M2PA notifies its peer by sending a corresponding link status *Processor recovered* on the user data stream. To resynchronize the sequence numbers the BSN in the link status *Processor recovered* message is set to the FSN of the last user data message received from the peer M2PA and which has not been discarded.

When the peer M2PA receives the link status *Processor recovered* it responds with the link status *Ready* message on the user data stream. For resynchronization the BSN in the link status *Ready* message is set to the FSN of the last user data message received from the peer M2PA and which has not been discarded.

Upon reception of the link status *Ready* message M2PA responds with a link status *Ready* message on the user data stream with the BSN set to the FSN of the last user data message received from the peer M2PA and which has not been discarded.

The BSN is used at both endpoints to resynchronize the sequence numbers before transmission of user data messages is resumed.

MTP Level 2 Flow Control

M2PA must provide the MTP Level 2 flow control (see Sect. 9.1.1). The purpose of the Level 2 flow control is to inform the peer endpoint about a receive congestion, so that the transmitting endpoint can distinguish between congestion and failure situations and to enable the peer to take appropriate actions, e.g., to trigger the SS 7 flow control (see Sects. 9.1.2 and 9.1.3) and to take the link *out of service* if the congestion situation lasts too long.

When M2PA detects a receive congestion it sends a link status *Busy* message to the peer M2PA. Again, this message is not sent continuously but may be repeated as long as the congestion situation persists. The termination of the receive congestion is indicated by sending a link status *Busy ended* message to the peer. During receive congestion M2PA continues transmitting messages but must not acknowledge the message that triggered the sending of the link status *Busy* message nor any messages received before the link status *Busy ended* message has been sent.

Upon receipt of the first link status *Busy* message the peer M2PA starts the remote congestion timer T6 (see Appendix A for timer values) and stops the excessive delay of acknowledgement timer T7 if there are messages in the retransmission buffer. Any other link status *Busy* messages received while T6 is running do not reset the timer T6. Furthermore, T7 shall not be started while T6 is running. The peer M2PA continues to receive and acknowledge messages while the other end is busy but must not send user data messages after receiving the link status *Busy* message. When the peer M2PA receives the link status *Busy ended* message while T6 is running it stops T6 and starts T7 if there are messages in the retransmission buffer to be acknowledged and restarts sending user messages. Should timer T6 expire a link failure indication is sent to the local MTP-3.

Data Retrieval

In the case of a link failure MTP-3 performs a changeover to an alternative link, which includes data retrieval from the failed link, if possible. This requires buffer updating, i.e., the identification of all user data messages in the retransmission buffer of the failed link which have not been received by the far end and untransmitted messages, as well as transferring these messages to the local MTP-3 for sending to the peer via an alternative link.

The retransmission buffer update is performed by exchanging the forward sequence number of the last user data message accepted by the remote M2PA (FSNC) between the peer M2PA. Given that the sequence numbers of M2PA are 24 bits long MTP-3 needs to use the extended changeover order (ECO) and extended changeover acknowledgement (ECA) messages [14] to transfer the FSNC.

Upon reception of an ECO or ECA message the MTP-3 sends a RETRIEVAL REQUEST AND FSNC primitive to M2PA. When M2PA receives this primitive it shall first retrieve and deliver in sequence any transmitted user data messages beginning with the first unacknowledged message with FSN greater than FSNC. After these, it sends in sequence any untransmitted user data messages.

There may be the case that it is impossible for an endpoint to determine the FSN of the last user data message accepted by the peer. In this case emergency changeover is performed. If M2PA receives a retrieval request with no FSNC or an invalid FSNC value, this indicates emergency changeover, in which case M2PA retrieves and delivers to MTP-3 any untransmitted user data messages.

7.4 MTP-2 User Adaptation Layer

The MTP-2 user adaptation layer (M2UA) protocol is designed for *backhauling* MTP-3 messages between a SG and a MGC over IP using the services of SCTP, i.e., to transport MTP-3 messages when the SG has no MTP-3 functionality. In this case, an SCTP association acts as a logical extension of the link set between the SG and the adjacent SS 7 SEP or STP. In other words, the M2UA allows remote control of the SS 7 links at the SG by the MTP-3 at the MGC. The protocol structure for the transport of MTP-3 messages between the SG and a MGC applying M2UA is shown in Fig. 5.3. In the following, we describe in more detail the functions and services provided by the M2UA.

7.4.1 M2UA Messages

The peer-to-peer communication is performed by M2UA using various messages which belong to different classes. The basic M2UA message format corresponds to the general adaptation layer message format which consists of the common message header, shown in Fig. 7.18, followed by the M2UA specific part.

The *VERSION* field contains the version of M2UA. For the current release 1.0 of M2UA the value is '01'. The *MESSAGE CLASS* field identifies the class an

M2UA message belongs to, where we distinguish management (MGMT), ASP state maintenance (ASPSM), ASP traffic maintenance (ASPTM), MTP-2 user adaptation (MAUP), and interface identifier management (IIM) messages. For each class the different messages are distinguished by the *MESSAGE TYPE*. Finally, the *MESSAGE LENGTH* field defines the length of the message in octets including the common header.

In addition to the common header, MAUP messages will use an M2UA-specific message header, as shown in Fig. 7.20.

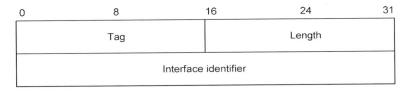

Fig. 7.20. M2UA message header

The M2UA message header contains the interface identifier, which identifies the physical interface at the SG for which the signalling messages are sent or received. The interface identifier can be text or integer, where the values assigned are according to the network operator policy.

Finally, an M2UA message contains zero, one or more variable-length parameters, depending on the message type, and which are defined in a tag-length-value format as shown in Fig. 7.21. The parameter *TAG* field identifies the type of the parameter, e.g., traffic mode type, interface identifier or error code. The length of the parameter, including the tag, length, and value fields, is contained in the parameter *LENGTH* field whilst the parameter *VALUE* field contains the actual information of the parameter. In an M2UA message mandatory parameters must come before optional parameters.

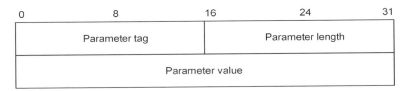

Fig. 7.21. Variable-length parameter format

The specific use of the ASPSM, ASPTM, and related MGMT messages is described in Sect. 6.2.3 whilst the M2UA-specific messages are introduced in the following sections.

7.4.2 Management of SCTP Associations

In order to avoid a single point of failure, at least two ASPs resident in separate hosts and therefore available over different SCTP associations, as shown in Fig. 6.3, should be part of an AS within a MGC, where the peer MTP-3 and MTP-3 User Parts are located.

Establishment of an SCTP Association

For the establishment of the SCTP association the peer M2UA should be configured so that one always takes on the role of the client and the other the role of the server. The default is that the ASP takes on the role of the client whilst the SGP is the server. When an ASP is responsible for initiating the setup of an SCTP association to the SGP, the M2UA layer at the MGC receives an M-SCTP_ESTABLISH request primitive from the layer management. The M2UA layer then tries to establish the SCTP association with the peer M2UA at the SG. Upon receipt of an eventual COMMU-NICATION UP notification primitive from the SCTP, the M2UA layer will invoke the M-SCTP_ESTABLISH confirm primitive to the layer management. In a similar way, the peer M2UA at the SG receives a COMMUNICATION UP notification primitive from the SCTP, which then invokes the M-SCTP_ESTABLISH indication primitive to its local layer management. Once the SCTP association is established the local ASP state and traffic maintenance function of the M2UA layer at the MGC then conveys the ASP state to the SG using the ASPSM and ASPTM messages (see Sect. 6.2.3).

The M2UA may also need to inform its local layer management about the status of an underlying SCTP association, which is performed using the M-SCTP_STATUS request and indication primitives; for example, the M2UA layer may inform the local management about the reason for the release of an SCTP association, determined either locally within the M2UA layer or by a primitive from the SCTP.

Management of Streams

A user-specified number of streams may be opened during the initialization of an SCTP association. The M2UA at the SG must maintain a map of an interface ID to a physical interface, e.g., E1 line/timeslot. At the SGP an interface ID is uniquely mapped onto a stream within an SCTP association, where this mapping may dynamically change due to a change of ASP states. For example, it would be natural that every incoming SS 7 link within a linkset at the SG is uniquely mapped onto a corresponding SCTP stream based on the SLC. In this case, there is a one-to-one mapping of the SLC to the interface identifier. Another possibility would be that an implementation splits an SS 7 link across several streams based on the SLS value so that, in this case, the correct stream is identified by the SLC and SLS.

Stream '0' should only be used for ASP maintenance messages and not for MAUP messages. M2UA is responsible for the proper management of streams allowed with each association.

Termination of an SCTP Association

If the layer management at the SG or MGC decides to bring down an SCTP association for management reasons, it sends an M-SCTP_RELEASE request primitive to its local M2UA layer. The M2UA then sends a SHUTDOWN or ABORT primitive to the local SCTP in order to gracefully or ungracefully close the association, depending on whether message discard should be avoided or not. On receipt of a SHUTDOWN COMPLETE notification from SCTP the M2UA layer informs the local layer management that requested the release of the association using the M-SCTP_RELEASE confirm primitive whilst the peer uses the M-SCTP_RELEASE indication primitive, respectively.

Active Association Control

At the SG an AS list may contain active and inactive ASPs to support ASP failover procedures and load sharing. This list of ASPs in an AS is dynamic, i.e., may change during operation, taking into account availability and traffic-handling capability. When the traffic-handling mode of the AS is not known via configuration it is indicated by the first ASP-ACTIVE message (see Sect. 6.2.3). There are three modes of AS traffic handling supported by M2UA: override, loadshare, and broadcast.

If the SGP receives an ASPAC message and if the override mode applies (see Sect. 6.2.4) then the SGP redirects the complete traffic for the AS to the ASP that sent the ASPAC. In addition, the SGP responds with an ASPAC ACK message to that ASP. Any previously active ASP in the AS list is considered to be *inactive* and will no longer receive traffic for the AS. Finally, the SGP sends a NOTIFY message with status information *alternate ASP active* to the previously active ASP after stopping all traffic to that ASP. On receipt of this NOTIFY message the previously active ASP considers itself to be in the *inactive* state. If the SGP receives an ASPAC message and if the loadshare mode applies then the SGP will send part of the traffic for the AS to the ASP that sends the ASPAC message in addition to all other active ASPs in the AS. The load sharing algorithm at the SGP is considered to be implementation dependent. An ASPIA message received by the SGP from an ASP causes that ASP to move to the *inactive* state. The SGP stops sending traffic to that ASP and continues to loadshare traffic to the remaining active ASPs in the AS. In the broadcast mode an ASPAC message received at the SGP causes the traffic to be sent to the ASP sending the ASPAC whilst the same traffic continues to be sent to the other active ASPs in the AS.

Finally, if the SGP determines that the traffic-handling mode indicated in the AS-PAC message does not correspond to the currently used AS mode, or if the indicated traffic-handling mode is not supported, the SGP responds with an ERROR message indicating an *unsupported* or *invalid traffic-handling mode*.

7.4.3 Interface Boundaries

M2UA–MTP-2

In order to enable seamless operation of MTP-3 peers in the SS 7 and IP domain M2UA supports the MTP-2/MTP-3 interface boundary. This means that all primitives between MTP-2 and MTP-3 are provided by the M2UA upper layer interface at the MGC and the NIF at the SGP to support the MTP-2/M2UA boundary.

The difference from the M2PA is that the M2UA does not itself provide the full MTP-2 functions and services offered to its local MTP-3 at the MGC but instead extends access to the MTP-2 functions and services available at the SG. In fact, the MTP-3 at the MGC is unaware that the expected MTP-2 services accessed via its lower layer interface are offered remotely from the MTP-2 layer at the SG. Similarly, the MTP-2 at the SG is also unaware that its local MTP-3 is actually located in the remote MGC and accessed via M2UA.

This remote access is performed by mapping a received primitive from MTP-3 at the MGC onto the corresponding MTP-2 user adaptation layer (MAUP) message. The MAUP message is then transferred by M2UA to its peer at the SGP via the SCTP stream that corresponds to the interface identifier of the link to which the primitive is related and which is also contained in the M2UA message header of the MAUP message. At the SGP, the MAUP message is transferred by the NIF to the corresponding link as the original MTP-3/MTP-2 primitive. In the same way, MTP-2/MTP-3 primitives received at the SGP via the NIF are transferred to the responsible ASP in the IP domain using the corresponding MAUP message.

M2UA–Layer Management

M2UA may be informed by its layer management to establish or terminate an SCTP association, to activate or deactivate ASPs or to request the current status of an SCTP association, ASP or AS. The corresponding messages and actions are described in Sects. 7.4.2 and 6.2.3.

M2UA–SCTP

Finally, the M2UA uses the SCTP services by passing primitives to SCTP and receiving notifications from SCTP, as described in Sect. 7.2.

7.4.4 M2UA-Specific Functions

In order to provide backhauling of MTP-3 messages between the SG and the MGC as well as a remote control of the SS 7 links at the SG by the MTP-3 at the MGC, the M2UA layer has to perform several functions, which are described below.

Link Activation and Deactivation

In order to activate an SS 7 link at the SG the MTP-3 at the MGC needs to send a corresponding START primitive, which is transferred to the SG as an ESTABLISH REQUEST message. The mode *normal* or *emergency* for bringing the link in service is default to *normal*. The STATE REQUEST message with the state parameter *request emergency alignment procedure* can be used to change the mode to *emergency*. When the link is *in service* the SG sends an ESTABLISH CONFIRMATION message to the MGC, which is transferred to the MTP-3 as a link IN SERVICE indication primitive. Equally, the RELEASE REQUEST message is used by the MGC to trigger a STOP primitive at the SGP to deactivate a link. When the link is deactivated the SG returns a RELEASE CONFIRMATION to the MGC. If the link is taken out of service for some reason, the SG can autonomously send a RELEASE INDICA-TION message to the MGC, which is transferred to the local MTP-3 as a link OUT OF SERVICE indication primitive.

Processor Outage

If the AS moves to the *inactice* or *down* state, i.e., if the MTP-3 at the MGC is un-available, while the SS 7 links are *in service* the Level 2 at the SG should apply local processor outage on the SS 7 links. Equally, if Level 2 at the SG is informed about the beginning or end of a remote processor outage situation at the adjacent SS 7 node this information is transferred to the MGC using the STATE INDICATION mes-sage with value *remote entered processor outage* or *remote exited processor outage*, respectively, which are transferred to the MTP-3 as REMOTE PROCESSOR OUT-AGE and REMOTE PROCESSOR RECOVERED indication primitives. At the end of a processor outage situation Level 2 is instructed by MTP-3 whether to flush its Level 2 buffers and to synchronize the Level 2 sequence numbers before the trans-mission of user traffic is resumed or to simply continue with sending messages. This information from MTP-3 at the MGC to the SS 7 links at the SG is transferred by M2UA using the STATE REQUEST message with value *flush receive, transmit, and retransmit queues* or *continue*.

M2UA Flow Control

If an implementation-dependent congestion onset threshold in the Level 2 transmit buffer at the SG is exceeded, Level 2 sends a corresponding CONGESTION ONSET primitive to its local MTP-3, which is transferred by M2UA to the MTP-3 at the MGC using the CONGESTION INDICATION message with value set to *congestion level 3*. Equally, if an implementation-dependent congestion abatement threshold is crossed, the CONGESTION INDICATION message with value *no congestion* is sent to the MGC. When the national option with congestion priorities applies this message may also be used to transfer the congestion status or discard status to MTP-3 (see Sect. 9.1). Furthermore, when the SG runs out of buffer space for MSUs received from the MGC the SG shall send a CONGESTION INDICATION message with the parameters congestion status and discard status set to *level 4 discarding* and discards MSUs received from the MGC.

Finally, M2UA may receive an indication from SCTP about an IP network con-gestion onset or abatement. Note that the handling of this congestion indication by M2UA is considered to be implementation dependent. However, in order to assure the function of the SS 7 flow control, the SG should initiate the Level 2 flow control at the SS 7 links when a transmit congestion exists towards the MGC. The other way round, if M2UA at the MGC receives a congestion indication from SCTP it must send a CONGESTION ONSET indication primitive to its local MTP-3.

Data Retrieval

In the case of a link failure MTP-3 performs a changeover to an alternative link, which includes data retrieval from the failed link, if possible. To this end MTP-3 at the MGC sends a RETRIEVE BSNT requests primitive to its M2UA, which is transferred to the SG by means of the RETRIEVAL REQUEST message with value *retrieve the backward sequence number*. When receiving the BSNT from the local link the SG sends the RETRIEVAL CONFIRM message in response with the retrieved BSNT. If the BSNT could not be retrieved the value of the *RESULT* field is set to *action failed*, otherwise it is set to *action successful*.

For data retrieval, the RETRIEVE REQUEST primitive from MTP-3 at the MGC is then transferred to the SG using the RETRIEVAL REQUEST message with value *retrieve the PDUS from the transmit and retransmit queues*. M2UA at the SG then sends a RETRIEVAL CONFIRM message where the value of the result field will indicate *success* or *failure*. In addition, the SG sends a RETRIEVAL INDICATION with a PDU from the transmit or retransmit buffer taking care of the sequence of the retrieved messages. Finally, the RETRIEVAL COMPLETE INDICATION message indicates that it contains the last PDU from the Level 2 buffers.

7.4.5 M2UA Management

When an error with an incoming message is detected, i.e., when an invalid version, an invalid interface or stream identifier, an unsupported message class or type, an unsupported traffic-handling mode or an unexpected message is received or when a protocol error occurs, the M2UA uses the ERROR (ERR) message to inform the peer of the error event, where the error code parameter is mandatory whilst the interface identifier and diagnostic information parameters are optional. Finally, it should be noted that an error message is not generated in response to other error messages.

In order to provide an autonomous indication of M2UA events to an M2UA peer the NOTIFY (NTFY) message, which contains the mandatory status type and status information parameters that yield more detailed information for the notification, is used. The ASP identifier, interface identifier, and info string parameters are optional.

7.5 MTP-3 User Adaptation Layer

The MTP-3 user adaptation layer (M3UA) protocol is designed to transport MTP-3 user (ISUP, SCCP, TUP, etc.) messages over IP using the services of SCTP and to enable seamless operation of MTP-3 User Parts in the SS 7 and IP domains. This protocol applies between a SG and one ore more MGCs or IPSPs, where the SG provides the MTP-3 functionality, which is terminated by the SG. The M3UA layer then extends access to the MTP-3 layer services to a remote IP-based application, i.e., the M3UA does not itself provide the full MTP-3 functions and services. The protocol structure for the transport of ISUP messages between the SG and MGCs applying M3UA is shown in Fig. 5.4, the transport of SCCP messages via the SG is shown in Fig. 5.5, and the transport of SCCP messages between IPSPs adapted to the simplified point-to-point relationship using M3UA is shown in Fig. 5.6. In the following, we describe in more detail the functions and services provided by M3UA.

7.5.1 M3UA Messages

The communication between peer M3UAs is performed by means of various messages, which belong to different classes. The basic M3UA message format corresponds to the general adaptation layer message format with the common message header shown in Fig. 7.18. The *VERSION* field contains the version of M3UA. For the current release 1.0 of M3UA the value is '01'. The *MESSAGE CLASS* field identifies the class, an M3UA message belongs to, where six classes are defined: management (MGMT), SS 7 signalling network management (SSNM), routing key management (RKM), ASP state maintenance (ASPSM), ASP traffic maintenance (ASPTM) and transfer messages. For each class the different messages are distinguished by the *MESSAGE TYPE* field. Finally, the *MESSAGE LENGTH* field defines the length of the message in octets including the common header.

The M3UA-specific part follows the common part of an M3UA message and consists of zero, one or more variable-length parameters, depending on the message type. All these parameters are defined in a tag-length-value format as shown in Fig. 7.21. The parameter *TAG* field identifies the type of the parameter, e.g., info string, routing context or ASP identifier. The length of the parameter, including the tag, length, and value fields, is contained in the parameter *LENGTH* field whilst the parameter *VALUE* field contains the actual information of the parameter.

The specific use of the ASPSM, ASPTM, and related MGMT messages is described in Sect. 6.2.3 whilst the M3UA-specific messages are introduced in the following sections.

7.5.2 Management of SCTP Associations

In order to avoid a single point of failure an AS should consist of at least two ASPs resident in separate hosts and therefore available over different SCTP associations. The ASPs may be addressed by the SPC of the SG or by their own SPC. In the first case, the SCTP association acts as an internal connection between MTP-3 and its SS 7 User Parts, actually located in the IP domain, so that from the SS 7 point of view the SG is an a SEP. In the second case, the SCTP association acts as an SS 7 route set towards the final destination, where the peer SS7 User Part is located so that, from an SS 7 point of view, the SG works as a transfer point for the concerned user messages.

Establishment of an SCTP Association

In order to avoid redundant SCTP associations from being established between two M3UA peers, the default is that the SGP takes on the role of the server whilst the ASP is the client. In the case of the simplified IPSP-to-IPSP communication it should be fixed by configuration which of the peer M3UA endpoints takes on the role of the client and which the role of the server. At the ASP, which is responsible for initiating the setup of an SCTP association, the M3UA layer at the MGC or IPSP receives an M-SCTP_ESTABLISH request primitive from the layer management. The M3UA layer then tries to establish the SCTP association with its peer M3UA. Upon receipt of an eventual COMMUNICATION UP notification primitive from SCTP, the M3UA layer will invoke the M-SCTP_ESTABLISH confirm primitive to the layer management. Similarly, the peer M3UA receives a COMMUNICATION UP notification primitive from the SCTP when the association is successfully set up, which then invokes the M-SCTP_ESTABLISH indication primitive to its local layer management. Once the SCTP association is established the local ASP state and traffic maintenance function of the M3UA layer at the MGC or IPSP then conveys the ASP state to the SG using the ASPSM and ASPTM messages (see Sect. 6.2.3).

The M3UA layer may also need to inform the local management about the status of an underlying SCTP association, which is performed using the M-SCTP_STATUS request and indication primitives. For example, the M3UA layer may inform the local management about the reason for the release of an SCTP association, determined either locally within the M3UA layer or by a primitive from the SCTP.

Management of Streams

A user-specified number of streams may be opened during the initialization of an SCTP association. With the objective to minimize transmission and buffering delays, the use of SCTP streams by M3UA is recommended as a further step towards providing the performance and reliability of SCN signalling transport. However, the distribution of SS 7 User Part messages over SCTP streams must be performed in such a way to avoid message missequencing. To this end, traffic that requires sequencing must be assigned to the same stream based on, for example, the signalling link selection (SLS) value of the MTP routing label, i.e., by using SCTP streams as normal SS 7 links. As a rule, DATA messages must not be sent via stream '0', ASPSM, MGMT, and RKM messages are sent via stream '0', whilst SSNM, ASPTM, BEAT, BEAT ACK, and NTFY messages can be sent on any stream. The heartbeat messages BEAT and BEAT ACK are optional and may be used to ensure that the M3UA peers are still available. It is the responsibility of the M3UA layer to ensure proper management of streams allowed with each association.

Termination of an SCTP Association

If the layer management at the SG, MGC or IPSP decides to close an SCTP association for management reasons, it sends an M-SCTP_RELEASE request primitive to its local M3UA layer. M3UA then sends a SHUTDOWN or ABORT primitive to the local SCTP in order to gracefully or ungracefully close the association, depending on whether message discard should be avoided or not. On receipt of a SHUTDOWN

COMPLETE notification from SCTP the M3UA layer informs its local layer management that requested the release of the association using the M-SCTP_RELEASE confirm primitive, whilst the peer uses the M-SCTP_RELEASE indication primitive.

Active Association Control

All MTP-3 user messages received at the SGP from an SS 7 originating node are assigned to a uniquely determined AS, using the SS 7 addressing information contained in the message and the provisioned routing keys. The AS list at the SGP normally contains one or more active ASPs, which are currently used to process the concerned traffic, and inactive ASPs. The M3UA layer on the SGP maintains the state of all configured remote ASPs in order to manage the SCTP associations and the traffic between the SGP and the ASPs. In the case of a failure of an active ASP, failover may be performed that leads to another ASP, where both load sharing and backup scenarios are supported. When the traffic-handling mode of the AS is not know via configuration it is indicated by the first ASP-ACTIVE message (see Sect. 6.2.3). There are three modes of AS traffic handling in the SGP M3UA: override, loadshare, and broadcast.

If the SGP receives an ASPAC message and if the override mode applies (see Sect. 6.2.4) then the SGP redirects the complete traffic for the AS to the ASP that sent the ASPAC. In addition, the SGP responds with an ASPAC ACK message to that ASP. Any previously active ASP in the AS list is considered to be *inactive* and will no longer receive traffic for the AS. Finally, the SGP sends a NOTIFY message with status information *alternate ASP active* to the previously active ASP after stopping all traffic to that ASP. On receipt of this NOTIFY message the previously active ASP considers itself to be in the *inactive* state. If the SGP receives an ASPAC message and if the loadshare mode applies then the SGP will send part of the traffic for the AS to the ASP that sends the ASPAC message in addition to all other active ASPs in the AS. The load sharing algorithm at the SGP is considered to be implementation dependent. An ASPIA message received by the SGP from an ASP causes that ASP to move to the *inactive* state. The SGP stops sending traffic to that ASP and continues to loadshare traffic to the remaining active ASPs in the AS. In the broadcast mode an ASPAC message received at the SGP causes the traffic to be sent to the ASP sending the ASPAC whilst the same traffic continues to be sent to the other active ASPs in the AS.

Finally, if the SGP determines that the traffic-handling mode indicated in the AS-PAC message does not correspond to the currently used AS mode, or if the indicated traffic-handling mode is not supported, the SGP responds with an ERROR message indicating an *unsupported* or *invalid traffic-handling mode*.

In the case of the simplified IPSP to IPSP communication shown in Fig. 5.6 the active association control is the same with the SGP replaced by the server ASP at the IPSP receiving the ASPAC message.

7.5.3 Interface Boundaries

M3UA–MTP-3

All services and primitives between MTP-3 and MTP-3 User Parts are provided by the M3UA upper layer interface. However, the M3UA does not itself provide the full MTP-3 functions and services offered to its local MTP-3 users at the MGC or IPSP but instead extends access to the MTP-3 functions and services available at the SG. On receiving an MTP-TRANSFER request primitive from an MTP-3 user via the upper layer at the MGC or IPSP, the M3UA will send a corresponding DATA message to its M3UA peer at the SGP, where it is transferred to the MTP-3 by the NIF for ongoing routing to its final SS 7 destination. In the same way, an MSU received at the SGP from the NIF is transported to the peer M3UA layer at the MGC or IPSP as a DATA message, which then transfers the message as an MTP-TRANSFER indication primitive to its local MTP-3 user. The MTP-PAUSE indication primitive is used by M3UA to inform the local User Parts about the total inability of providing the MTP-3 services to the specified destination, whilst the MTP-RESUME indication primitive is used to inform the user that the MTP-3 services are now available again to the specified destination. Furthermore, the MTP-STATUS indication primitive is used by M3UA to indicate the partial inability of providing the MTP-3 services, because of User Part unavailability or SS 7 network congestion towards the affected destination.

M3UA–Layer Management

M3UA may be informed by its layer management to establish or terminate an SCTP association, to activate or deactivate ASPs or to request the current status of an SCTP association, ASP or AS. The corresponding messages and actions are described in Sects. 7.5.2 and 6.2.3.

M3UA–SCTP

Finally, M3UA uses the SCTP services by passing primitives to SCTP and receiving notifications from SCTP, as described in Sect. 7.2.

7.5.4 M3UA-Specific Functions

7.5.4.1 Routing Key Management

The routing key management provides the means for an ASP to dynamically register or deregister one or more routing keys with the peer M3UA at the SGP.

Registration

A REGISTRATION REQUEST (REG REQ) message is sent by an ASP to indicate to the remote M3UA peer on the SGP that it wishes to register one or more routing keys as contained in the REG REQ message. On receipt, the SGP examines the contents of the routing key parameters and compares it with the available routing keys at the SGP.

On the one hand, if the ASP is not currently included in the list of ASPs serving an AS and if a received routing key matches an existing routing key entry, then the ASP is added to the AS list. On the other hand, if a routing key contained in the REG REQ message currently does not exist and if the received routing key data is valid and unique, an SG supporting dynamic configuration may create a new routing key and a related AS and add the concerned ASP to the new AS list. In either case, the SG returns a REGISTRATION RESPONSE (REG RSP) message to the ASP indicating a successful registration. In the case of an error condition, i.e., if the routing key data is invalid, the SG returns a REG RSP message to the ASP where the registration result status field now indicates the reason for the failure of the registration.

Finally, an ASP may include a routing context parameter in a REG REQ message. When the SGP receives a REG REQ message with a routing context and if the routing context applies to an existing routing key, the SGP may modify the existing routing key according to the new information provided in the routing key parameter. A REG RSP is returned indicating a successfull registration or that the SGP does not support the re-registration.

Deregistration

In the same way a DEREGISTRATION REQUEST (DEREG REQ) message is sent by an ASP to indicate to the remote M3UA peer at the SGP that it wishes to dereg- ister a given routing key, which is specified by a routing key and routing context parameters. After receipt of a DEREG REQ message the SGP examines the contents of the routing key and routing context parameters. If the ASP is currently registered in the AS related to the included routing context, the ASP is deregistered as an ASP in the concerned AS. Note that the deregistration does not necessarily imply the dele- tion of routing key and AS configuration data at the SGP since other ASPs may be associated with that AS, in which case the routing key cannot be deleted. However, if no more ASPs are in an AS list the SGP may delete the routing key data. In any case, the SG acknowledges the deregistration request by returning a DEREGISTRA- TION RESPONSE (DEREG RSP) message, indicating success or failure with the cause.

7.5.4.2 Interworking of Network Management Functions

The purpose of MTP-3 signalling route management (SRM) is to ensure reliable exchange of information between the signalling points about the availability of the underlying signalling routes. In order to allow seamless operation between peer User Parts in the SS 7 and IP domains, it is required that the SGP also provides an exten- sion of the MTP-3 network management functions into the IP domain.

User Parts in the IP domain must be informed about the unavailability or avail- ability of relevant SS 7 destination points, the congestion of route sets towards SS 7 destination points or the unavailability or availability of peer User Parts in the SS 7 network. In the same way, User Parts in the SS 7 network must be informed about a congestion situation regarding the transport of SS 7 messages to an SPMC or the unavailability or availability of a peer User Part in the IP domain. In order to exchange the relevant information between the SGP and the relevant ASPs in the IP domain, the M3UA layer uses the SS 7 signalling network management (SSNM) messages DUNA, DAVA, DRST, SCON, DUPU, and DAUD. Note that DUNA, DAVA, DRST, and SCON messages should arrive in order so that they must be sent on a sequenced stream. For DUPU and DAUD messages sequencing is not required so that they may be sent unsequenced. In the following, we describe the use and function of these messages in more detail.

The SSNM messages function in a different way depending on whether an AS is addressed by the same SPC of the SG or by an individual SPC. In the first case, the MTP-3 User Part in the SS 7 network considers the AS to be a peer user located at the SG so that the SG acts as an SEP. The SSNM message exchange is then nothing other than an internal communication between the MTP-3 at the SG and its local User Parts, i.e., the network management messages from the SS 7 network are transferred to the relevant ASPs in the IP domain as MTP-PAUSE, MTP-RESUME or MTP-STATUS primitives. Furthermore, no TFP and TFA messages will be sent in this case by the SG to adjacent SS 7 nodes, since they will not take any action on the receipt of these unexpected SRM messages. In the second case, when the peer MTP-3 User Part in the IP domain is addressed by its own SPC, the SG acts as an STP. All SRM messages are then mapped onto the corresponding SSNM messages, now functioning as SRM messages in the IP domain, which are mapped again by the M3UA layer at the final ASP onto the corresponding MTP-PAUSE, MTP-RESUME or MTP-STATUS primitives.

Transfer Prohibited

An STP sends a transfer prohibited (TFP) message to an adjacent node via any available route when it has to notify the adjacent nodes that they must no longer route messages addressed to a specified destination node via that STP. Thus when a SG, acting as a transfer node, determines that the transport of SS 7 messages to all ASPs in a particular SPMC is interrupted, the MTP-3 route management at the SG is informed, which then initiates the sending of corresponding TFP messages to the relevant adjacent nodes in the SS 7 network.

When the SG, acting as an SEP or STP, determines that a destination point in the SS 7 network is inaccessible, it sends a corresponding destination unavailable (DUNA) message to all concerned ASPs in the IP domain. A DUNA is also sent in response to a message from an ASP to an unreachable SS 7 destination. It may contain more than one affected DPCs and can also refer to a complete region or cluster of inaccessible signalling points. This is of use if due to a route set failure a larger region of an SS 7 network becomes inaccessible. Finally, the DUNA message may contain an optional network appearance parameter. This parameter may be used when the SG is part of different SS 7 networks and when the SS 7 network indicator, as contained in the SIO of an SS 7 message, does not provide sufficient information. In this case, the network appearance parameter defines the format of the affected DPCs, the DPC point code length, and specific sub service field definitions of the SIO.

Transfer Allowed

An STP sends a transfer allowed (TFA) message to an adjacent node via any available route when it has to notify the adjacent nodes that they may start to route messages addressed to a specified destination node via that STP. Thus when a SG, acting as a transfer node, determines that the transport of SS 7 messages to an ASP in a particular SPMC can be resumed, the MTP-3 route management at the SGP is informed, which then initiates the sending of corresponding TFA messages to the relevant adjacent nodes in the SS 7 network.

When the SG, acting as an SEP or STP, determines that a destination point in the SS 7 network is accessible again, it sends a corresponding destination available (DAVA) message to all concerned ASPs in the IP domain. A DAVA message is also sent in response to a DAUD message, if appropriate. The parameters of the DAVA message and their format are the same as for the DUNA message.

Transfer Controlled

The purpose of signalling traffic flow control is to limit signalling traffic at its source in the case when the SS 7 network is not capable of transferring all signalling traffic offered by the User Parts, because of failure or congestion situations. For the international network, a transfer controlled (TFC) message is sent by a signalling transfer point for every eight messages, when congestion is detected, to one or more originating nodes in order to convey the congestion indication regarding the concerned destination node (see Sect. 9.1). In the same way, when an MSU from a local User Part is received for a congested route set, a congestion indication primitive is sent to all local User Parts for every eight messages [4]. According to the national option with congestion priorities, an STP sends a TFC message when it has to notify one or more originating nodes that they should no longer send messages with a given priority or lower to the concerned destination node via that STP. In the case when the congestion status of a signalling route set changes as a result of either the receipt of a TFP message relating to a particular destination or an indication of local signalling link congestion or due to the signalling route set congestion test procedure, an indication is given from the MTP-3 to the local User Parts informing them about the current congestion status of the signalling route set. Messages received from local User Parts with congestion priorities lower than the current signalling route set congestion status are discarded by the MTP-3 [4].

Thus when an SG, acting as a transfer node, determines that the transport of SS 7 messages to an SPMC is encountering congestion, the MTP-3 route management at the SG is informed, which marks the route to the affected SPMC as *congested* and triggers the sending of corresponding TFC messages to the originating nodes in the SS 7 network as well as congestion indication primitives to local User Parts, if present. When the SG acting as an SEP or STP determines that the congestion status of a signalling route set towards a destination point in the SS 7 network changes to *congested* then it sends a signalling congestion (SCON) message to all concerned ASPs in the IP domain. The SCON message may also be sent from the M3UA of the ASP to an M3UA peer, indicating that the M3UA or the ASP is congested. The format of the network appearance and affected DPC parameters is the same as for the DUNA message. In addition, the SCON message may contain the optional congestion level parameter, used for the national option with congestion priorities.

Signalling Route Set Test and Signalling Route Set Congestion Test

A signalling route set test is performed at a signalling point to test whether or not signalling traffic towards a certain destination may be routed via an adjacent transfer node. To this end, a signalling route set test (RST) message is sent by a signalling point to an adjacent STP, from which a TFP message was received, every 30–60 s, until a TFA message is received indicating that the concerned destination node is available again.

The signalling route set congestion test is performed at an originating signalling point to update the congestion status associated with a route set towards a certain destination. The purpose is to test whether or not signalling messages destined towards that destination with a given congestion priority or higher may be sent [4].

For both tests an ASP sends a destination state audit (DAUD) message to audit the availability or congestion state of an SS 7 route set to one or more affected destination nodes. The parameters of the DAUD message and their format are the same as for the DUNA message.

User Part Unavailability

If the MTP-3 is unable to distribute a received message to a local user because that user is unavailable, the MTP-3 sends a User Part unavailability (UPU) message to the MTP-3 at the originating signalling point of that message. When the originating signalling point's MTP-3 receives a UPU message, it sends an MTP-STATUS primitive with parameter

- *Unequipped remote user*, if no such user exists
- *Inaccessible remote user*, if the user exists but the MTP-3 cannot currently distribute messages to it.

The destination User Part unavailable (DUPU) message is used by the SGP to inform a concerned ASP that a remote peer MTP-3 User Part at a node in the SS 7 network is unavailable. The format of the network appearance and affected destination parameters are the same as for the DUNA message. The unavailability cause parameter provides the reason for the unavailability of the MTP-3 User Part, its values are

- *Unknown*
- *Unequipped remote user*
- *Inaccessible remote user*

Finally, the MTP-3 user identity parameter identifies the specific MTP-3 user, e.g., ISUP or SCCP, that is unavailable. Its values correspond to those provided in the UPU message and the SS 7 service indicator.

Transfer Restricted

In national networks the transfer restricted procedure is performed at a signalling point acting as a signalling transfer point for messages relating to a given destination, when it has to notify one or more adjacent signalling points that they should, if possible, no longer route the concerned messages via that STP. This is done by sending a corresponding transfer restricted (TFR) message to the concerned adjacent nodes.

Equally, the SGP optionally sends a destination restricted (DRST) message to all concerned ASPs to indicate that one or more SS 7 destinations are now restricted, or in response to a DAUD message, if appropriate. The M3UA at the ASP should then send traffic to the affected destination via an alternate SGP of equal priority, if such an alternate route exists and is available. If an ASP has marked the affected destination to be *unavailable*, a received DRST causes traffic to the affected destination to be resumed via the SGP initiating the DSRT message. The parameters of the DRST message and their format are the same as for the DUNA message.

7.5.5 M3UA Management

The ERROR (ERR) message is used by M3UA to indicate errors associated with a received M3UA message to the peer, e.g., when an invalid version, invalid network appearance, unsupported message class or type, unsupported traffic-handling mode, invalid routing context, stream identifier or parameter value is received as well as when a protocol error occurs. The ERROR message contains the mandatory error code parameter, which indicates the reason for the ERROR message. The parameters routing context, network appearence, and affected point code are only mandatory for specific error codes. Finally, it should be noted that an error message is not generated in response to other error messages.

In order to provide an autonomous indication of M3UA events to an M3UA peer the NOTIFY (NTFY) message is used, which contains the mandatory status type and status information parameters that yield more detailed information for the notification. The ASP identifier parameter is conditional whilst the routing context and info string parameters are optional.

7.6 SCCP User Adaptation Layer

The SCCP user adaptation layer (SUA) protocol is designed to transport SCCP user messages over IP using the services of SCTP and to enable a seamless operation of

SCCP users in the SS 7 and IP domains. This protocol applies between a SG and one ore more IPSPs, e.g., an IP resident database, where the SG provides the SCCP functionality, which is terminated by the SG, or between IPSPs. The protocol structure for the transport of SCCP user messages between the SG and an IPSP applying SUA is shown in Fig. 5.7. The transport of SCCP user messages between two IPSPs adapted to the simplified point-to-point relationship using SUA is shown in Fig. 5.8. Depending upon the upper layer protocol supported, SUA will need to support SCCP connectionless services, SCCP connection-oriented services, or both. In the following, we describe in more detail the functions and services provided by SUA.

7.6.1 SUA Messages

Two peer SUA layers use for their communication various messages, which are asigned to different classes. The basic SUA protocol message format corresponds to the general adaptation layer message format with the common message header shown in Fig. 7.18. The *VERSION* field contains the version of SUA. For the current release 1.0 of SUA the value is '01'. The *MESSAGE CLASS* field identifies one of seven classes, a SUA message belongs to: management (MGMT), SS 7 signalling network management (SSNM), routing key management (RKM), ASP state maintenance (ASPSM), ASP traffic maintenance (ASPTM), connectionless (CL) and connection-oriented (CO) messages. For each class the different messages are distinguished by the *MESSAGE TYPE* field. Finally, the *MESSAGE LENGTH* field defines the length of the message in octets, including the common header.

The SUA-specific part follows the common part of a SUA message and consists of zero, one or more variable length parameters, depending on the message type. All these parameters are defined in a tag-length-value format as shown in Fig. 7.21. The parameter *TAG* field identifies the type of the parameter, e.g., info string, routing context or ASP identifier. The length of the parameter, including the tag, length, and value fields, is contained in the parameter *LENGTH* field whilst the parameter *VALUE* field contains the actual information of the parameter.

The specific use of the ASPSM, ASPTM, and related MGMT messages is described in Sect. 6.2.3, whilst the SUA-specific messages are introduced in the following sections.

7.6.2 Management of SCTP Associations

Like the other adaptation layers SUA needs to manage the underlying SCTP associations.

Establishment of an SCTP Association

In the case of the transport of SCCP user messages from an SS 7 SEP to an IPSP via the SG, as shown in Fig. 5.7, it is assumed that the ASP at the IPSP initiates the establishment of the SCTP association with the SGP. In the case of the simplified

IPSP-to-IPSP communication shown in Fig. 5.8, it should be fixed by configuration which of the peer SUA endpoints takes on the role of the client and which the role of the server. At the ASP, which is responsible for initiating the setup of an SCTP association, the SUA layer receives an M-SCTP_ESTABLISH request primitive from the layer management. The SUA layer then tries to establish the SCTP association with its peer SUA. Upon receipt of an eventual COMMUNICATION UP notification primitive from SCTP, the SUA layer will invoke the M-SCTP_ESTABLISH confirm primitive to the layer management. Similarly, the peer SUA receives a COMMUNI-CATION UP notification primitive from the SCTP when the association is success-fully set up, which then invokes the M-SCTP_ESTABLISH indication primitive to its local layer management. Once the SCTP association is established the local ASP state and traffic maintenance function of the SUA layer at the IPSP then conveys the ASP state to the SGP using the ASPSM and ASPTM messages (see Sect. 6.2.3).

The SUA layer may also need to inform the local management about the status of an underlying SCTP association. This is done using the M-SCTP_STATUS request and indication primitives. For example, the SUA layer may inform the local man-agement about the reason for the release of an SCTP association, determined either locally within the SUA layer or by a primitive from the SCTP.

Management of Streams

SUA supports the use of multiple SCTP streams. SCCP user messages requiring sequenced message transfer need to be sent over the same stream supporting se-quenced delivery. The stream selection is based on the protocol class. For protocol class 0 SUA uses the unordered delivery where the selected stream depends on the available traffic information. For protocol class 1 SUA must select ordered delivery where the selected stream is based on the sequence parameter received from the up-per layer and available traffic information. Finally, for protocol classes 2 and 3 SUA will select ordered delivery where the selected stream depends on the source local reference of the connection and other traffic information available.

All nontransfer messages, except ASPTM, BEAT, and BEAT ACK, are sent via stream '0'. In order to minimize possible message loss ASPTM messages should be sent via one of the streams used to carry data traffic related to the routing context. All nontransfer and non-SSNM messages should be sent with sequenced delivery to ensure ordering, with the exception of BEAT and BEAT ACK messages, which may be sent using unsequenced delivery and on any stream. The heartbeat messages BEAT and BEAT ACK are optional and may be used to ensure that the SUA peers are still available. It is the responsibility of the SUA layer to ensure proper management of the streams allowed with each association.

Termination of an SCTP Association

If the layer management at the SG or IPSP decides to close an SCTP association for management reasons, it sends an M-SCTP_RELEASE request primitive to its local SUA layer. SUA then sends a SHUTDOWN or ABORT primitive to the local SCTP in order to gracefully or ungracefully close the association, depending on whether message discard should be avoided or not. On receipt of a SHUTDOWN COM-PLETE notification from SCTP the SUA layer informs its local layer management that requests the release of the association using the M-SCTP_RELEASE confirm primitive whilst the peer uses the M-SCTP_RELEASE indication primitive.

Active Association Control

As described in Sect. 6.1.1 an AS can be considered as a list of ASPs configured to handle a certain range of SCCP user messages defined by the routing key. One or more ASPs in the list may normally be active, i.e., currently processing traffic, while others may be inactive but may be activated in the event of a failure or unavailabil-ity of an active ASP. In order to support a high availability of transaction process-ing capabilities SUA supports ASP failover and failback functions, as described in Sect. 6.2.4. The traffic-handling mode parameter in the ASPAC message indicates the traffic handling-mode used in a particular AS (see Sect. 6.2.3). Like M2UA and M3UA, SUA uses three modes of AS traffic handling in the SGP: override, loadshare, and broadcast.

If the SGP receives an ASPAC message and if the override mode applies (see Sect. 6.2.4) then the SGP redirects the complete traffic for the AS to the ASP that sent the ASPAC. In addition, the SGP responds with an ASPAC ACK message to that ASP. Any previously active ASP in the AS list is considered to be *inactive* and will no longer receive traffic for the AS. Finally, the SGP sends a NOTIFY message with status information *alternate ASP active* to the previously active ASP after stopping all traffic to that ASP. On receipt of this NOTIFY message the previously active ASP considers itself to be in the *inactive* state. If the SGP receives an ASPAC message and if the loadshare mode applies then the SGP will send part of the traffic for the AS to the ASP that sends the ASPAC message in addition to all other actice ASPs in the AS. The load sharing algorithm at the SGP is considered to be implementation dependent. An ASPIA message received by the SGP from an ASP causes that ASP to move to the *inactive* state. The SGP stops sending traffic to that ASP and continues to loadshare traffic to the remaining active ASPs in the AS. However, when TCAP messages are transported, load sharing is only possible for the first message in a TC dialogue, i.e., TC_BEGIN, TC_QUERY or TC_UNIDIRECTIONAL. All other TCAP messages in the same dialogue must be sent to the same ASP that was selected for the first message. In the broadcast mode an ASPAC message received at the SGP causes the traffic to be sent to the ASP sending the ASPAC whilst the same traffic continues to be sent to the other active ASPs in the AS.

Finally, if the SGP determines that the traffic-handling mode indicated in the AS-PAC message does not correspond to the currently used AS mode, or if the indicated traffic-handling mode is not supported, the SGP responds with an ERROR message indicating an *unsupported* or *invalid traffic-handling mode*.

7.6.3 Interface Boundaries

All services and primitives between SCCP and SCCP users are provided by the SUA upper layer interface. Depending upon the SCCP user, SUA provides the four SCCP protocol classes, two for connectionless services and two for connection-oriented services:

- *Protocol class 0* provides the basic connectionless service of transferring one User information block in the DATA parameter of a unitdata (UDT), extended unitdata (XUDT) or long unitdata (LUDT) messages called SCCP service data units (SDU) to the peer User Part without guaranteed in-sequence delivery.
- *Protocol class 1* provides the sequenced connectionless service used by an SCCP user when a stream of SCCP SDUs shall be delivered in sequence. When a UDT message is not sufficient to convey the user data message a segmenting/reassembly function for protocol classes 0 and 1 is provided. In this case, the SCCP at the originating node or in a relay node provides segmentation of the information into multiple segments, which are transferred in the data field of XUDT messages to the peer node. At the destination node reassembly is performed before the user message is passed to the local SCCP user.
- *Protocol class 2* provides the means for a bidirectional transfer of a number of related user data messages called network service data units (NSDU) between the SCCP users by setting up a temporary or permanent signalling connection as well as the segmenting and reassembling capability.
- *Protocol class 3* provides the same features of class 2 extended by flow control measures and additional capabilities to detect message loss or missequencing. In such a circumstance, the signalling connection is reset and a corresponding notification is given to the SCCP user.

On receiving an N-UNITDATA request primitive from the upper layer at the IPSP, the SUA layer will send a corresponding connectionless data transfer (CLDT) message to its SUA peer at the SG, where it is transferred to the SCCP by the NIF for the ongoing routing to its final SS 7 destination as an SCCP UDT, XUDT or LUDT message. In the same way, an N-UNITDATA indication primitive received at the SG from the NIF is transported as a CLDT to the peer SUA layer at the IPSP, which then transfers the message as an N-UNITDATA indication primitive to the local SCCP subsystem. The CLDT message is also used to transfer SCCP user data between peer SUA layers located at different IPSPs. If an SCCP service data unit could not reach the final destination and if the return option *return SCCP-SDU on error* is set, then the SDU is sent back to the originating node as a unitdata service (UDTS), extended unitdata service (XUDTS) or long unit data service (LUDTS) message, which is then transported to the corresponding SCCP user as an N-NOTICE primitive. This purpose is served by the connectionless data response (CLDR) message, i.e., if the SG receives a UDTS, XUDTS or LUDTS message, it is transported as a CLDR message to the peer SUA at the IPSP, which then transfers the message as an N-NOTICE primitive to the corresponding local subsystem.

The SCCP user at an IPSP requests the transfer of data on a temporary or permanent signalling connection by invoking an N-DATA request primitive, or an N-EXPEDITED DATA request primitive in the case of protocol class 3, to bypass the flow control mechanism. The transfer of data from one SUA to another for connection-oriented services is performed using the connection-oriented data transfer (CODT) message. For example, if the SG acts as an SEP, an N-DATA or N-EXPEDITED DATA request primitive received from the local SCCP user at an IPSP is transferred as a CODT message to the SUA layer at the SG, where it is forwarded by the NIF for ongoing routing to the final SS 7 destination as a data form 1 (class 2), data form 2 (class 3) or expedited data message. In the same way, an N-DATA indication primitive received at the SG from the NIF is transported as a CODT message to the peer SUA at the IPSP, which then transfers the received message to the local subsystem as an N-DATA indication primitive. Finally, the connection-oriented data acknowledgement (CODA) message is sent between peer SUA layers to acknowledge the receipt of data by the peer for protocol class 3. It covers the SCCP data acknowledgement message, used to control the window flow control mechanism, and the expedited data acknowledgement message, used to acknowledge an expedited data message. The connection-oriented error (COERR) message corresponds to the protocol data unit error message sent by SCCP on detection of any protocol errors.

An SCCP user at an IPSP may initiate the setup of a temporary signalling connection by means of the N-CONNECT request primitive. On receipt of this primitive SUA then sends a connection request (CORE) message to the SG, acting as an SEP or a relay node. However, if the SG acts as a relay node, the CORE message is used to establish a first connection section between the IPSP and the SG. The SCCP at the SG then sends a connection request (CR) message to the SS 7 destination node to establish the SS 7 connection section. The other way round, a CR received at the SG is transferred to the IPSP as a CORE message. At the SG, local resources and source local reference numbers are allocated to keep/retrieve the required address information and the connection state in order to format and route subsequent messages for the connection based on reference numbers only. The existing SCCP procedures may be deployed at the SG to perform this coupling. At the destination node a connection request from the peer endpoint is transferred to the local SCCP user as an N-CONNECT indication primitive, which answers with an N-CONNECT response primitive. This is transferred by the SCCP as a connection confirm (CC) message and via the SUA layer as a connection acknowledge (COAK) message to the node initiating the establishment of the SCCP signalling connection. At that node, an N-CONNECT confirm primitive is sent to the calling SCCP user.

Equally, in order to initiate the release of a signalling connection, an SCCP user invokes an N-DICONNECT request primitive, which is transported as a connection released (RLSD) message via the SCCP and as a release request (RELRE) message via the SUA layer. The peer endpoint acknowledges the release of the signalling connection by sending a release complete (RELCO) message via the SUA layer, which corresponds to the SCCP release complete (RLC) message sent via the SS 7 section.

The peer SCCP users are informed about the release of the signalling connection by means of the N-DISCONNECT indication primitive.

Furthermore, the N-RESET primitive can occur in the data transfer state of a connection with protocol class 3, including flow control. The N-RESET overrides all other activities and causes the start of the reinitialization procedure for sequence numbering. The reset request is transported via the SUA layer as a reset request (RESRE) message that corresponds to the SCCP reset request (RSR) message, whilst the reset confirmation is transported via the SUA layer as a reset confirm (RESCO) message and as a reset confirmation (RSC) message via the SCCP section.

Finally, SUA uses the SCTP services by passing primitives to SCTP and receiving notifications from SCTP, as described in Sect. 7.2.

7.6.4 SUA-Specific Functions

7.6.4.1 Addressing

SCCP addressing makes use of the destination point code (DPC), global title (GT) and subsystem number (SSN) where one, two or all of these elements may be present in the called and calling party address. In addition, SUA users may use the hostname and IPv4 or IPv6 addresses to identify their peer IP endpoints. In order to uniquely identify the source and destination, a SUA message contains the source address and destination address parameters, respectively. The general format of these parameters is shown in Fig. 7.22.

The following combinations of address parameters are valid:

- GT + optional DPC and/or SSN, where the SSN may be zero when routing is done on GT
- SSN (nonzero) + optional DPC and/or GT when routing is done on DPC + SSN. The DPC is mandatory in the source address when a message is sent from the SGP to the ASP and in the destination address when a message is sent from the ASP via the SGP to a final SS 7 SEP.
- Hostname + optional SSN, when routing is done on hostname
- SSN (nonzero) and optional IP address (IPv4 or IPv6) when routing is done on IP address + SSN

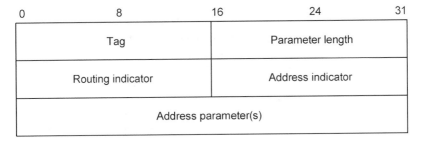

Fig. 7.22. Source and destination address parameter format

The *ROUTING INDICATOR* determines which address parameters need to be present in the *ADDRESS PARAMETER* field and may take on the following valid values:

- Route on GT
- Route on SSN + DPC
- Route on hostname
- Route on SSN + IP address

Finally, the *ADDRESS INDICATOR* is needed for interworking with SS 7 networks. It specifies which address parameters are received in the SCCP address from the SS 7 network or have to be included in the SCCP address when the message is sent into the final SS 7 SEP.

7.6.4.2 Routing Key Management

Routing key management provides the means for an ASP to dynamically register or deregister one or more routing keys with the peer SUA at the SGP.

Registration

A REGISTRATION REQUEST (REG REQ) message is sent by an ASP to indicate to the remote SUA peer on the SGP that it wishes to register one or more routing keys as contained in the REG REQ message. On receipt, the SGP examines the contents of the routing key parameters and compares it with the available routing keys at the SGP.

On the one hand, if the ASP is not currently included in the list of ASPs serving an AS and if a received routing key matches an existing routing key entry, then the ASP is added to the AS list. On the other hand, if a routing key contained in the REG REQ message does not currently exist and if the received routing key data is valid and unique, an SGP supporting dynamic configuration may create a new routing key and a related AS and add the concerned ASP to the new AS list. In either case, the SG returns a REGISTRATION RESPONSE (REG RSP) message to the ASP indicating a successful registration. In the case of an error condition, i.e., if the routing key data is invalid, the SG returns a REG RSP message to the ASP, where the registration result status field now indicates the reason for the failure of the registration.

Finally, an ASP may include a routing context parameter in an REG REQ message. When the SGP receives an REG REQ message with a routing context and if the routing context applies to an existing routing key, the SGP may modify the existing routing key according to the new information provided in the routing key parameter. An REG RSP is returned indicating a successful registration or that the routing key change was refused.

Deregistration

In the same way a DEREGISTRATION REQUEST (DEREG REQ) message is sent by an ASP to indicate to the remote SUA peer at the SGP that it wishes to deregister a given routing key, which is specified by a routing key and routing context parameters. Before attempting to deregister the routing key an ASP should move into the *inactive* state. After reception of a DEREG REQ message the SGP examines the contents of the routing key and routing context parameters. If the ASP is currently registered in the AS related to the included routing context, the ASP is deregistered as an ASP in the concerned AS. Note that the deregistration does not necessarily imply the deletion of routing key and AS configuration data at the SGP since other ASPs may be associated with that AS, in which case the routing key cannot be deleted. However, if no more ASPs are in an AS list the SGP may delete the routing key data. In any case, the SG acknowledges the deregistration request with a DEREGISTRATION RESPONSE (DEREG RSP) message, indicating success or failure with the cause.

7.6.4.3 Interworking of Network Management Functions

The purpose of SCCP management (SCMG) is to provide capabilities to handle the congestion or failure of a peer SCCP, SCCP user or the signalling routes to a peer SCCP, i.e., to maintain network performance by rerouting or throttling traffic in the event of failure or congestion situations in the network. The SCCP at the SG is informed by MTP-3 about an SS 7 signalling point inaccessibility through the MTP-PAUSE primitive, indicating the affected destination point. In this case, the SCCP management initiates

- A local broadcast of N-PCSTATE primitives with signalling point status *signalling point inaccessible*
- A local broadcast of N-PCSTATE primitives with remote SCCP status *remote SCCP inaccessible*
- A local broadcast of N-STATE primitives with user status *User-out-of-service* for each subsystem at the affected SS 7 node

to all concerned and available SCCP users. When a corresponding MTP-RESUME primitive is received the SCCP performs a similar broadcast of the accessibility information to all concerned SCCP users. Equally, the SCCP at the SG is informed by MTP-3 about a remote SCCP unavailability by means of an MTP-STATUS primitive with cause *remote SCCP unavailable*. In this case, the SCCP initiates

- A local broadcast of N-PCSTATE primitives with remote SCCP status *remote SCCP inaccessible*
- A local broadcast of N-STATE primitives with user status *User-out-of-service* for each subsystem at the affected SS 7 node

to all concerned and available SCCP users. In addition, the SCCP initiates a subsystem status test (SST) with SSN = 1 (SCMG). When a corresponding subsystem allowed (SSA) message related to SSN = 1 is received, the SCCP performs a similar broadcast of the availability information to the concerned SCCP users. Finally, when the SCCP management receives

- A subsystem prohibited (SSP) message for an unavailable subsystem or
- An N-STATE request primitive with user status *User-out-of-service* from the concerned local subsystem or
- If the SCCP management detects that a local subsystem is unavailable

then the SCCP management initiates a local broadcast of N-STATE primitives with user status *User-out-of-service* to all concerned and available users. In addition, it starts the subsystem test procedure. When the SCCP management receives

- A subsystem allowed (SSA) message for an unavailable subsystem with SSN $\neq$ 1, i.e., not for the SCCP management, or
- If an N-STATE request primitive with user status *User-in-service* from a local subsystem marked unavailable is received

then the SCCP management initiates a local broadcast of N-STATE primitives with user status *User-in-service* regarding the newly available subsystem to all concerned and available users.

In order to provide seamless operation between SCCP users in the SS 7 and IP domain, the SUA layer at the IPSP needs to support the SCCP management primitives N-COORD, N-STATE, and N-PCSTATE, and should provide interworking with SCCP management functions at the SG. In particular, when an SCCP management (SCMG) message is received from the SS 7 network the SG has to determine whether there are concerned AS interested in subsystem status changes. The SUA management function is then informed with the N-STATE indication primitive upon which it formats and transfers the applicable network management messages to the list of concerned ASPs using stream '0'.

When an MTP-PAUSE, MTP-RESUME or MTP-STATUS indication primitive is received, the SCCP subsystem management at the SG determines whether there are concerned local SCCP users. SUA management is informed with the N-PCSTATE indication primitive when these local SCCP users are application servers. In this case, SUA formats and transfers the applicable network management messages to the concerned ASPs as described in the following. Due to the fact that DUNA, DAVA, SCON, and DRST messages are sent sequentially and processed at the receiver in the order sent, the SCTP stream '0' should not be used.

When the peer SUA receives an SS7 signalling network management (SSNM) message the SUA at the ASP invokes the appropriate primitive indications to the SUA users and informes the local management.

Destination Unavailable/Available

In the scope of SUA the N-PCSTATE and N-STATE indication primitives passed to local SCCP users are covered by the destination unavailable (DUNA) and the destination available (DAVA) messages. When an SS 7 destination point, SCCP or SCCP user has become unavailable the DUNA message is sent from the SG or relay node to all concerned ASPs serving all SCCP users which are considered to be local to the SG or relay node. At the ASP the SCCP users are informed with the appropriate primitive and should stop sending traffic to the affected destination or SCCP user via the SG or relay node sending the DUNA. Equally, the DAVA message is sent from the SG or relay node to all concerned ASPs, serving local SCCP users, to indicate that an SS 7 destination point, SCCP or SCCP user is now available again. The SCCP users at the ASP may resume traffic to the affected destination or SCCP user via the SG or relay node sending the DAVA.

Destination State Audit

A destination state audit (DAUD) message is sent periodically from an ASP to the SG or relay node to query the availability state of an affected destination. The sending of DAUD messages is stopped when the ASP receives a DAVA message. Furthermore, it may happen that an ASP is isolated from the SG or relay node for some time. After recovery, the ASP can also sent a DAUD message to verify the status of an SS 7 destination node, SCCP or subsystem marked prohibited.

When the DAUD message is received at the SGP from an ASP, the SGP checks the status of the specified SS 7 destination and returns DAVA, DUNA or SCON messages depending on the result of the check. The SGP initiates subsystem status test procedures following the SCCP procedures, which are not triggered by the receipt of a DAUD message. The SCCP subsystem management procedures may also be triggered in the case of an AS state change.

Remark: A duplicated SCCP subsystem may be withdrawn from service without degrading the performance of the network. When a duplicated subsystem wishes to go out of service, it invokes an N-COORD request primitive, which is transferred to the backup system. If the backup system and its local SCCP have sufficient resources to allow the duplicate to go out of service, then the initiating subsystem will receive the corresponding information as an N-COORD confirm primitive. This coordinated state change and the related primitives are not supported between SUA and SCCP users.

◇

SS 7 Network Congestion

If the restricted importance level variable (see Sect. 9.3.3), used by the SCCP management to inform local SCCP users about the severity of a congestion situation, changes because the SCCP at the SG

- Encounters congestion or
- Continuously receives MTP-STATUS indication primitives with cause *network congestion* or

- When it is informed by SCCP/subsystem congestion (SSC) messages of a remote SCCP congestion,

then the SCCP management of the SG should inform all concerned and available SCCP subsystems at the IPSP about the congestion situation by invoking an N-PCSTATE indication primitive with the *new restricted importance level* value. When the user is able to identify the affected remote signalling point or SCCP, it may decide not to send any primitives of importance numerically below the level indicated that will result in messages towards the SCCP at that remote signalling point. Primitives of importance numerically equal to or greater than the level indicated will still be sent.

With this respect the SS 7 network congestion (SCON) message can be sent from the SG to all concerned ASPs to indicate that the congestion level in the SS 7 network to a specified destination has changed. Equally, the SUA layer at an ASP or IPSP may indicate local congestion to the SUA peer at the SG with an SCON message. When the SGP receives an SCON message from the peer SUA, indicating that the peer endpoint is now encountering congestion, it should trigger the SCCP congestion procedures (see Sect. 9.3).

MTP Restart

When the SG is isolated from the SS 7 network the SGP sends a DUNA message for the concerned SS 7 destinations to all concerned available ASPs.

At the end of the MTP restart procedure (see Sect. 10.4) the SGP informs all concerned and available ASPs about the accessibility of SS 7 destinations using the DAVA message, and in the case of restricted destinations the DRST message. For those destinations which are still inaccessible after the MTP restart no message is sent.

When the SUA peer at an ASP receives a DUNA message, indicating SS7 destination unavailability at the SG, SUA will inform its SCCP users with an N-PCSTATE indication primitive, which causes any affected traffic to this destination to be stopped. When the SUA receives a DAVA or DRST message it informs the SCCP users with an N-PCSTATE indication primitive, which may resume traffic towards the newly available SS7 destinations via the SG, provided the ASP is in the *active* state. In addition, the ASP may audit the availability of unavailable destinations by sending corresponding DAUD messages.

7.6.5 SUA Management

SUA management messages are used for managing SUA and the representations of the SCCP subsystems in the SUA layer.

The ERROR (ERR) message is used by SUA to indicate errors associated with a received SUA message to the peer. It contains the mandatory error code parameter that indicates the reason for the ERROR message, e.g., invalid version, invalid stream identifier, unsupported message class or type, unsupported traffic-handling mode, unexpected message or parameter and destination status or subsystem status unknown. The parameters routing context, network appearence, and affected point code are only mandatory for specific error codes. Finally, it should be noted that an error message is not generated in response to other error messages.

In order to provide an autonomous indication of SUA events to an SUA peer the NOTIFY (NTFY) message is used, which contains the mandatory status type and status information parameters that yield more detailed information for the notification. The ASP identifier, routing context and, info string are optional.

8

SS 7 Network Outages

Let us now concentrate on the question how an SS 7 network outage can occur. Concerning the isolation and outage of wide network areas or an outage of the whole network, there are a lot of more or less likely reasons. In this book, however, we will only consider protocol-relevant network outages and those caused by network planning.

First of all, the question of SS 7 network outages might seem a bit curious because, in the case of local outages of single signalling links and/or exchanges and thus signalling routes, the specified changeover and rerouting procedures within the MTP specification cater for proper diversion of the signalling traffic towards alternative links and routes. In addition, the SS 7 flow control caters for a reduction of the signalling traffic in the case of a congestion situation until this congestion situation ceases. So, how do SS 7 network outages actually occur?

If, by suitable network planning, bidirectionality and loop-freeness of the routing data is assured and sufficient links and routes are available to handle single failures, these local failures and problems will not lead to an SS 7 network outage.

For an SS 7 network outage, it is required that *local problems* spread throughout the network very fast and create *global problems* within the nodes of the network *at nearly the same time*, which then lead to an outage of the nodes.

Now the question is, how can local problems spread throughout the network, and which of the MTP procedures will lead to an outage of an exchange when problems are present?

8.1 On the Failure of Links and Exchanges

Concerning a failure of links and exchanges there are a lot of reasons, of which we summarize the most important in the following.

Out of Service of Links

Single links may be taken out of service, for example, in the case of an excessive signal unit error rate. In addition, congestion situations may cause a failure of single links. If a congestion situation at the receiving end of a signalling link does not terminate within 3–6 s, then the Level 2 timer T6 expires, which leads to an out of service of the concerned link. Furthermore, there is an out of service of links due to a loss or delay of network management messages. If a changeover order (COO) is delayed so that it is received at the remote end when the link is *in service* again, this leads to an *out of service* of the link. If, after a link activation, the link test is not successful due to a delay or loss of link test messages and if a single repetition of the test is again not successful, the link is taken *out of service* and management is informed. Note that the link may then remain out of service for a longer time.

Finally, a loss of transfer prohibited messages (TFP) leads to elementary routing loops, causing a congestion situation and a related *out of service* of the concerned links.

On the Outage of Exchanges

Due to faulty internal processes caused, for example, by faulty software, hardware failures or a loss of internal messages, the exchange may run into an undefined state which may be ended merely by an *out of service* of the exchange followed by a restart. Furthermore, congestion situations are also of importance concerning an outage of an exchange.

Due to the load sharing mechanism there is a high probability that in a high signalling traffic load situation, not only one but many, if not all, links within a route set are congested. Due to the fact that both directions of a route are nearly equally loaded, a lot of links of an exchange may be concerned. Note that a Level 3 congestion may lead to a congestion of *all* links of the exchange. Related link failures lead to the fact that, in a high signalling traffic load situation, the status of the exchange gets worse, so that more and more links are taken out of service. Thus, at some stage, the exchange is completely isolated or performs a restart because of too many failed links.

8.2 The Spread of Local Problems within the SS 7 Network

Congestion situations are crucial with respect to SS 7 network outages because they may spread within the SS 7 network. Such a spread of local congestion situations within the network may be caused by a nonfunctioning flow control or by masses of network management messages.

The Role of the Flow Control

Due to the nature of SS 7, local congestion situations *will* spread within the network. This is because one of the fundamental objectives of the MTP is to avoid a loss of MSUs to be transferred. In order to meet the specified requirement that not more than one in 10^7 MSUs will be lost, exchanges strive to avoid message loss. Thus, in the case of route set and Level 3 congestion situations, exchanges buffer received messages internally. If there is no flow control or if the flow control does not work, there are problems because the internal buffers fill up. What should be done with the MSUs?

Correlated Congestion Situations

On the one hand the Level 3 could drastically reduce or stop the MSU rates received from its local User Parts or links. As a consequence, a congestion situation is caused at the receiving end of *all* links of the exchange, and the messages are stored back to the neighboring nodes. In a short time the concerned Level 2 buffers within these nodes are filled up and route set congestion is caused. If the flow control does not work, and if, according to the MTP philosophy, no messages are discarded, the MSUs are stored back to the Level 3 causing, in addition, Level 3 congestion within these nodes, and so on.

In this way, starting from an initial node, there is a wave-like and, due to the filling of internal buffers, time-delayed spread of route set and Level 3 congestion situations into the surrounding network *before* links and exchanges fail. This situation is what we call a correlated congestion situation.

Notes:

(1) Due to a Level 3 congestion, *all local links* of a node and, thus, *all neighboring nodes* as well as *all signalling routes* via this node are affected.
(2) The higher the traffic load is, the faster the internal buffers fill up, and the faster the spread of the congestion situation within the network.

$\diamond$

Uncorrelated Congestion Situations

On the other hand, the Level 3 may discard continuously received messages when the internal buffers are filled up. Due to this, messages are not buffered back to the adjacent nodes and, in addition, the very fast correlated spread of the congestion situation within the network is avoided. However, in this case, a temporary loss of bidirectionality occurs at the user level and within the MTP, causing the problems described in Sect. 12.6.

In particular, a loss of TFPs leads to elementary routing loops (see Sect. 12.7). A loss of transfer allowed messages (TFA) means that available alternative routes are not used in time, so that congestion situations may occur in other network areas. A loss of transfer controlled messages (TFC) means that the flow control does not work properly so that, again, in other parts of the network congestion situations may arise. Furthermore, if during a changeback of signalling traffic on a newly available link changeback declaration (CBD) or changeback acknowledgement (CBA) messages are delayed or lost, the concerned MSUs have to be buffered up to 2.4 s, which in conjunction with a high signalling traffic load, will lead to a dangerous Level 3 congestion and/or to message loss. In addition, when the timers expire, a lot of messages are sent via the newly available link so that link and route set congestion may be caused. If a changeover order (COO) message is delayed it may be received at the adjacent node when the concerned link is in the *in service* state again, causing a renewed failure of the link. In critical situations the sending of large amounts of old COOs may cause a large number of link failures and in some circumstances an outage of the whole exchange. Finally, an outage of links can also be caused by a delay or loss of link test messages.

Due to those events uncorrelated congestion situations may be caused within different nodes somewhere in the network.

Notes:

(1) Discarding messages actually does not solve the problem of congestion situations.
(2) In those situations of a high signalling traffic load, when the MTP procedures are essential to remove problems, they do not work properly.

◇

The Influence of Extensive Network Management Activities

Related to an outage of a large network area, there is the reception, the processing, and the sending of a large number of TFP messages, a corresponding routing data update as well as signalling route set tests (RST) for a large number of inaccessible destination nodes. The availability of this network area is indicated again by a broadcast of a large number of TFA messages. Finally, depending on the network structure, a similar mass problem may occur in the case of a route set or Level 3 congestion due to the sending of TFC messages.

Caused by these masses of signalling route management messages there may be congestion situations in a large number of nodes within the network at nearly the same time. Nevertheless, if these events do not cause a congestion situation within an exchange on their own, they will lead to a correlated spread of congestion situations within the network in conjunction with a high signalling traffic load.

8.3 The Outage and Isolation of Large Network Areas

We distinguish between correlated and uncorrelated network outages.

Correlated Network Outage

If, starting from an initial node, a correlated congestion situation is caused in a large number of, if not all, nodes within the SS 7 network at nearly the same time and if the Level 2 timers T6 expire, leading to an out of service of the links, then there is an outage of the concerned nodes within a short time. This is what we call a correlated network outage.

Uncorrelated Network Outage

In a similar way, uncorrelated congestion situations may cause an outage of exchanges somewhere in the network. In those situations of a high signalling traffic
load, the restart procedure plays an important role. In large SS 7 networks, a complete routing data update might not be completed within the available time, so that
faulty routing data within the restarting node as well as the network may cause congestion situations and a renewed failure of the restarted node.

Due to the fact that the situation within the network, caused by these failures, is
deteriorating, the number of uncorrelated outages of exchanges may increase in time,
which may result in an SS 7 network outage. This is what we call an uncorrelated
network outage.

Isolation of Large Network Areas

Finally, in hierarchical networks, an isolation of large network areas may occur due
to the unavailability of the interconnecting routes, e.g., caused by an outage of central
transfer nodes.

To summarize, we see that a functioning flow control and a coordinated and protected restart of an exchange are of crucial importance regarding SS 7 network security and reliability. Thus, in order to provide deeper understanding, we first describe
in the following two chapters the SS 7 flow control and the MTP restart procedure,
before discussing potential problems with MTP procedures in real SS 7 networks.

9

SS 7 Flow Control

There is a need for flow control within the signalling system to maintain the required signalling performance and network availability.

Due to the outage of signalling links and exchanges or due to internal difficulties of exchanges, congestion situations within the SS 7 network may be caused, which means that the network is not able to handle the occurring signalling traffic and to perform the necessary network management activities. Signalling System No. 7 (SS 7) in common with other transport mechanism needs to limit traffic at its source when congestion onset is detected. The nature of SS 7 leads to route set, signalling point or signalling transfer point congestion being spread through the signalling network if no specific actions are taken. This will result in impaired signalling performance, message loss or an outage or isolation of wide network areas or an outage of the whole SS 7 network, as discussed in the previous chapter.

Thus, the objective of the SS 7 flow control is to reduce the signalling traffic at its source until the problems are removed and the congestion situation ceases, so that normal traffic may be resumed. In the following sections we describe in some detail the procedures of the MTP and User Part flow control, the SCCP, ISUP, and other application part signalling congestion control procedures as well as the function of the SS 7 flow control. Finally, for a discussion of the SS 7 flow control within the SS 7 over IP environment, we summarize the IP and SCTP flow control.

9.1 MTP Flow Control

In the following, we consider the general network structure as shown in Fig. 9.1. For the originating nodes $O_1, \ldots, O_m$, not necessarily adjacent to the transfer node A, signalling relations via A to the destination node Z are realized. The set of all routes from A to Z form the route set (A,Z).

We now consider the case that, for any reason, the network is not able to transfer the signalling traffic to the destination node Z originated at the signalling points $O_1, \ldots, O_m$ so that congestion occurs.

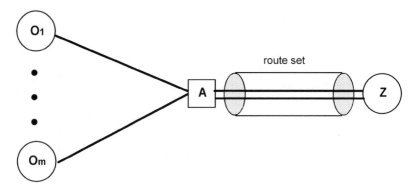

Fig. 9.1. On the function of the SS 7 flow control

9.1.1 Level 2 Flow Control

If the Level 2 cannot transfer received messages to its Level 3 congestion occurs at the receiving end of the considered signalling link. Note, that the mechanism for detecting congestion at the receiving end of a signalling link is implementation dependent [32].

After congestion is detected, both positive and negative acknowledgements to message signal units are withheld and link status signal units (LSSU) with indication *busy* (SIB) are periodically sent from the receiving end of the link to the remote end at time interval T5 (80–120 ms). Note that the receiving end may continue to accept MSUs. At the remote end of the signalling link, every reception of a SIB causes the excessive delay of acknowledgement timer T7 (0.5–2 s) to be restarted and the first received SIB starts the longer supervision timer T6 (3–6 s). If timer T6 expires this leads to an *out of service* of the concerned link. Due to the Level 2 flow control the message signal units to be transferred are stored back to the sending end of the link, where the Level 2 transmission and retransmission buffers fill up. Note that such a filling of the Level 2 buffers may also be caused at the sending end of the link if, for example due to changeover processes of signalling traffic to the considered link, the traffic streams to be transferred exceed the transmission rate of the link.

9.1.2 Signalling Traffic Flow Control

Congestion Status of Signalling Links

According to the MTP flow control, as specified for the international network which, in fact, is also used in a large number of European networks, two congestion states are defined: congested and uncongested. When a predetermined implementation-dependent congestion onset threshold (O) of MSU fill in the transmission (or retransmission) buffer is crossed then the link is considered to be congested (see Fig. 9.2). Since the Level 2 is not the source of the signalling traffic the only possibility is to give an indication to Level 3 advising of congestion. When the buffer occupancy

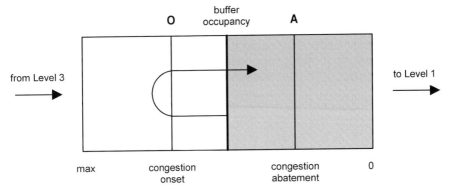

Fig. 9.2. Level 2 congestion and buffer occupancy

decreases and crosses an implementation-dependent congestion abatement threshold (A) then congestion is terminated. The congestion abatement threshold should be placed lower than the congestion onset threshold in order to provide hysteresis during the process of recovering from congestion. The criterion for setting the congestion thresholds is based on the proportion of the total buffer capacity and the total number of messages contained in the transmit and retransmit buffers. The buffer capacity below the threshold should be sufficient to overcome load peaks due to signalling management functions, and the remaining buffer capacity should allow User Parts time to react to congestion indications before message discard occurs.

Congestion Status of Signalling Route Sets

If at least one link within a route set towards a given destination Z becomes congested, the congestion status of the signalling route set towards the affected destination is changed to *congested*. In fact, a route set congestion is nothing else than Level 2 congestion. Since the Level 3 is not the source of the signalling traffic the only thing that may be done is to inform the relevant User Parts about the congestion. This is done locally using MTP STATUS primitives with cause *CONGESTION*, called congestion indication (CI) primitives, or in the case of remote User Parts using transfer controlled (TFC) messages that contain the destination point code (DPC) of the affected destination. Within the originating points of the signalling traffic, the local User Parts are again informed about the congested destination point using CI primitives.

Signalling Traffic Flow Control

With respect to the creation of the CI primitive and TFC rates we distinguish between the route set method (RSM), the congested link method (CLM), and the octet method (OM) [21]. According to the RSM method, *all MSUs received for the congested route set* are taken into consideration. In more detail, let us consider the first MSU received by MTP-3 since the beginning of congestion. If it is received from a local User Part for the congested route set, a congestion indication primitive will be returned to each local User Part. However, if the first MSU is received from a User Part located in the originating points $O_1, \ldots, O_m$, then a transfer controlled (TFC) message including the signalling point code of the affected destination point Z is sent to the originating point. At the originating point a corresponding CI primitive is sent to each local User Part. Furthermore, for every eight MSUs, received for the congested route set, a congestion indication is sent. This is done by considering one out of the eight MSUs. If it is received from a local User Part, a congestion indication primitive is again returned to each local User Part. Instead, if it is received from a User Part located in the originating points $O_1, \ldots, O_m$, then a transfer controlled (TFC) message is sent to that originating point. At the originating point a corresponding CI primitive is again sent to each local User Part.

According to the CLM method, however, only those MSUs are used to create the CI primitive and TFC rates which are received *for the congested links of the congested route set*. The improvements of the CLM are that, on the one hand, User Parts that do not send any signalling traffic via the congested links of the congested route set are not forced to reduce their traffic (no impact on the performance) and, on the other hand, that User Parts which have a major contribution to the congested links are forced to reduce their traffic much more than according to the RSM method (congestion situation is removed faster). Furthermore, the octet method allows taking into consideration the message length, since for every N octets ($N = 279$–300) a TFC message is sent so that *for long messages more than one TFC message may be sent*.

Notes:

(1) For the relevant User Parts, the received CI primitive rate contains the information about their actual contribution to the congestion and, thus, how much they should reduce their traffic towards the concerned destination point.
(2) The SS 7 flow control does not distinguish between the individual User Parts within a signalling point. They are all informed by the same CI primitive rate, independent of their actual load contribution to the congested route set.

$\diamond$

9.1.3 National Option with Congestion Priorities

Congestion Status and Discard Status of Signalling Links

In national signalling networks, each MSU may be assigned by its generating User Part a congestion priority, with 0 being the lowest and N ($1 \leq N \leq 3$) the highest congestion priority. These congestion priorities are used by the MTP to determine whether or not an MSU should be discarded under link congestion, as well as whether the traffic streams created by the User Parts are stopped or not in the case of

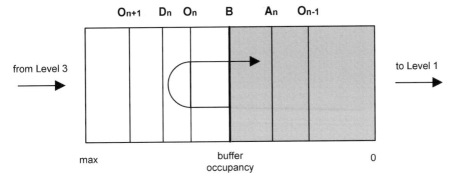

Fig. 9.3. Congestion status and discard status of signalling links

a congestion situation. In this respect, the signalling link congestion status and the discard status are important, which are defined as follows.

For every link there are N ($1 \leq N \leq 3$) different congestion onset O_n, congestion abatement A_n and congestion discard D_n thresholds defined with

$$O_{n-1} < A_n < O_n < D_n \leq O_{n+1}, \quad 1 \leq n \leq N$$

If the buffer occupancy B is increasing and located within the interval $O_n \leq B < O_{n+1}$ or if the buffer occupancy is decreasing and located within the interval $A_{n+1} > B \geq A_n$, then the link is assigned the congestion status n. Under normal operation, when the signalling link is uncongested, the signalling link congestion status is assigned the zero value. Furthermore, if the buffer occupancy B is located within the interval $D_n \leq B < D_{n+1}$, the current signalling link discard status is assigned the value n. In the case $B < D_1$ the signalling link discard status is zero.

Finally, if the congestion priority of an MSU is greater than or equal to the discard status of the link, which is used to transfer the MSU, then the MSU is sent, otherwise the MTP discards the MSU.

Congestion Status of Signalling Route Sets

At each originating signalling point, there is associated with the route set towards destination point Z a congestion status within the range 0 to N, which indicates the degree of congestion in the signalling route set. Normally the congestion status of the signalling route set is zero, indicating that the signalling route set is uncongested. If a link in the route set becomes congested, the congestion status of the route set is assigned the value of the link congestion status, if it is higher than the current signalling route set congestion status.

Signalling Traffic Flow Control

If an MSU is received at a transfer node for a concerned destination point Z and when a signalling link has been selected for transmitting the MSU, comparison of the congestion priority of the message is made with the congestion status of the selected link. If the congestion priority is less than the current signalling link congestion status, a TFC message is sent in response to the originating node O of that message, indicating that the relevant User Parts should no longer send messages to the concerned destination point with a given priority or lower. This TFC message contains the congestion status of the concerned link.

When the originating point receives the TFC message relating to the destination point Z and if the current congestion status of the signalling route set towards Z is less than the congestion status in the TFC message, the congestion status of the route set is updated with the value as contained in the TFC message. Furthermore, if within T15 (2–3 s) after the receipt of the last TFC message relating to Z, the originating node O receives another TFC message relating to Z and if the value of the congestion status carried in the new TFC message is greater than the current value of the congestion status of the signalling route set towards Z, then the current value is updated to the new value.

When T15 expires, the signalling route set congestion test (SRSCT) procedure is invoked at the originating point O, which is used to update the congestion status associated with the route set towards Z. According to this procedure, the originating point O sends a signalling route set congestion test (RCT) message to the destination point Z. If within T16 (1.4–2 s) a TFC message relating to Z is received, the originating point O updates the congestion status of the route set towards Z with the value of the congestion status carried in the TFC message. However, if T16 expires without a TFC relating to Z having been received, the originating node changes the congestion status associated with the route set towards Z to the next lower status. After the congestion status has been decremented by one, the test is repeated unless the congestion status is zero.

Finally, when the congestion status of a signalling route set changes within the originating point O, as a result of either the receipt of a TFC message relating to Z or an indication of local signalling link congestion or due to the SRSCT procedure, an indication is given from the MTP to the local User Parts, informing them about the current congestion status of the route set towards Z. Each User Part then takes appropriate actions in order to stop generation of signalling messages destined for Z with congestion priorities lower than the specified congestion status. MSUs received from local User Parts with congestion priorites lower than the current route set congestion status are discarded by the MTP.

9.2 ISUP Congestion Control

ISUP load reduction [5] is based on a stepwise reduction of the ISUP traffic by reducing new call attempts (see Fig. 9.4). When the first congestion indication primitive is received, the traffic load towards the affected destination point is reduced by one step and two timers T29 (300–600 ms) and T30 (5–10 s) are started at the same time. In order not to reduce traffic too rapidly and to react too sensitive on statistical fluctuations, all received CI primitives received during T29 for the concerned destination are ignored. However, the reception of a CI primitive after the expiry of T29, but

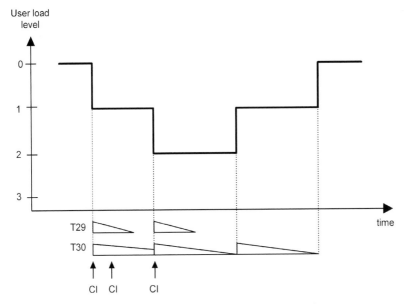

Fig. 9.4. The ISUP signalling congestion control

still within T30, will decrease the traffic load by one more step and restart T29 and T30. This stepwise reduction of the ISUP traffic is continued until maximum load reduction is obtained by arriving at the last step or if within the time period since expiry of T29 and T30 no CI primitive is received. In the latter case, traffic load will be increased by one step and T30 restarted. This is repeated, unless the full traffic load has been resumed or a new CI primitive is received, which leads to a renewed reduction by one step as well as a restart of T29 and T30, and so on.

However, the number of steps and their size are not fixed. The reason for this is that these parameters are, in fact, network dependent. As a consequence, it is not generally fixed how fast the load reduction and enhancement has to be performed.

Notes:

(1) A CI - primitive rate of $2s^{-1}$ results in a maximum load reduction. Higher primitive rates have no other influence.
(2) Primitive rates lower than $0.1s^{-1}$ do not cause any load reduction.

◇

In the case of the national option with congestion priorities, the load reduction consists in stopping the transmission of MSUs towards the concerned destination point with congestion priorities less than the route set congestion status.

9.3 SCCP Congestion Control and Load Reduction of Application Parts

Related to the introduction of mobile communications, the intelligent network or operations, maintenance, and administration services are the new application parts MAP, INAP, and OMAP. All these new applications use the transaction capabilities (TC) [11] protocol for the non-circuit-related information exchange, e.g., a database inquiry, which directly accesses the connectionless SCCP services [6] (see Sect. 2.3.2). The TC users are application service elements (ASEs). An ASE is the basic component of an application entity (AE), which are the subsystems or users of the SCCP. The subsystems are locally identified by the subsystem number (SSN).

These new applications may be addresses using a global title (GT), which may consist of dialled digits or another form of address that will not be recognized in the SS 7 network. Therefore, a translation is required, which results in a DPC and possibly also a new SSN and GT. Thus, an application part may not use a SPC that identifies a specific signalling point. How are the new application parts informed about a congestion situation within the SS 7 network?

The SCCP is informed about an SS 7 route set or signalling point congestion by MTP-STATUS primitives with cause *SIGNALLING NETWORK CONGESTED*, which we call in the following congestion indication (CI) primitives. The rate of the congestion indications reflects the contribution of the receiving SCCP to the congestion situation. In addition, SCCP is informed about a peer SCCP congestion by an SCCP/subsystem congested (SSC) message. Since the SCCP is not the source of the traffic it has to notify its users correspondingly in order to reduce their traffic, if possible, and to discard messages, if necessary.

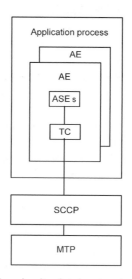

Fig. 9.5. Non-circuit-related protocol architecture

9.3.1 SCCP Congestion

The detection of SCCP congestion is implementation dependent. When a message arrives at a congested SCCP, the SCCP routing control (SCRC) informs the SCCP management (SCMG). The SCMG then returns an SSC message to the originating point of the received message, identified by the OPC in the MTP routing label, for the first message since congestion onset and then for every eighth (provisional value) message received until congestion abates. The congested SCCP is identified in the SSC message by the signalling point code (SPC) of the congested SCCP node in the *AFFECTED DPC* parameter and $SSN = 1$ (SCMG) in the *AFFECTED SSN* parameter. Furthermore, the SSC contains the CONGESTION LEVEL parameter, which indicates the severity of congestion to the originating SCCP and which may take on the values 1–8. Any reaction towards a local originator of a received message is implementation dependent.

The SCCP management locally marks the congestion status of a remote congested SCCP using the congestion level (CL_S) variable. The CL_S may take on nine levels 0–8 with 0 indicating that no congestion is present. When a first SSC message is received from a congested SCCP, locally marked *uncongested*, the corresponding CL_S variable is set to the congestion level value contained in the SSC, and the timer T_{CON} is started. When another SSC is received for the considered congested SCCP, while T_{CON} is running, SCCP management compares the value of the associated CL_S variable with the congestion level contained in this SSC. If the congestion level in the SSC is higher than the current CL_S value than CL_S is updated with the new, received congestion level. Otherwise CL_S is unchanged. Finally, if the congestion level of the SSC message was not less than the value of CL_S, then T_{CON} is restarted. If T_{CON} expires, the value of CL_S is decremented by 1 and T_{CON} is restarted until CL_S reaches 0. In this case, T_{CON} is stopped.

9.3.2 SCCP Flow Control

SCCP management locally marks the congestion status of a signalling route set or signalling point using the restriction level (RL_M) variable. RL_M may take on the nine levels 0–8 with 0 indicating that no congestion is present. Every restriction level, except the highest level 8, consists of four sublevels. The actual sublevel is denoted in the following by $RL_M.RSL_M$. When the first CI primitive from MTP is received for an affected DPC, then the timers T_a and T_d are started and RSL_M is set to 1 (see Fig. 9.6). If another CI is received while T_a is running, this CI is ignored. If a CI is received when T_a has expired but T_d is still running, the timers T_a and T_d are restarted and RSL_M is incremented by 1. If RSL_M reaches 4, RSL_M is reset to 0 and RL_M is incremented by 1. When the highest value $RL_M = 8$ is reached, the reception of a CI does not cause any further actions. When the timer T_d expires, RSL_M is decremented by 1. In the case, when RSL_M takes on the value -1, it is reset to 3 and RL_M is decreased by 1. The timer T_d is restarted unless the uncongested state $RL_M.RSL_M = 0.0$ is reached.

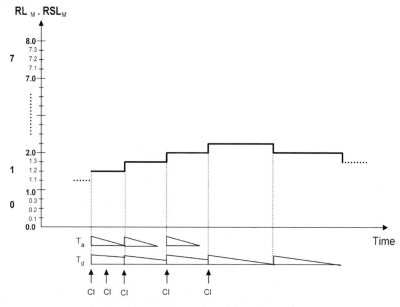

Fig. 9.6. SCCP signalling congestion control

Notes:

(1) Timer T_a avoids a too fast reaction on CI primitives received and limits the positive slope of the restriction level curve, i.e., how fast the restriction level is increased during the beginning of a congestion situation. The shorter T_a is, the faster may the restriction level increase.

(2) Timer T_d determines how fast the restriction level decreases, i.e., how fast normal traffic load may be resumed. The shorter T_d is, the faster decreases the restriction level, i.e., the faster normal traffic load can be resumed.

(3) The timer values T_{CON}, T_a, and T_d are considered to be administrable and are currently provisional.

⬦

9.3.3 Congestion Report

The SCCP management uses the RL_M, RSL_M, and CL_S variables as inputs to compute the values of the restriction level (RL), restriction sublevel (RSL), and restricted importance level (RIL) variables. The RL and RSL variables are used by the SCCP routing control to determine whether a message is discarded or routed in the case of a congestion situation, as described in the next section. If there is a change in RL or RSL, SCCP routing control is informed by the SCCP management of the new RL and/or RSL values. The RIL variable is used by the SCCP management to inform local users about the severity of a congestion situation. If there is any change in the restricted importance level, a local broadcast of N-PCSTATE indication primitives with the new *RESTRICTED IMPORTANCE LEVEL* value is invoked.

Note: The computation of the RL, RSL, and RIL variables is left for further study.

◇

9.3.4 Traffic Limitation

In the case of a congestion situation towards an affected destination point or a remote SCCP, the SCCP has to reduce concerned signalling traffic appropriately. If a local SCCP user receives an N-PCSTATE indication primitive with a new *RESTRICTED IMPORTANCE LEVEL* value and when the user is able to identify the affected remote signalling point or SCCP, it may decide not to send any primitives of importance numerically below the level indicated that will result in messages towards the SCCP at the remote signalling point. Primitives of importance numerically equal to or greater than the level indicated will still be sent.

Furthermore, if the SCCP routing control receives a message for a congested destination, it has to decide whether this message is sent or discarded. In order to take that decision each affected destination is associated with an RL and RSL value, provided by the SCCP management as described above. In addition, every message is assigned an importance value: on the one hand, every SCCP message is assigned a default importance value as summarized in table 2/Q.714 [6]. On the other hand, messages originated by an SCCP user may be assigned a higher importance value contained in the optional *IMPORTANCE* parameter which, however, must not exceed the specified maximum importance value. The default value is used by the SCCP if no *IMPORTANCE* parameter is contained in the message.

When a message has to be sent towards a congested destination, the importance of the message is compared to the RL value of the affected destination. If the importance value of the message is greater than the RL value, then the message is sent. If the importance value of the message is lower than the RL value, then the message is discarded. If, however, the importance value of the message is equal to the RL value, then the RSL value is considered. The RSL value indicates the portion of the considered traffic that should be discarded:

- RSL = 0 indicates that none of the considered messages are discarded,
- RSL = 1 indicates that 25% of the concerned traffic is discarded,
- RSL = 2 indicates that 50% of the concerned traffic is discarded, whilst
- RSL = 3 indicates that 75% of the concerned traffic is discarded

Note: The portion of traffic reduction is considered to be network specific.

◇

If the message is discarded, then the message return procedure is initiated for a connectionless message, the connection refusal procedure is initiated for an SCCP connection request (CR) message and no additional actions are taken for connection-oriented messages other than the CR message.

9.4 The Function of the SS 7 Flow Control

For a quantitative description of the function of the SS 7 flow control we consider the originating points $O_1,\ldots,O_m$, where we assume in the following, without loss of generality, that only one User Part is located at every originating point and which we denote by $U_1,\ldots,U_m$ (see Fig. 9.7). These originating points have a signalling relation to the destination point Z via the transfer point A. The total number of links within the route set (A,Z) is L. At time t, the User Part i creates a traffic load of $X_{il}(t)$ in MSU/s and, if we consider the MSU length, a traffic load of $Y_{il}(t)$ kbit/s, respectively, that is transmitted via the link 1 of the route set. The total traffic load created by the User Part i at time t, which is sent via the route set to destination node Z, is given by:

$$X_i(t) = \sum_{l=1}^{L} X_{il}(t) \quad \text{(in MSU/s)} \quad or \quad Y_i(t) = \sum_{l=1}^{L} Y_{il}(t) \quad \text{(in kbit/s)} \quad (9.1)$$

The total traffic load of the route set (A,Z) at time t, created by the User Parts $U_1,\ldots,U_m$, is then

$$X(t) = \sum_{i=1}^{m} X_i(t) = \sum_{i=1}^{m}\sum_{l=1}^{L} X_{il}(t) \quad \text{(in MSU/s)} \quad (9.2)$$

or

$$Y(t) = \sum_{i=1}^{m} Y_i(t) = \sum_{i=1}^{m}\sum_{l=1}^{L} Y_{il}(t) \quad \text{(in kbit/s)}. \quad (9.3)$$

Finally, the normal traffic load created by User Part i for the destination point Z in the absence of failures or if no congestion exists, is given by X_i^0 or Y_i^0, respectively. The normal traffic load of the route set is given by the following expressions

$$X^0(t) = \sum_{i=1}^{m} X_i^0(t) \quad \text{(in MSU/s)} \quad or \quad Y^0(t) = \sum_{i=1}^{m} Y_i^0(t) \quad \text{(in kbit/s)}. \quad (9.4)$$

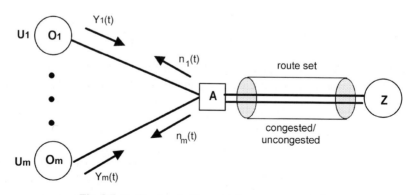

Fig. 9.7. Traffic flow in the case of route set congestion

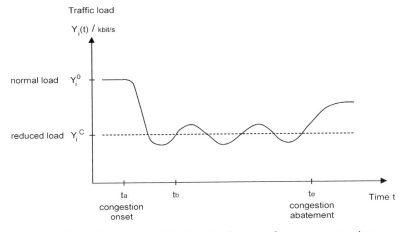

Fig. 9.8. Load reduction of User Part i in the case of route set congestion

Let us now consider the case that, at time t_a, L_1 links within the route set become congested so that the route set itself becomes congested. Such a congestion of the route set may be caused by outages of local links and signalling routes towards destination point Z as well as an awkward network planning. According to the RSM or CLM method, the transfer point A creates for User Part i at $t > t_a$ the TFC rate

$$n_i^{RSM}(t) = \sum_{l=1}^{L} \frac{X_{il}(t)}{8} \quad \text{or} \quad n_i^{CLM}(t) = \sum_{l=1}^{L_1} \frac{X_{il}(t)}{8}, \quad i = 1, \ldots, m. \quad (9.5)$$

According to the received TFC rate, User Part i reduces its traffic load towards the concerned destination point Z (see Fig. 9.8).

At time t_b User Part i has reached an average load level X_i^c or Y_i^c, respectively, which should be dimensioned such that the sum of all reduced load contributions of all User Parts $U_1, \ldots, U_m$ is less than or equal to the current capacity X^c or Y^c of the route set (A,Z).

$$X^c = \sum_{i=1}^{m} X_i^c \quad \text{(in MSU/s)} \quad \text{or} \quad Y^c = \sum_{i=1}^{m} Y_i^c \quad \text{(in kbit/s).} \quad (9.6)$$

Figure 9.9a shows the case that a reduction of the capacity within route set (A,C), caused by link failures, leads to a load reduction below the normal route set loading Y^0 whilst in Fig. 9.9b the case is shown that, due to temporarily increasing traffic load, the current capacity Y^C of the route set is exceeded and a load reduction on that value is performed. Around Y^C a small oscillation of the user load occurs, which is a consequence of the flow control procedure. The reason is that, due to the load reduction of the User Parts, the received TFC rate is reduced. Then, timer intervals may exist within which no TFC messages are received so that an enhancement of the traffic load occurs which, again, is reduced by an increased TFC rate and so on.

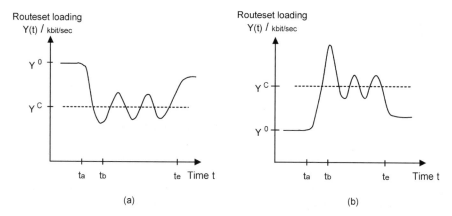

Fig. 9.9. Route set loading and SS 7 flow control set congestion

At time t_e the congestion situation is removed. Since the User Parts do not receive any further TFC messages, they are increasing their traffic load until the normal load level is reached (see Fig. 9.9a), whilst Fig. 9.9b shows the case that the normal route set loading is reached due to changeback or rerouting processes.

9.5 SS 7 over IP and Flow Control

Various approaches exist to develop telecommunication networks further. On the one hand, in order to replace the older network technologies by new and cost-effective transport protocols some network operators would like to migrate completely to an IP-based network. On the other hand, because of the emerging demand for broadband services, a network operator would like to introduce an IP-based multimedia network to support a wide range of data, voice, audio, video, and multimedia applications in one network as currently specified in IETF. Further applications of SS 7 over IP are foreseen like, for example, to realize IP-based high-speed links, to perform the PSTN and IP network convergence in order to improve the Internet and PSTN network transition, to allow switched circuit network (SCN) signalling points to have access to databases and other devices in the IP domain that do not employ SS 7 links, and likewise to provide IP telephony applications access to SS 7 services. SS 7 over IP is designed to provide the signalling system needed for these applications. Since the SS 7 user and application parts are used unchanged, the SS 7 flow control must also be realized in the IP domain.

Thus, in the case of a congestion situation, an SS 7 User part located in a media gateway controller (MGC) or an IP signalling point (IPSP) shall perform an appropriate load reduction as specified in the corresponding ITU recommendations and as described in the previous sections. Since the flow control actions taken by an SS 7 User Part are based on the information about the load contribution of the considered User Part to a congestion situation, the SS 7 flow control must be enhanced into the IP domain. In order to avoid problems with the flow control (see Sect. 12.3) the required congestion indication primitive rate must be provided by the lower layer protocols. In the following we describe the flow control actions taken by IP and SCTP and work out the commonalities and differences between SS 7 and IP networks as far as this is relevant to the SS 7 flow control.

9.5.1 IP Flow Control

Both types of networks offer to their user the basic message delivery service between any two nodes in the network. However, compared to SS 7, IP is connectionless where each message, called a datagram, is delivered in isolation, even with reference to other related datagrams, i.e., with IP there are no connections nor logical circuits [17] (see Sect. 7.1). Furthermore, the datagram delivery service is unreliable since no guarantees are made that a datagram will ever arrive at its destination, so that reliability must be provided by the upper layer protocols. In the SS 7 network signalling messages are transferred via signalling links, which are separated from the data transmission circuits. Thus, in the IP network a mixing of data and signalling messages occurs so that the signalling traffic might be affected by the data traffic.

   In both networks, a route that a message takes from the originating node to the destination node consists of a set of transfer nodes called signalling transfer points (STP) in SS 7 or routers in IP and interconnecting transmission paths. When a transfer node receives a message it determines whether it can deliver the message directly to a destination to which it is connected. If not, it will pass the message to another transfer node to onward route the message. In this way, the message is passed from transfer node to transfer node until it eventually arrives at the destination.

ICMP Source Quench Message

In Sect. 9.1 we discussed an SS 7 link or route set as well as signalling point congestion. In the same way a LAN, router or host congestion may occur in the IP network so that internal buffers fill up (see Sect. 7.1). In contrast to SS 7, further received datagrams are discarded if the internal buffers are exhausted. In this case, ICMP source quench messages are sent to the corresponding source hosts informing them that the datagrams must be resent. Upon reception of a source quench message, a source host will also slow down the transmission rate of datagrams until no source quench messages are received. Hosts will then begin to increase the sending rate again. In this way, similar to the SS 7 flow control, equilibrium will be achieved between the rate at which a host sends datagrams and the rate at which a router or destination host can process the datagrams, thus providing some kind of flow control.

   Notes:

(1) As with SS 7 networks, the IP network size can have an influence on the function of the IP flow control (see Sect. 12.3.2).
(2) Implementations may send source quench messages when the buffer capacity is approached.

◇

Type of Service Concept

Because of the high IP transmission rate of several Mbit/s (depending on the underlying network technology) it is rather unlikely that for SS 7 signalling message transfer severe congestion situations will occur during normal operation. However, there might be situations like, for example, that a receiving SS 7 node runs slower than the sending IP signalling point or that huge amounts of data traffic sent via the IP network cause router or host congestion, thus affecting the signalling traffic sent via the IP network. In order to avoid this transfer of problems from data traffic streams to signalling traffic streams the type of service concept of IP should be used. The type of service concept allows applications to request that particular routes are chosen such meet specific requirements on throughput, reliability or delay. This feature allows IP users to request a certain quality of service provided by the network between the source and destination host regarding delay, throughput, and reliability. To this end, the *Type of Service* field of the datagram is used. It contains three precedence bits that allow a user to specify the importance of the considered datagram and may therefore give priority to signalling traffic over normal user data. Thus, in order to avoid problems with the SS 7 flow control, the precedence level 7 should be used for SS 7 signalling traffic, the delay bit should be set to $D = 1$ (low delay), the throughput bit to $T = 1$ (high throughput) and the reliability bit should be set to $R = 1$ (high reliability), respectively (see Sect. 7.1). Where multiple routes exist to a given network these bits should be used in determining the best path in an attempt to provide better overall SS 7 performance.

9.5.2 SCTP Flow Control

Whichever protocol structure is used to realize a specific SS 7 over IP application, the SCTP [18] provides the basic reliable message transport service. In order to realize the function of SS 7 flow control in the IP domain and to avoid the spread of problems the SCTP needs to perform specific flow control actions. In the following, we describe in more detail potential problems with the specified SCTP congestion control and how they could be avoided by stream-based flow control.

9.5.2.1 SCTP Streams

Compared to SS 7, user data are transferred as DATA chunks in SCTP packets via the SCTP connection, called association (see Sect. 7.2). An association consists of a positive number of streams in one direction and a possibly different number of streams in the other direction. The number of streams per direction is negotiated during the setup of the association. The maximum number of streams per direction is 2^{16}. When the upper layer sends data it also has to specify the stream to which this data belongs. SCTP then makes sure that on the receiving side the User data of each stream is delivered to the upper layer in the same sequence it was sent. Therefore in-sequence delivery is guaranteed only per stream and not per association. There is an additional option for the upper layer to send data without requesting the ordered delivery. The user data still belongs to a stream but it is up to the receiving SCTP engine when to deliver such data to the upper layer. To summarize, SCTP streams are unidirectional and provide the in-order delivery function.

If we would wait for a DATA chunk to be acknowledged before we are allowed to send the next, this would not make best use of the available bandwidth. So, instead of acknowledging each DATA chunk and waiting for the acknowledgement, the SCTP is allowed to have multiple DATA chunks unacknowledged. However, under adverse conditions, this could lead to filling of the receive buffer at the peer SCTP endpoint. In this case, the transmitting SCTP is not allowed to transmit further DATA chunks. Since the transmitting SCTP is allowed to accept further DATA messages from its local user this may lead, in addition, to filling of its transmit buffer and, if no messages are discarded, to the fact that the traffic is stored back to its upper layer. In order to avoid the problems with receive and send buffer overflow the SCTP employs the congestion window mechanism (see Sect. 7.2.4). A window is placed over the data such that any DATA chunk to the left of the window has been transmitted and acknowledged, data chunks under the window have been transmitted but an acknowledgement has not yet been received for all of them, and all DATA chunks to the right outside the window are untransmitted. By adjusting the congestion control window size, the transmitting SCTP can control its data flow such that filling of the receive buffer of its peer and, thus, receive congestion at the peer endpoint can be avoided and that it can react appropriately to IP network congestion. A transmit congestion at its local side is avoided by adapting the rate it accepts data from its local user to the transmission rate to the peer SCTP.

9.5.2.2 Traffic Mixing and Flow Control

Using multiple streams for independent user data resolves the receiver-side head of line blocking problem between the independent user data streams. However, the streams were not introduced to assure a separation of different traffic streams. In fact, SCTP can also bundle multiple user data chunks, even if the user data belong to different streams, into one SCTP packet. As a consequence, if an SCTP packet is lost, all streams for which user data are transferred in that packet are affected.

For the SCTP upper layer protocols it is important to classify the user data into independent classes and transport these classes using different streams. The basic idea behind the framework architecture for SCN signalling message transport over IP [16] (see Sect. 4.3) is that the SCN adaptation modules can make use of the multiple streams in order to realize SS 7 signalling links or signalling routes. This, however, causes problems as described in the following.

Congestion control is one of the basic functions provided by SCTP. A congestion situation can occur at the receiving and sending SCTP endpoint as well as the interconnecting IP path. In those situations the SCTP receive and/or transmit buffers fill up. In order to avoid message loss and a spread of congestion situations into the network the SCTP congestion control is specified which, however, is applied to the SCTP association and not to individual streams. As is shown in Sect. 10.3 there are serious reasons to perform the SS 7 flow control on a link basis, which has been introduced during the ITU-T White Book study period. With the objective of mini-mizing transmission and buffering delays, M2UA and M3UA use SCTP streams as normal SS 7 links or routes, respectively, i.e., MTP-3 user traffic is assigned to the individual streams based on, for example, the SLS value of the MTP routing label. Since different traffic streams are distributed by the SLS value and normally sent via different streams, this separation of different traffic streams and their independence should not be destroyed by the SCTP.

However, one problem with the SCTP is that all messages are stored in one com-mon receive buffer so that different traffic streams are mixed at the receiving end-point. Thus, bulk data sent via a specific stream can lead to complete filling of the receive buffer at the peer SCTP, which causes a blocking of other messages sent via other streams. Although one of the fundamental ideas behind the introduction of streams was to avoid the head of line blocking, the stream idea does not in itself pre-vent blocking of other traffic streams, if one common receive buffer for all streams is realized. Another problem is that, due to the mixing of different traffic streams, the SS 7 flow control actions are also triggered for those traffic streams, which are not the source of the problems. Thus, on the one hand, one traffic stream can monopolize the whole receiver window space and in this way affect the other traffic streams and, on the other hand, the SS 7 flow control does not work properly in the SS 7 over IP environment, which may lead to a spread of problems into the SS 7 network.

To summarize, the crucial differences between SS 7 links/routes and SCTP streams are that signalling links/routes are physically independent, i.e., they are real-ized via different transmission paths and they have their own separated transmit and receive buffers. In addition, the SS 7 flow control can be performed on a link basis. This means that in the case of link congestion only those traffic streams which are sent via that link are reduced.

Note: The SS 7 problem presented here is only an example. The problem itself is of general nature.

◇

9.5.2.3 Stream-Based Flow Control

In order to avoid these problems, the easiest thing would be that the SCTP provides a stream-based flow control, which was extensively discussed in IETF [33]. As for SS 7 links, the SCTP receive and transmit buffers should be (logically) subdivided on a stream basis, i.e., during the association initialization a fixed stream-buffer or stream portion of the transmit/receive buffer should be allocated to every stream where the stream buffer size may be different for the individual streams based on the type of traffic to be transferred via the considered stream and which may be instructed by the SCTP user. In addition, the traffic flow limitation in units of bytes/messages on a per-stream basis allows the receiving SCTP to communicate to the sending SCTP a limit on how much outstanding data may be sent within a particular stream as follows.

Whenever an implementation dependent congestion onset threshold is exceeded regarding one of the receiving SCTP stream buffers or if a specified stream portion

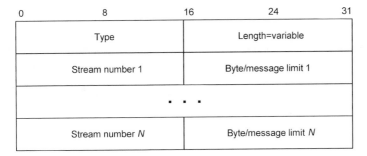

Fig. 9.10. Stream byte/message limit change parameter set congestion

of the receive buffer is exhausted by the stream-specific messages, the sending end-point should be informed about the peer's receive congestion through the use of a corresponding congestion information. This was proposed to be done by sending an address/stream configuration change (ASCONF) chunk with a *STREAM FLOW LIMIT CHANGE* or *STREAM FLOW MESSAGE CHANGE* parameter to the sending SCTP (see Fig. 9.10).

These parameters contain a sequence of one or more parameter values, each of which consists of a specific stream number and a byte or message limit to be applied to that stream. When a stream byte/message limit request is received at the sending SCTP it must record each limit with its appropriate stream.

When a byte limit is set on a stream and when the SCTP user attempts to send messages to its peer via that stream, the sending SCTP checks whether the number of outstanding bytes sent to that stream, i.e., those belonging to messages buffered at the sending end which are not yet acknowledged by the cumulative TSN, plus the number of data bytes received from the SCTP user for transmission is greater than the current stream limit. If so, the SCTP endpoint must reject the request and not queue the data for transmission. Instead it should return an error to the sending SCTP user. However, if the number of outstanding bytes plus the number of bytes of the message to be transferred is smaller than or equal to the limit, the SCTP accepts the message for transmission and queues the user data, which increases the number of outstanding data bytes on this stream.

When a message limit is set on a stream and when the SCTP user attempts to send messages to its peer via that stream, the sending SCTP checks whether the number of outstanding messages sent to that stream, i.e., those messages buffered at the sending end which are not yet acknowledged by the cumulative TSN, is greater than or equal to the current stream limit. If so, the SCTP endpoint must reject the request and not queue the data for transmission. Instead it should return an error to the sending SCTP user. However, if the number of outstanding messages is less than the current limit, the SCTP accepts the message for transmit and queues the user data, which increases the number of outstanding messages on this stream.

In particular, a receiving SCTP should be able to stop the message transfer via a specific stream in order to prevent the receive buffer from being monopolized by that stream or when the SCTP detects problems with its local user, e.g., failure or inaccessibility. This should be done by setting the byte/message limit to '0'[1]. In this case, the sending SCTP must immediately sent a corresponding primitive to its upper layer so that it can take appropriate actions. In addition, the SCTP should not accept further SEND primitives from its user.

Note: Although it is possible to negotiate byte/message limits during the association initialization by adding the corresponding parameters to the INIT and INIT ACK chunks, this is not recommendable. The reason is that, as a side effect, an upper limit is imposed on the size of messages that may be sent via the concerned streams. The use of stream specific flow limits should be restricted to congestion situations and peer SCTP user inaccessibility.

◇

Whenever the sending SCTP receives a byte/message limit information from its peer, indicating a receive congestion at the receiving endpoint or when an implementation-dependent congestion onset is exceeded for one or more transmit stream buffers at the sending endpoint, the SCTP should send a congestion indication primitive to its upper layer, which should take further actions. When the congestion situation at the receiving SCTP terminates or if the problems with the local SCTP user are removed, e.g., it is available again, the SCTP should remove the byte/message limit for the concerned streams. This should be done by sending an AS-CONF chunk with the byte/message limit fields all set to '1'. If the sending SCTP receives the information about the termination of a stream flow limit or if it detects that a local stream transmit congestion terminates it informs its local user using a corresponding primitive.

Unfortunately, the described stream-based flow control could not solve the problems without changing the SCTP specification, so the suggested protocol extension was not accepted by IETF. However, the separation of different traffic streams must be realized by implementations in order to avoid the spread of problems into the SS 7 network. If multiple streams are used as different SS 7 links or routes a new approach called *fair treatment of multiple SCTP streams concept* could be implemented [34]. It is based on having separate send queues for each stream as well as on the local behavior at the sender and receiver of an SCTP association to provide fair sharing of the bandwidth between the traffic of different streams. The data chosen from these queues affect the bandwidth assigned to each stream. Another approach is to realize the separation of different traffic streams at the SCTP upper layer by introducing IP-based links or by using the MTP-3 user adaptation layer, as discussed in Sects. 13.3.1 and 13.3.2.

---

[1] Note that the meaning of the values '0' and '1' as presented here differs from what is specified in [33]. Within the draft, the value '0' means that no flow limit is set to a stream whilst the value '1' has no meaning. The procedure described above corresponds to Level 2 flow control.

MTP Restart Procedure

In Sect. 3.4 we, in short, described the development of the MTP restart procedure. Given that an unprotected restarting node may be the source of correlated and uncorrelated network outages (see Sect. 8.3), the overall objective of the restart procedure is to protect the node whose MTP is restarting and the network. Since the specified restart procedure can only solve the problems of the MTP, further problems are present at the user level so that, in addition to the activities within the MTP, some kind of user restart at the user level is necessary.

In order to gain a deeper understanding of the problems present during the restart of an exchange we describe in the following in more detail the problems that were recognized with the Blue Book signalling point restart procedure as well as their solutions that eventually led to the improved White Book restart procedure.

In Sect. 10.1 we discuss the problems of the Blue Book restart procedure and the changes agreed to remove them. Unexpected traffic restart allowed messages, short-term isolations as well as late events caused further problems with the restart procedure, which are described in Sect. 10.2. Furthermore, interworking problems were present which are discussed in Sect. 10.3. In particular, it is shown that the interworking problems could not be solved in a satisfactory way since solving the interworking problems means switching off the restart procedure. Finally, we end with a short description of the White Book restart procedure.

10.1 Problems with the Blue Book Restart Procedure

In this section we first review the Blue Book restart procedure before we concentrate on the main problem with this procedure: that only a stand-alone STP is fully protected but not an STP with user functionality or an SEP. The solution of this problem, however, caused a loss of bidirectionality of about 30 s, which had to be solved, as described in the following.

10.1.1 The Blue Book Restart Procedure

A signalling point restarts when it becomes available. In the following we describe the actions taken by a restarting node as well as an adjacent node according to the Blue Book procedure [35].

Actions in a Restarting Node

At the beginning of a restart, a signalling transfer point (STP) starts timer T18 (20 s) and activates its signalling links. When all signalling links are available T18 is stopped. During that time the STP takes into account any transfer prohibited TFP, transfer restricted TFR, and traffic restart allowed TRA messages received. In addition, when the first link of a link set is available again, message traffic terminating at the far end of the link set is immediately restarted.

When T18 is stopped or expires the STP starts timer T19 (4 s) during which it expects to receive additional TFP, TFR, and TRA messages, which are merely sent by adjacent STPs. During this time the restarting node is informed about the current network status by the adjacent nodes. T19 is stopped when all TRA messages are received.

When T19 is stopped or expires the STP starts timer T20 (4 s) during which it informs the adjacent nodes about its updated knowledge of the network status by broadcasting eventually TFP and TFR messages, taking into account links which are not available and any TFP and TFR messages eventually received. After that, the timer T20 is stopped. When T20 is stopped or expires, the STP broadcasts TRA messages to all adjacent signalling points and restarts the remaining traffic.

A signalling end point (SEP), which restarts, starts timer T21 (30 s) during which it activates its links. Furthermore, it takes into account any TFP and TFR messages received. In addition, when the first link of a link set is available again, message traffic terminating at the far end of the link set is immediately restarted. If a TRA message is received, which are merely sent by adjacent STPs, T21 is stopped. When T21 is stopped or expires, the SEP restarts the remaining traffic.

Actions in a Node Adjacent to a Restarting Signalling Point

A signalling node X knows that an adjacent node Y is restarting when Y becomes accessible again. If X and Y have the transfer function and if the restarting node Y becomes accessible because the direct link set becomes available again, then X starts timer T21, immediately restarts traffic terminating in Y, sends any eventual TFP and TFR as well as a TRA messages to Y, and takes into account the eventual TFP and TFR messages received from Y.

When X receives a TRA message from Y, T21 is stopped. When T21 is stopped or expires, X restarts any remaining traffic to Y and broadcasts TFA messages concerning Y and all signalling points made available via Y. However, when Y becomes accessible on the reception of a TFA or TFR message, X merely sends any required TFP and TFR messages to Y on the available route and no TRA. If X has the transfer function and the restarting node Y does not, then X performs the above activities. The only exception is that X does not start T21, because it does not expect to receive a TRA message from the restarting adjacent SEP.

If X does not have the transfer function, it immediately restarts traffic terminating at the restarting adjacent node Y, which may have the transfer function or not, it starts timer T21, and takes into account any eventual TFP and TFR messages received. On the receipt of a TRA message, T21 is stopped. When T21 is stopped or expires, X restarts any remaining traffic.

Notes:

(1) A first major point of the Blue Book restart procedure is, that we distinguish between signalling points having the transfer function and signalling points having no transfer function. Only signalling points having the transfer function send a traffic restart allowed (TRA) message. Thus, the general formulation *when all traffic restart allowed messages are received* actually means, that the restarting node only expects to receive TRAs from adjacent points having the transfer function. The reason behind this kind of asymmetry is that, during the Blue Book study period, problems were only foreseen for signalling points having the transfer function. To solve these problems of an STP, the restart procedure was aimed to guarantee a systematic restart, i.e., some time was foreseen to activate the links and to perform the network synchronization.

(2) If the adjacent node X and the restarting node Y are SEPs, then both immediately restart their user traffic and, at both sides, timers T21 expire, because no TRA messages are received. In fact, no restart procedure is performed. Thus, the problems described above in the restarting node are present, i.e., the restarting SEP is not protected.

(3) At the beginning of the procedure, the restarting node considers all routes to be available. The unavailability of individual routes may be recognized by unavailable links directly connected to the restarting point, i.e., using their own information, or by TFP messages received during the procedure. Finally, a restarting STP informs the network about unavailable routes, if necessary. When all these measures are performed a restarting STP broadcasts traffic restart allowed (TRA) messages telling the adjacent nodes that the restart has terminated, i.e., that the problems are gone now, and that the network nodes may start to route user traffic via the restarted node.

(4) Furthermore, if we look at a signalling point having the transfer function, which is adjacent to a restarting node, it first has to send any necessary transfer prohibited messages in order to inform the restarting node of failures within the network and, finally, sends a traffic restart allowed message. Thus, the TRA message indicates that the information needed to route traffic via the adjacent transfer point is now complete. Note, that adjacent signalling end points (SEP) without the transfer function do not sent TRA messages. Thus, when the restarting point has received all expected TRAs its routing data update should be complete and user traffic which has to be routed via the adjacent transfer points may now be sent.

10.1.2 Problems with Early User Traffic

According to the Blue Book restart procedure, however, merely restarting signalling points having the transfer function and no user functions, i.e., stand-alone STPs, are fully protected. This may be seen from the fact that the restarting and adjacent signalling points are allowed to immediately restart traffic terminating in the neighboring node. The remaining transfer traffic may not be sent according to the Blue Book procedure before a traffic restart allowed (TRA) message is received. Thus, a signalling point having user functions is not fully protected. What are the consequences?

Let us consider a restarting signalling point having user functions in addition to the transfer function. Then the following problems are present when user traffic is immediately restarted to available adjacent nodes [36]:

- Depending on the network structure there may be some hundreds of destinations available at nearly the same time. The user synchronization can then cause a considerable traffic load during the signalling point restart.
- If the first link in the direct link set towards an adjacent node is available again, user traffic terminating in the adjacent node, and vice versa user traffic from the adjacent node terminating in the restarting node, is restarted immediately and sent via this link. This early user traffic can cause a link or route set congestion which, however, is not stopped since due to the Blue Book procedure no measures are taken to remove the congestion situation. Thus, an extensive message loss and network outages could be the consequence.
- In addition, related to this early user traffic are a large number of parallel changeover and changeback processes (the time-controlled diversion has to be performed) which, in addition to the link activation, the routing data update and network synchronization due to the reception and the sending and processing of signalling route management (SRM) messages, lead to unnecessary loading of the restarting node during the restart.
- In addition, links of the restarting signalling point which are still unavailable can exist so that user traffic may not be transferred to final destinations. Thus, a user congestion situation can occur within the restarting signalling point due to unsuccessful calls. Again, depending on the network structure, the resulting traffic load may be considerable.

In order to avoid the problems with early user traffic it was first agreed during the White Book study period to restart the whole user traffic at the end of the signalling point restart procedure instead of at the beginning, i.e., it was agreed not to restart any user traffic unless the restarting node has sent a TRA message to all of its available adjacent nodes or corresponding timers expire. The TRA should indicate that no problems are present anymore.

10.1.3 Problems with Restarting Signalling Points with no Transfer Function

Finally, in the case of a restarting signalling end point (SEP) having only user functions and no transfer function, the restart procedure is immediately terminated if the

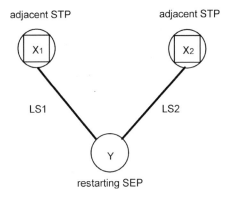

Fig. 10.1. Problems with restarting signalling points with no transfer function

first link to an adjacent node is available again. This means that, according to the Blue Book procedure, no restart procedure is performed after failure of an SEP so that a signalling end point is not protected [37].

Let us consider a restarting signalling end point (SEP) with adjacent nodes having the transfer function as well as user functions, as shown in Fig. 10.1.

According to the Blue Book specification the restarting signalling point Y with no transfer function stops its timer T21 if a traffic restart allowed message is received. In order to reveal the resulting problems let us consider in detail the activities performed within Y and the adjacent node X1 during the restart.

Activities of X1

Let us consider the case that the first link becomes available in link set LS1. According to the Blue Book specification X1 will immediately start user traffic terminating in Y. Furthermore, it eventually sends TFP messages and, finally, a TRA message. In addition, it informs the network that Y is accessible again by sending TFA messages. On the reception of a TFA, remote users start sending traffic towards Y.

Activities of Y

When the first link in LS1 becomes available, Y starts the restart procedure. In detail, it starts timer T21 (30 s) and continues activating remaining links. Y also starts immediately those user traffic terminating in X1 but traffic towards more distant destinations, which may be reached via X1, is not sent. A very short time after Y has started the restart procedure, it may receive the TRA from X1. If, according to the Blue Book procedure, a traffic restart allowed message is received, Y stops timer T21 and restarts the remaining traffic. In fact, the restart procedure is terminated. This, however, does not make any sense, because Y has just started activating its links and may still receive routing data information from other adjacent STPs like X2.

Furthermore, let us consider the routing data update within the restarting node. In general, neighboring signalling points may have the transfer function so that they have to inform the restarting node about the inaccessibility of destination points due to some failures within the network by sending TFP messages. The final TRA message indicates that the relevant information has been transmitted with respect to the concerned adjacent node. Thus, in order to have complete routing data and to avoid problems with message loss, the restarting node has to wait with the sending of the remaining user traffic until all expected TRA messages are received.

These were the reasons why we changed the restart procedure during the White Book study period so that Y has to wait for all expected TRA messages before T21 is stopped. Unfortunately, although this solves the above described problems, a new one occurred leading to a loss of bidirectionality for up to 30 s. This is described in the following.

10.1.4 Loss of Bidirectionality

According to the changes to the restart procedure described above the actions in X1 are still as described above. Y is allowed to restart user traffic terminating in X1 immediately but, differing from the Blue Book specification, Y now has to wait with the sending of the remaining traffic until all expected TRA messages are received. Thus, because remote users are immediately informed by X1 via TFA messages that they may start to send traffic via X1 to Y, bidirectionality is lost for up to 30 s.

We are now faced with a fundamental problem. To solve the loss of bidirectionality described above, X1 must not broadcast TFA messages to neighboring nodes unless the restart activities within Y are terminated. This leads to the question: how does the adjacent node X1 know when the restart activities within Y are finished? According to the Blue Book procedure, X1 assumes that the difficulties within Y are removed when the first link in LS1 is available. This assumption may no longer be true. There is only one signalling point which knows exactly when the difficulties are gone and the traffic may be sent again: the restarting point itself. Thus, the most natural thing is that Y tells its adjacent points when its restart activities are terminated and user traffic is started. This led to the following further change to the restart procedure:

When all restart activities within a restarting node are finished it sends a TRA message to all of its adjacent signalling points. When an adjacent signalling point with the transfer function receives a TRA message it broadcasts TFA messages to its neighboring nodes, indicating that traffic may again be routed towards the restarted signalling point.

Notes:

(1) With respect to the sending of TRA messages, we no longer distinguish between signalling points with the transfer function and those without the transfer function.

(2) The above described problem of a loss of bidirectionality is also present when a signalling point (with the transfer function or not) considers an adjacent point

(with no transfer function) to be available when a TFA message is received concerning the previously inaccessible adjacent point (see Q.704, section 3.6.2: Signalling point availability). Again, the reason for the problem lies in the fact that, for the described configuration, the received TFA does not indicate the end of the restart activities within the restarting node so that the neighboring node actually does not know when to restart user traffic.

(3) The described loss of bidirectionality, which may occur in various situations, is solved by the above proposal because traffic is restarted nearly simultaneously by the concerned users.

(4) According to the Blue Book procedure, a restarting signalling point has to wait for all expected TRA messages, which will only be sent by signalling points with the transfer function. Thus, a signalling point must know the type of all of its adjacent nodes. Although the relevant information is contained within the local routing data, it may be not so easy to extract this information. We note that, as an additional feature, this difficulty was removed by the proposal above.

(5) In order to solve the overall restart problem, it was suggested that the user traffic not sent abruptly but that it be smoothly increased up to the maximum traffic load. In addition, it was suggested that a User Part should take appropriate actions in order to open all directions nearly simultaneously to avoid congestion situations.

$\diamond$

10.2 Further Problems with the Restart Procedure

So far the main changes discussed were that no premature user traffic is restarted before the restart procedure is terminated and that TRA messages are also sent by SEPs. Nevertheless, further open issues had to be clarified. On the one hand, we discuss in the following how to handle a situation where the two sides of a link set are of a different opinion on whether the restart procedure has to be performed or not and, on the other hand, how to handle short-term isolations. As a final issue we discuss in this chapter the accessibility of signalling routes during the restart procedure [38].

10.2.1 Unexpected TRA Messages

There is an important issue within the restart procedure concerning different views of adjacent nodes on whether a restart procedure has to be performed or not. As an example, consider a situation where, due to link failures and link restorations, different views on the availability of the adjacent signalling point at each side of the link set occur. Another situation is that a node simply forgets the inaccessibility of an adjacent node. Thus, one side might start the restart procedure whilst the other acts normally, which is the source of a loss of bidirectionality.

As a consequence a received TRA message is unexpected on the side of the link set not performing the restart procedure. There is a section within the Blue Book specification describing what to do in the case of the reception of an unexpected TRA message (Q.704 section 9.4: Actions in signalling point X on receipt of unexpected TRA message). However, the specified measures will, in general, not avoid one-way signalling relations.

Thus, in order to handle the above described situations it was agreed to change Q.704, section 9.4 so that, when an unexpected TRA message is received, any necessary TFP and TFR messages (in the case of an STP) and a TRA should be sent once to the adjacent node from which the unexpected TRA message was received. The reason is that this TRA message will stop T21 at the adjacent node, thus avoiding a one-way signalling relation. It should only be sent once, within a certain time interval supervised by timer T19, in order to avoid a possible ping-pong of TRA which might occur if, due to some failures, a signalling point forgets that an adjacent node performs a restart so that the terminating TRA is unexpected.

10.2.2 Short-Term Isolations

Other cases where adjacent nodes might have different views whether a restart procedure has to be performed or not result from short-term isolations of less than 1 s due to a short-term processor outage, which is nearly simultaneously performed on all links of a node. It was agreed that in this case the isolated node should not start the restart procedure. The reason is that an adjacent node will start the time-controlled changeover timer T1 when it is of the opinion that an alternative route exists. If the processor outage condition is removed before T1 expires, the adjacent node cannot know that the considered node was inaccessible so that it does not start the restart procedure.

Thus, in order not to have different views on whether the restart procedure has to be performed, the restarting node should not start the restart procedure in the case of short-term isolations due to blocking of its links. To determine whether the isolation is short term or not may be done by the processor outage timer at the local side.

In the case that the adjacent node has no alternative route it considers the concerned adjacent node to be inaccessible. No timer T1 is started. Thus, whether the blocking was short term or not, this adjacent node starts timer T21 and sends any necessary TFP and TFR messages as well as a TRA message towards the other node when the direct link set becomes available again. This TRA message is considered to be unexpected when the isolation was short term. According to the measures specified above, the previously isolated node returns a TRA, which immediately terminates the restart procedure at the adjacent node so that no problems are present.

If the isolation is long term, i.e., it lasts longer than 1 s, an adjacent node will, in any case, consider the concerned node to be inaccessible. In this case, it was agreed to perform the restart procedure on all adjacent nodes as well as the restarting node.

10.2.3 Late Events

Within the Blue Book specification we distinguish between two kinds of late events: links becoming available after T18 has expired and TFP and TFR messages received after T19 has expired. According to the Blue Book specification, these events are treated after the restart procedure has terminated. The reason behind this rule was to stop traffic-disturbing changebacks on newly available links after T18 and time-consuming routing data updates after T19 expire, in order to come to a proper termination of the restart procedure.

However, according to the changes described in Sect. 10.1.2, there is no user traffic started unless the restart procedure has finished, so that the actual reason for this rule was no longer valid. Unfortunately, the above rule has the drawback that when user traffic is restarted after the restart procedure has terminated, a lot of parallel changebacks on the late available links as well as an update of the routing data according to the late TFPs and TFRs have to be performed. This results in possible message loss as well as an unnecessary burdening of the MTP within the restarting node, i.e., problems which were thought to be removed by the restart procedure.

This is the reason why we changed the rule on late events in accordance with the changes agreed during the White Book study period, i.e., it was agreed that any links becoming available and any TFP and TFR messages received during the restart procedure would be handled.

As a final issue, we would like to discuss the question of how to handle signalling points becoming accessible during the restart procedure and which earlier were declared to be inaccessible. Let us suppose that an adjacent node to a restarting STP has recognized a distant signalling point Z as inaccessible. At the beginning of the restart procedure this information is transferred by sending a TFP message referring to Z towards the restarting node. However, during the restart procedure, the adjacent node might receive information on the new accessibility of Z. Should this information be forwarded during the restart procedure?

It was agreed that, while the restart procedure is running, an adjacent node should send a TFA message concerning the new accessibility of a signalling point previously declared to be inaccessible due to the sending of a corresponding TFP message, immediately after it receives this information. Accordingly, the restarting node should take this TFA message into account during the first phase of the restart procedure, supervised by the White Book timer T18. When T18 is stopped or expires, the second phase of the restart procedure begins, which includes as a major part a broadcast of nonpreventive transfer prohibited messages taking into account signalling link sets which are not available and any TFP, TFA, and TFR messages received during phase 1.

The reception of TRA messages or link restorations during phase 2 at a node whose MTP is restarting after the node has sent out TFPs or TFRs referring to the concerned signalling points are called late events, and they are treated outside the restart procedure as normal events. The handling of late events in phase 2 before sending out TFPs or TFRs referring to the concerned signalling points was considered to be an implementation-dependent matter. In addition, it was considered to be an implementation-dependent matter whether the reception of TFPs or link set failures during phase 2 should be handled within or after the termination of the restart procedure.

Thus, it was agreed that the restarting node should not send TFA messages during the restart procedure but, instead, performs the broadcast of TFA messages immediately after the restart procedure has terminated. Note, that no loss of bidirectionality will occur because user traffic from Z towards other destinations via the restarted node and vice versa is restarted nearly simultaneously.

10.2.4 Link Activation and Routing Data Update

During the first phase of the restart procedure a restarting STP activates its links and performs an update of the routing tables, according to the routing information received, supervised by timer T18. However, depending on the network structure, central stand-alone STPs may have port capacity for several hundred links so that, on the one hand, for these STPs a large value for T18 is necessary. However, it was difficult to generally fix an appropriate value for T18. On the other hand, there were concerns about the possible length of a signalling point restart because of one-way signalling relations due to the loss of a TRAs as well as the drawbacks in the case of interworking with older nodes (see Sect. 10.3.3). Therefore, it was agreed that an upper bound on the total length of a signalling point restart must exist, in order to avoid the described problems. Thus, we were forced to fix the value of T18, but the only question was, which value should be taken?

In order to keep the restart time as short as possible, the available time should be used in an efficient way. Thus, it was agreed that all link sets should be made available at nearly the same time, by activating first one link per link set, and by applying emergency alignment for at least the first link in each link set. Because of this measure, the routing data update can be started for all routes at the very beginning of the restart procedure. These links, however, which cannot be activated due to some transient error conditions on transmission facilities for one or more minutes, should not prevent a signalling point from becoming accessible again.

Based on these agreements, there was no longer the need foreseen to specify a specific value for the timer T18, which then was regarded as implementation and network dependent. It was finally agreed to stop T18 if sufficient links and link sets are available to carry the expected signalling traffic and enough TRA messages and therefore routing data have been received to give a high level of confidence in the received routing data.

10.2.5 Network Outages

Network synchronization is a major part of the restart of an exchange. If every accessible signalling point within the network would be indicated to the restarting node by the sending of a corresponding TFA message and the inaccessibility of other nodes by the sending of TFP messages then the sending, reception, and processing of signalling route management (SRM) messages would cause a lot of problems, especially in large SS 7 networks. On the one hand, user traffic should only be restarted if the routing information within the restarting node as well as the network is complete. On the other hand, the overall restart procedure should not take too much time, so that the network status does not change during the restart procedure and in order to fulfil the outage time objectives for exchanges, which are very low in many networks, i.e., only a few minutes per year.

Thus, the objective was to reduce the number of SRM messages to be transferred during the restart procedure. In principle, two possibilities exist:

- We assume that all nodes within the network are accessible and indicate the inaccessibility of nodes by the sending of corresponding TFP messages.
- We assume that all nodes within the network are inaccessible and indicate the accessibility of nodes by the sending of corresponding TFA messages.

In the normal case, when nearly all nodes of the network are accessible and only a few are inaccessible, the first assumption would be the best, while it causes considerable trouble in the case of a network outage. In the case of an SS 7 network outage, the second assumption would clearly be more appropriate in order to reduce the number of SRM messages to be exchanged. However, this measure will cause considerable problems in the normal case. Thus, both cases are conflicting so that we had to take a decision.

Because it was considered to be more likely that the normal case will occur, it was eventually decided that, at the beginning of the MTP restart procedure, a restarting signalling point assumes all signalling routes to be allowed. As a consequence, the values of the MTP restart timers T18 and T21 are defined for use during normal operation. However, it might be advantageous for the network operator to define an alternative value for each timer, for use during potential network failures, since network synchronization will take much longer in these situations. This emergency timer set depends on the network size. Thus, it was decided that the selection and use of the appropriate emergency timer set is within the responsibility of the network administration.

10.3 Interworking Problems with the MTP Restart Procedure

As discussed in Sect. 10.1 major changes to the MTP restart procedure have been agreed in order to remove incompatibilities within the restart procedure entailing one-way signalling relations. In addition, there are other sources of a loss of bidirectionality resulting from the interworking between Red, Blue, and White Book nodes. In the following, these are referred to as the interworking problems with the MTP restart procedure [39]. Due to the fact that, in general, more than two nodes are concerned with an MTP restart, we have in fact to deal with a multi color problem, which makes the situation very complex. We start with a detailed discussion of general multi color interworking. After that we concentrate on the most important interworking problem, between Red Book and White Book versions. Those inter-working problems appear as a loss of bidirectionality leading, in special cases, to the isolation of SEPs. Finally, we discuss possible approaches to solve these interworking problems, especially the traffic restart waiting method.

There is, however, a fundamental difference between the two types of problems. Whilst the loss of bidirectionality within the White Book procedure could be solved, so that the White Book procedure now works well, this is actually not the case for the interworking problems. The reason is that the general way to avoid a loss of bidirectionality due to the interworking of different versions of the procedure is to switch off the restart procedure. However, this means that all of the Red Book problems of a restarting node, whether an SEP or STP, are present. Thus solving the interworking problems of the restart procedure does not solve the problems of the restarting node.

10.3.1 Problems with a Restarting SEP

In the following we consider the restart of a signalling point Y with no transfer function which is interconnected to adjacent Red Book (RB), Blue Book (BB), and White Book (WB) nodes with the transfer and user functionality (see Fig. 10.2). When the restarting node Y becomes available again, the adjacent Red Book as well as Blue Book nodes immediately restart traffic terminating in Y and broadcast TFA messages concerning signalling point Y. This means that the Red Book and Blue Book nodes will restart the whole user traffic towards Y when it becomes available regardless of its color version, i.e., Red, Blue or White. An adjacent White Book node, however, starts timer T21 to wait for the TRA message and restarts user traffic when a TRA message is received or T21 expires.

10.3.1.1 Problems with a Restarting Red Book Node

A restarting Red Book SEP will immediately restart traffic when an adjacent node becomes accessible. Thus, no loss of bidirectionality occurs for adjacent Red Book and Blue Book nodes. However, the disadvantage is that the restarting Red Book SEP is not protected. This is the well known Red Book problem.

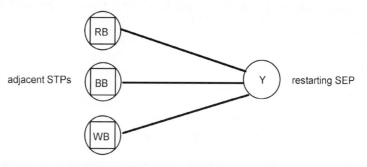

Fig. 10.2. Restart of a signalling end point

A loss of bidirectionality for up to T21, however, occurs between the restarting Red Book node and the adjacent White Book node, which is waiting for the TRA message. A possible way to avoid the one-way signalling relation is that the White Book terminates the restart procedure and restarts user traffic towards Y. In fact, no new problem is created by this measure. The only question to be answered is: how does the adjacent White Book node determine whether the restarting SEP is a Red Book node or not? Four possibilities to treat the problems are described below.

Solution 1: Traffic Restart Waiting Method

The first possibility, as introduced by ANSI [40], is to use a new network management message called traffic restart waiting (TRW) (see Sect. 10.3.3.1). The idea is that a restarting White Book node sends a TRW message towards an adjacent node immediately after it becomes available via the direct link set. Thus, if the adjacent WB node does not receive a TRW message during a very short time period (in fact, much less than T21), this means that the restarting node Y is not a White Book version. As a consequence, the restart procedure within the WB node is terminated and user traffic towards the restarting node Y is immediately restarted.

Solution 2: MSU Method

Instead using a new network management message we may use as an indicator the traffic sent by the restarting signalling point. If the adjacent WB node receives messages from Y during the restart procedure, this indicates that the restarting node has finished the restart procedure. As a consequence, the adjacent WB node should terminate the adjacent restart procedure and restart user traffic immediately towards Y. The MSU method, in addition, avoids the loss of bidirectionality for up to T21 that occurs if a TRW message is lost.

Solution 3: Change the Red Book Side

If the one-way signalling relation is considered to be problematic and should be avoided, then this might also be performed by a simple measure at the restarting Red Book node Y. If, during a restart, the adjacent WB node becomes available, the restarting RB node Y sends a TRA message via the direct link set and restarts traffic as normal.

Solution 4: Do Nothing

Ignore the loss of bidirectionality.

10.3.1.2 Problems with a Restarting Blue Book Node

A restarting Blue Book SEP Y as well as an adjacent Blue Book node immediately restarts traffic terminating in the neighboring node when the direct link set becomes available. Furthermore, an adjacent BB STP sends TFA messages concerning Y to other nodes as well as a TRA message towards Y. This TRA stops the restart procedure within the restarting Blue Book node (if not yet done by another TRA message) and the remaining User traffic is immediately restarted. Thus, no loss of bidirectionality occurs.

Concerning an adjacent Red Book STP there is, in general, a one-way signalling relation, because distant signalling points may send traffic towards Y via the RB node whilst Y is not allowed to answer. This problem occurs if a BB node is surrounded exclusively by Red Book nodes which do not send a TRA message, so that the BB node does not restart traffic to remote destinations unless T21 expires. However, if in addition to RB nodes at least one BB or WB node is present, the restart procedure within the restarting BB node Y is terminated because of the received TRA message. If this Red Book–Blue Book interworking problem may not be ignored it might be solved by the following additional measure at the Blue Book side.

Solution 5: MSU Method

If a restarting Blue Book SEP Y receives traffic during the restart procedure, regardless of where it comes from, it terminates the restart procedure and immediately restarts its user traffic. Note, that an adjacent Blue Book node will start sending its traffic in any case, after possible TFPs and the TRA message are sent to Y. Thus, no loss of bidirectionality occurs.

A similar problem exists with a White Book adjacent node because the WB node will send a TRA message towards Y when the direct link set becomes available again so that the BB node Y immediately stops the restart procedure, if this has not yet been done due to the reception of another TRA message, and restarts the whole user traffic without broadcasting TRA messages. Thus, an adjacent WB node will wait to restart user traffic until its timer T21 expire, i.e., a loss of bidirectionality of about 60 s occurs.

There is one puzzling issue concerning the appropriate measures to avoid the problems because they have to be adapted to the solutions specified in Sect. 10.3.1.1. If solution 1 is implemented within the WB node, it has to be assured that the restart procedure within the WB node is not terminated (because of the missing TRW messages) unless the TRA message is sent by the WB node. In this case, whether further adjacent BB or RB nodes are present or not, this TRA message will terminate the restart procedure within Y, so that within the WB and the restarting BB nodes the procedure is terminated at nearly the same time, thus avoiding a loss of bidirectionality. If solution 2 above is adopted, the TRA send by the WB node will terminate the restart procedure within Y, if it has not already been stopped by another TRA. The traffic sent by the restarting BB node towards the adjacent WB node will stop the restart procedure within the adjacent WB node. As another possibility, we could also adopt solution 3 for the BB node, i.e., before starting its user traffic, after receiving a TRA message, it should broadcast TRA messages to all of its adjacent nodes.

To summarize, the above proposals to avoid a loss of bidirectionality are combinations of the solutions 1, 2 or 3 with solution 5. Again, another valid view might be to simply ignore the loss of bidirectionality.

10.3.1.3 Problems with a Restarting White Book Node

The cases discussed so far have in common that the restarting signalling end point is not protected during its restart. However, during the White Book study period it has been agreed to protect SEPs, too. Thus, concerning interworking problems with a restarting WB node the objective should be to avoid the termination of the restart procedure within the WB exchange as well as a loss of bidirectionality.

The restarting WB node Y starts timer T20 and waits for all TRA messages. If at least one adjacent RB node is present, Y will not receive a TRA message from the RB node so that the restarting WB node has to wait until T20 expires before user traffic can be restarted. However, adjacent RB nodes as well as BB nodes restart the complete user traffic towards Y. As a consequence, there is a loss of bidirectionality for up to 60 s. The question is whether it is possibile to stop traffic sent by adjacent RB or BB nodes.

For the restarting WB SEP Y, the only way to stop traffic sent by adjacent RB nodes is to use the signalling point congestion procedure, which allows the sending of TFC messages relating to Y itself. However, it is doubtful whether this measure would work because the signalling point congestion procedure as well as the adaptation of the TFC rate to the user load reduction is considered to be network specific and, thus, is normally not performed in real SS 7 networks. In addition, this method is unsuitable to stop traffic from BB nodes, because at the BB side TFC messages are ignored during the restart procedure. Another approach might be to shorten the restart time of the WB node which, however, would deteriorate the restart procedure in large networks. If the loss of bidirectionality is not acceptable the only alternative is to terminate the restart procedure, as is done for a restarting BB node.

Solution 6: MSU Method

If a restarting White Book SEP Y receives traffic during the restart procedure, this indicates the presence of adjacent RB or BB nodes. In order to avoid a loss of bidirectionality, the WB node should terminate the restart procedure, broadcast TRA messages to available adjacent nodes and restart user traffic.

Note: The discussion shows that we have to choose between the protection of the restarting node and the avoidance of one-way signalling relations, i.e., both objectives are conflicting. The termination of the restart procedure within the restarting node, in order to avoid a loss of bidirectionality, does not solve the problems within the restarting node. Thus, no ideal solution to solve the interworking problems exists.

◇

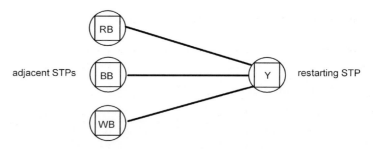

Fig. 10.3. Restart of a signalling transfer point

10.3.2 Problems with a Restarting STP

In this section we consider the restart of a signalling point Y with the transfer function which is interconnected to Red Book (RB), Blue Book (BB), and White Book (WB) nodes as shown in Fig. 10.3. When the restarting node Y becomes available again, the adjacent RB node restarts the whole user traffic for Y and those destination points which can be reached via Y and broadcast TFA messages concerning Y as well as all signalling points made accessible via Y. An adjacent BB node immediately restarts user traffic terminating at the restarting STP Y and starts timer T21 to supervise the reception of the TRA from Y. On reception of the TRA the BB node restarts the remaining user traffic and broadcasts TFA messages concerning Y and all other destinations made accessible via Y. An adjacent WB node, however, merely starts timer T21 to wait for the TRA message. When the TRA message is received from Y or T21 expires it restarts the whole user traffic and broadcasts corresponding TFAs to other nodes.

10.3.2.1 Problems with a Restarting Red Book Node

A restarting RB STP Y will immediately restart traffic when an adjacent node becomes accessible. Thus, no one-way signalling relation occurs for adjacent RB nodes. However, the disadvantage is that the restarting node is not protected, the well-known Red Book problem.

A loss of bidirectionality for up to T21, however, can occur between the restarting RB and an adjacent BB or WB node, which are waiting for the TRA message. The only way to avoid the one-way signalling relation is that the BB or WB nodes terminate the restart procedure and restart traffic towards Y. In fact, no new problem is created by this measure. For an adjacent WB node again solutions 1 and 2 are possible whilst for an adjacent BB node solution 2 may be the best. As an alternative, the restarting RB node could send TRA messages via the available direct link sets before user traffic is restarted, according to solution 3.

10.3.2.2 Problems with a Restarting Blue Book Node

A restarting BB STP Y as well as an adjacent BB node immediately restarts traffic terminating in the neighboring node when the direct link set becomes available again. Thus, no one-way signalling relation exists.

Concerning an adjacent RB STP there is, in general, a one-way signalling relation, because distant signalling points may send traffic towards Y via the RB STP whilst Y is not allowed to answer. This problem is relevant in the case where the BB node Y is surrounded only by RB nodes which do not send TRA messages. In this case, the BB node will not restart traffic to remote destinations unless T19 expires. Again, the solution depends on what is more preferred: the avoidance of loss of bidirectionality or the protection of the restarting STP.

If one-way signalling relations should be avoided, the restart procedure has to be terminated when user traffic from nonadjacent originating points is received during the restart procedure, indicating that an adjacent RB node is present. The termination should include the sending of the TRA messages to the adjacent nodes in order to terminate the restart procedure within adjacent BB/WB nodes. Note, that when solution 1 is implemented within the WB version, this node would in any case terminate the restart procedure, because the restarting node is not a WB version.

If, however, the protection of the restarting node is preferred, the restart procedure within the BB node Y should not be terminated. As a consequence, solution 1 must not be implemented within the WB node. In addition, user traffic received by the RB node should be discarded. Only for the described traffic streams does there exists a loss of bidirectionality, of about 30 s.

10.3.2.3 Problems with a Restarting White Book Node

The restarting WB node Y starts timer T18 as well as T20 and activates the local links. When all (sufficient) links are available and all (enough) TRA message have been received, T18 is stopped. If at least one adjacent RB node is present, Y will not receive all TRA messages so that Y normally waits until T18 expires. After T18 expires, the second phase begins, which includes as a major part a broadcast of nonpreventive TFP messages. When all TFP or TFR messages have been sent, the overall restart timer T20 is stopped and phase 2 is finished. When T20 is stopped or expires, the restarting node sends TRA messages to all adjacent signalling points via corresponding available direct link sets and restarts any user traffic.

An adjacent RB node, however, restarts the complete user traffic towards Y immediately after the direct link set becomes available again. As a consequence, there is a loss of bidirectionality of about 60 s. In addition, such a loss of bidirectionality occurs in the case of adjacent BB nodes, because they immediately restart user traffic terminating in the WB node Y.

To solve these problems there are two different approaches. Again, the chosen solution depends on what is more preferred: the protection of the restarting STP or the avoidance of loss of bidirectionality.

To avoid one-way signalling relations completely means to terminate the restart procedure when, within the WB STP, user traffic is received. Before sending user traffic the WB STP Y should broadcast TRA messages to the adjacent nodes in order to terminate the restart procedure within these nodes. The disadvantage is that the restarting node is not protected and the well-known problems, as mentioned in Sects. 3.4 and 10.1, are present.

Another approach is to stop the traffic received during the restart procedure. With respect to adjacent RB nodes TFPs may be sent for received transfer traffic. In this case, before broadcasting TRA messages, corresponding TFAs should be sent to those nodes to which a TFP message was sent in order to restart traffic immediately and to avoid another one-way signalling relation. Using TFP messages, however, is not appropriate to stop traffic terminating in the restarting White Book node. Therefore, we may try to use TFCs, but this seems to be an inappropriate measure, because user traffic from Blue Book nodes cannot be stopped and, as mentioned earlier, it might not work at all.

To summarize, if we compare the effort of implementing the described methods to protect the restarting node with the result that they actually do not solve the whole problems but at most improve the situation, they do not appear to be worthwhile. Again, we might argue that the loss of bidirectionality may be ignored. If not, the best way to solve the interworking problems is to introduce the White Book restart procedure within the adjacent Red and Blue Book nodes.

10.3.3 White Book STP and Red Book SEP Interworking Problems

Since the Blue Book restart procedure has not been introduced within real SS 7 networks the most important interworking problem is that between Red Book and White Book nodes. The interworking problems appear in the form of a loss of bidirectionality leading, in special cases, to the isolation of SEPs. The restart procedure cannot be introduced in all nodes of the network at the same time, so that for the network change a considerable time must be foreseen. Since there are many more signalling end points in an SS 7 network than signalling transfer points, the restart procedure should be introduced first within the STPs. During the introduction of the restart procedure, the major concern might be to avoid extensive outage times of SEPs when some nodes have the restart procedure implemented and others not, since outage objectives for exchanges of only a few minutes per year exist in many networks.

The impact on a restarting Red Book node of being surrounded by nodes that have implemented the White Book restart procedure will depend on the network configuration and the types of calls handled by the exchange. If there is no source of calls other than IAMs received over the SS 7 network, the exchange simply gets no calls until the procedures for being adjacent to a restarting node have timed out at the adjacent points. If the exchange has other sources for calls, e.g., directly connected subscribers or trunks employing signalling other than SS 7, it may launch IAMs into the SS 7 network. No responses will be received for these IAMs and the calls will time out. Since calls that time out tie up memory and perhaps other resources within the exchange for far longer than the average call setup time which is used in engineering the exchanges, there would be a potential for overloading the exchange, perhaps even leading to renewed outage if a sufficient fraction of the calls require the use of the SS 7 network for completion.

Thus, we concentrate in this section on the discussion of how to solve this White Book STP–Red Book SEP interworking problem. Especially, we discuss the use of a method specified within ANSI called the traffic restart waiting method (see also Sect. 10.3.1.1) to solve the interworking problems.

10.3.3.1 The Traffic Restart Waiting Method

In nonhierarchical networks the central stand-alone STPs are connected to a large number of SEPs, so that those STPs need port capacity for several hundred links and, maybe, in future still more (see Sect. 13.2.1). Thus, it might be difficult to generally find an appropriate value for the restart timer T18, which supervises the link activation during phase 1. In this respect, the traffic restart waiting method was first introduced within ANSI [40] into the restart procedure to allow a restarting transfer point to take more time, if needed, to activate its links.

When a signalling transfer point Y restarts, it starts the timer T26[1]. If the first link in a previously unavailable link set becomes available for a restarting STP Y within phase 1, during which it activates links and expects to receive TFP, TFR or TFA messages, a traffic restart waiting TRW message is sent to the adjacent node X at the far end of the link. Whenever timer T26 expires, the restarting signalling point restarts T26 and broadcasts a TRW message to those adjacent signalling points connected by an available link. If, at an adjacent node X, the first link in the previously unavailable link set to Y is in the *in service* state at Level 2, X starts a traffic restart waiting timer T28. If a TRW message is received at the adjacent node X, timer T28 is stopped and the overall restart timer T21 is started. If X receives a further TRW messages from Y while T21 is running, X restarts T21. When sufficient links are available for Y to carry the expected signalling traffic and the sending of the actual routing information by the broadcast of TFP and TFR is finished, T26 is stopped and the restarting STP Y broadcasts TRA messages to all adjacent signalling points. If X receives a TRA message from Y, X stops T21 or T28, whichever is running, and restarts traffic on the link set to Y. In the case that T21 or T28 expire, X restarts user traffic on the link set towards Y. Then T21 can be set to a reasonable small value, but a signalling point that requires more time to restart, e.g., because it has a large number of signalling links, can still complete its restart procedure before adjacent points time out and restart traffic. Thus, the restarting STP Y has the possibility to enhance the overall restart time as needed without causing a loss of bidirectionality.

Note: With the TRW method, there is a fundamental change in the philosophy of the original restart procedure. The adjacent timer T21 was conceived to terminate the restart procedure in failure situations, e.g., when a TRA message is not received.

---

[1] Note, that the timers T26 and T28 are not ITU timers. Their function is described within the text.

With the TRW method this no longer holds. There is no longer any method to terminate the restart procedure at an adjacent node when it, due to some failures, continuously receives TRW messages from the restarting node. Thus, the restart procedure might never terminate in such a situation.

◇

10.3.3.2 Reducing the Outage Time of Restarting Red Book SEPs

Another use of the TRW message within ANSI is to solve the interworking problem between a restarting Red Book SEP and adjacent White Book STPs, which can result in unwanted outage times within the network as discussed in Sect. 10.3.1.1 and above.

Timer T21 is used as a guard timer at signalling points adjacent to a restarting point so that adjacent points will not wait forever to restart traffic if a TRA message is lost or not sent because the restarting point is a Red Book node. Restarting signalling points with different implementations and different numbers of signalling links may take quite different amounts of time to complete the restart procedure. Therefore, it was considered difficult to determine what value timer T21 should have. If timer T21 is too short, traffic will be sent to a restarting point before it is ready to handle it. If timer T21 is too long, outages are extended unnecessarily when TRAs are lost or when they are not sent by Red Book nodes.

In ANSI, it was agreed to use the periodic broadcast of the traffic restart waiting TRW message to adjacent points to avoid those outage times while older nodes were not changed. As described for the restarting STP, a restarting signalling end point SEP Y starts timer T26. If the first link in a previously unavailable link set becomes available for a restarting SEP, a TRW message is sent to the adjacent node X at the far end of the link. Whenever timer T26 expires, the restarting SEP Y restarts T26 and broadcasts a TRW message to those adjacent signalling points connected by an available link. If, at an adjacent node X, the first link in the previously unavailable link set to Y is in the *in service* state at Level 2, X starts a traffic restart waiting timer T28 and sends to Y a TRW message, or if X has the transfer function, a TRW message followed by TFP and TFR messages and a TRA message. If a TRW message is received at the adjacent node X, timer T28 is stopped and the overall restart timer T21 is started. If X receives a further TRW message from Y while T21 is running, X restarts T21. When sufficient links are available for Y and the routing data update has been performed, T26 is stopped and the restarting SEP Y broadcasts TRA messages to all adjacent signalling points. When the STP X receives the TRA message from Y, X stops T21 or T28, whichever is running, and restarts traffic on the link set to Y. In the case that T21 or T28 expire, X restarts user traffic on the link set towards Y.

Thus, if the restarting SEP Y is a Red Book node, it will not send TRW or TRA messages, so that at the adjacent STP X the traffic restart waiting timer T28 expires. If T28 expires, the STP X assumes that the restarting point is a Red Book node that has not implemented the restart procedure. The adjacent point X then restarts traffic and notifies its neighbors of the restarting SEP's availability. Thus, if the timer T28 is set to a reasonable small value, e.g., 4 s, the adjacent restart procedure is terminated very soon, when no TRW message is received at the adjacent node X. In this way the TRW method may also help to reduce the time during which bidirectionality is lost.

10.3.3.3 Restarting White Book STP and Adjacent Red Book SEPs

As described above, the TRW method avoids unwanted outage times in the case of restarting Red Book SEPs. Furthermore, the advantage is that the older Red Book nodes do not have to be changed in order to avoid the loss of bidirectionality.

However, there are further problems that could not be neglected. So far, we have only discussed problems with a restarting SEP. In addition, we have to investigate in more detail the case of a restarting White Book STP with adjacent Red Book SEPs. Unfortunately, there are unwanted effects, which are summarized in the following.

Message Loss and Loss of Bidirectionality

Due to the restart of a neighboring White Book STP, a Red Book SEP is, in general, not isolated. However, a loss of messages will, in general, occur due to the fact that, when the first link in the link set towards the restarting STP becomes available, the Red Book SEP considers this node to be accessible again and performs a changeback of (or in presence of further failures restarts) normal traffic towards the restarting STP. However, especially at the beginning of the restarting phase, links towards more distant destinations might not be available so that such traffic is discarded. This results in a loss of bidirectionality when destination points use other available routes towards the considered Red Book SEP.

As a special example let us consider the case that there is a long-term failure of the STP transmission equipment towards a destination point so that this point remains inaccessible via the STP. According to the White Book restart procedure the originating Red Book SEP will only be informed about this unavailability due to a received TFP message at the end of the restart procedure. Since the received messages are discarded within the restarting White Book STP, message loss and a loss of bidirectionality will occur for the whole restarting time.

Note: If a restarting White Book STP enhances the overall restart time by using the TRW method, the above described loss of bidirectionality in the case an adjacent Red Book node is increased.

◇

The ANSI TFP Method

In order to solve this loss of bidirectionality, it is specified within the ANSI specification that the restarting White Book STP has to send TFP messages in order to stop premature user traffic, for example, sent by an adjacent Red Book SEP resulting in the above described message loss and loss of bidirectionality. This traffic is discarded when no routes are available at the restarting STP during the early restarting phase. Due to the TFP this traffic is stopped and possibly rerouted at the SEP.

Inconsistent Treatment of Signalling Routes

However, the disadvantage is an inconsistent treatment of signalling routes by this method, which may result in another loss of bidirectionality. Consider the case that, due to some additional failures, two Red Book SEPs are exclusively interconnected via the restarting White Book STP. Depending on how this restarting node performs its link activation, one of the SEPs will first consider the restarting node to be accessible again and, thus, restarts its traffic. But because no route towards the other SEP is available, the STP stops this traffic by sending a TFP. Some time later, the other SEP becomes accessible due to further link activation. The restarted traffic by this SEP, however, may be routed to the other SEP so that a loss of bidirectionality will occur, which lasts for the rest of the restart procedure, because no TFA messages are sent by the STP before the restart procedure is terminated. To summarize, although the TFP method solves one of the above interworking problems it may create another one under other circumstances.

Implementation Problem

Another drawback of this TFP method is an implementation one. The described method requires that for each TFP message a TFA message has to be sent after the restart procedure has terminated. As a consequence, besides the normal routing information, the additional information describing to which signalling points a TFP message referring to a special destination point has been sent must be retained.

A Restarting White Book STP Is Not Protected

Although, due to the implementation, routes may be opened during phase 1 of the restart procedure via the restarting White Book STP at nearly the same time, an unwanted effect remains: when a lot of Red Book SEPs are connected via the restarting White Book STP, they will reroute their normal traffic via the restarting node. As a consequence, a considerable traffic load has to be handled (routed or discarded) by the restarting STP. As a consequence, although it performs the White Book, i.e., the ideal, restart procedure it is not protected and problems as in the pure Red Book network are present.

10.3.3.4 Conclusions

Avoiding Loss of Bidirectionality Does Not Solve the Problems

During the White Book study period, major changes to the MTP restart procedure were agreed in order to remove incompatibilities within the restart procedure entailing one-way signalling relations. In addition, there were other sources for one-way signalling relations resulting from the interworking between Red, Blue, and White Book nodes. There is, however, a fundamental difference between the two types of problems.

Whilst the loss of bidirectionality within the White Book procedure could be solved, so that the procedure now works well, this is actually not the case for the interworking problems. The reason is that the general way to avoid a loss of bidirectionality due to the interworking of different versions of the procedure is to switch off the restart procedure, which is actually the result of the TRW method. However, this means that all of the Red Book problems of a restarting node, whether this is an SEP or STP, are present. Thus, solving the interworking problems of the restart procedure does not solve the problems of the restarting node.

Avoiding Loss of Bidirectionality and Protecting the Restarting Node Are Conflicting Objectives

As discussed previously, a restarting White Book node does not resume sending user traffic unless the restart procedure is terminated, whilst an adjacent Red Book node immediately restarts user traffic when the restarting node becomes available. As a consequence, there is a loss of bidirectionality for up to 60 s. However, avoiding the one-way signalling relations, in general, means terminating the restart procedure so that we can no longer protect the restarting node. In fact, protecting a restarting node and avoiding one-way signalling relations due to the interworking of different color versions are conflicting objectives. We cannot have both at the same time.

The Problem of Isolating SEPs

Due to the interworking problems with the restart procedure a consequence of one-way signalling relations might be the isolation of an SEP for T21. As discussed in Sect. 10.3.3, the most important interworking problem is that of a restarting White Book STP and Red Book SEP. As discussed in Sect. 10.3.3.2, the TRW method could be used to reduce the outage time of a restarting Red Book SEP. However, as discussed in Sect. 10.3.3.3, the TRW and TFP methods cannot solve all of the interworking problems. The objective should be to look for a solution which solves all of the problems in a satisfactory way and not only parts of them.

If we say that avoiding one-way signalling relations is of higher priority than protecting the restarting node and because we cannot achieve this in all cases, we may ask whether the implementation effort is worthwhile. We may then further argue, that the interworking problems are removed in a natural way by the network evolution towards the White Book network. On the other hand, if we say that protecting the restarting node is the first objective, we would like to emphasize the positive effect of the one-way signalling relation, i.e., because the adjacent White Book nodes will not restart traffic unless T21 expires, which means some kind of protection of the restarting Red Book node. Furthermore, the 60 s have to be compared to the overall isolation time: if the isolation lasts a few minutes than the isolation of the SEP for 60 s does not seem to be so relevant.

The TRW Method Makes No Sense in the Final White Book Network

If the TRW method is used in order to avoid the interworking problem between a restarting Red Book SEP and an adjacent White Book STP, i.e., to reduce the outage time of the restarting Red Book SEP, then the TRW method will be present in the final White Book network. This means that the TRW messages will be sent as described above and their arrival supervised which, within the final White Book network, does not make any sense at all. Moreover, it may have negative effects in the case that a TRW message gets lost or an unexpected TRW is received, leading to a termination of the restart procedure or yielding undefined states. Should we really replace the drawbacks during the time-limited interworking phase with the drawbacks within the final White Book network?

The Final Decision

At this point, the general question is raised of whether we should spend time and money to specify and implement procedures which are aimed to solve, in general, only parts of the interworking problems, which possibly create other problems under other circumstances, and which are only considered for the time-limited conversion phase of the network. In this respect, it was eventually decided not to introduce a new network management message within the MTP, i.e., not to introduce the TRW method within ITU. Indeed, since not all of the interworking problems could eventually be solved, the best approach was seen to avoid them by the introduction of the White Book restart procedure within all nodes of the network as fast as possible and to ignore the interworking problems during this conversion phase, which was eventually agreed at the end of the White Book study period. This is the only measure that really solves all interworking problems and which leaves the procedure simple.

Note, that the introduction of the restart procedure does not mean that each node is switched to the full White Book level.

As a summary of the previous detailed discussion we describe in the following section the MTP restart procedure that was eventually agreed at the end of the White Book study period [41].

10.4 The White Book Restart Procedure

When the first link is *in service* at Level 2, the restarting node Y starts the MTP restart procedure. At the beginning of the restart procedure, Y considers all concerned routes to be available and starts timer T20 (59–61 s) (for timer values see Appendix A), which defines an upper limit on the overall restart time. If Y has the transfer function it, in addition, starts timer T18, which is considered to be implementation and network dependent. Both timers subdivide the overall restart time into two phases.

Within the first phase, supervised by timer T18, links are activated and the routing tables within the restarting node Y are updated according to the TFP and TFA messages received from the adjacent nodes. In addition, Y takes into account any traffic restart allowed (TRA) messages received from adjacent nodes, where the number of received TRAs is a measure of the completeness of the received routing data. Timer T18 is stopped and, thus, the first phase terminated when:

- Sufficient links and link sets are available to carry the expected signalling traffic, and
- Enough TRA messages and, thus, routing data have been received to give a high level of confidence in the updated routing data.

When T18 is stopped or expires the second phase begins, which lasts until T20 expires or is stopped. A major task to be performed by Y during this phase is a broadcast of nonpreventive TFP messages regarding unavailable route sets, taking into account information about local link sets which are not available and any TFP and TFA messages received during phase 1. Note that timer T18 is determined such that during phase 2 the broadcast of TFP messages can be completed in normal situations.

TFPs and TFAs, received by Y during phase 2, are considered to be late events and should be treated as follows. If Y has declared a destination node Z to be inaccessible during a corresponding broadcast of TFPs and if Z becomes accessible during phase 2, this new reachability is treated outside the restart procedure, i.e., corresponding TFAs are sent when the restart procedure is terminated. The handling of the new accessibility of Z before the sending of TFPs referring to that destination is an implementation-dependent matter. Note that the restarting node Y never sends TFAs during the restart procedure.

When the broadcast is finished, timer T20 is stopped. If the restarting node Y has no transfer function, this broadcast of TFPs is not performed, i.e., the second phase is not present, so that timer T18 can be set equal to T20. Therefore, for the first phase the overall restart time is available so that in this case T18 and T20 are stopped at the same time according to the above criteria. When T20 is stopped or expires, Y stops the restart procedure and sends a TRA message to all adjacent signalling points via corresponding available direct link sets and an indication of the end of the MTP restart is sent to all local User Parts showing each signalling point's accessibility or inaccessibility.

A signalling point X, which is not completely isolated from the network, considers that a previously inaccessible adjacent node Y is restarting when the first link in a direct link set is in the *in service* state at Level 2 or when another route to Y becomes available. Then, X starts timer T21 (63–65 s), which defines an upper limit on the overall restart time and takes into account any TFP and TFA messages received from the restarting node Y. If X has the transfer function, it sends any necessary TFP messages to Y informing Y about inaccessible destination nodes. After that, X sends a TRA message to Y via the direct link set, indicating that Y has received all relevant inaccessibility information from X. If X has no transfer function it directly sends to Y a TRA message.

If a signalling point, previously declared to be inaccessible, becomes accessible again before T21 is stopped or expires, a corresponding TFA message is sent to Y. If a signalling point becomes inaccessible to X after a TRA message has been sent to Y, X sends a corresponding TFP to Y. Such a late event is treated normally by X. When a TRA message has been received by X from Y, indicating the end of the restart at the restarting node Y, and when a TRA message has been sent by X to Y, X stops timer T21. In the case where X is still sending TFP messages to Y when it receives the TRA from Y, X finishes the sending of TFPs to Y before it sends its TRA to Y and stops timer T21. However, if X is sending TFPs to Y and T21 expires, i.e., X does not receive a TRA from Y within T21, then X stops sending TFPs to Y and sends no TRA message to Y.

When T21 is stopped or expires, X sends an MTP-RESUME primitive concerning Y and all signalling points made available via Y to all local User Parts. If X has the transfer function, it broadcasts to adjacent available signalling points TFA messages concerning Y and all signalling points made accessible via Y (broadcast method).

11

Real SS 7 Networks

The SS 7 network will have a significant impact on the MTP, since the MTP forms the interface at a node with the rest of the SS 7 network. In this respect it is specified in Q.701, section 3 [42] that *"the MTP procedures must be independent of the signalling network in that it has to be capable of performing its set functions and attaining its objective no matter what network structure or status prevails."* However, the network structure and network planning has an impact on the function of the MTP procedures, like for example the SS 7 flow control (see Chap. 12). Therefore, the network structure must be carefully selected and the routing data designed to fulfill specific requirements.

On the one hand, the signalling network structure must be chosen to meet the most stringent availability requirements of any User Part served by the network. The availability of the individual components of the network must be considered in determining the network structure. The unavailability of a signalling route set is determined by the unavailability of the signalling links and signalling points belonging to that routes set and by the structure of the signalling network. According to Q.706 the unavailability of a signalling route set should not exceed a total of 10 min per year [43]. The MTP signalling network procedures are provided in order to effectively operate a signalling network with different degrees of complexity. They provide for reliable message transfer across the network and for reconfiguration of the network in the case of failures. Nevertheless, protection against transmission errors cannot be absolute and missequencing and a loss of signalling messages in the MTP cannot be excluded in extreme cases. With this respect it is specified in Q.706 that

- Not more than one in 10^{10} of all MSUs will contain an error that is undetected by the MTP
- Not more than one in 10^{10} messages will be lost due to failure in the MTP and
- That not more than one in 10^{10} messages will be delivered out of sequence to the User Parts due to failure in the MTP, including duplication of messages.

On the other hand, the MTP procedures were specified based on the assumption that the SS 7 network is bidirectional and loop-free, under normal operation as well as in case of failures within the network (see Sect. 2.1). Thus, in order to assure a correct operation of the MTP, routing data must be defined in such a way

- To prevent circular routing of signalling messages,
- To assure bidirectionality between any two nodes of the network, also in the case of failure situations and
- To provide sufficient node-disjoint routes between the nodes of the network.

(see Sect. 11.2.1). Considerable attention is drawn to STP routing tables to ensure that circular routing does not occur. A lot of planning and testing tools are available to avoid circular routing but they do not care about bidirectionality. A violation of the assumptions in conjunction with improper network planning may lead to the fact that the MTP procedures do not work properly so that it is hard to fulfill the overall availability requirements and local problems may spread within the SS 7 network, leading to the risk of an SS 7 network outage. The only way to avoid these problems is to select a suitable network structure and to carefully plan the routing data. However, the problem is that no underlying network topology exists which allows all three objectives to be reached at the same time [44]. So the question is what to do?

In Sect. 11.3 we describe suitable network topologies that enable one to realize bidirectionality and loop-freeness of the routing data, even in failure situations, as well as fixed number of node-disjoint routes between most nodes of the network. Furthermore, we describe the general structure of real SS 7 networks, which consists of the *physical* and *logical network*. Since the underlying topology is the basis of the logical network we describe different network topologies and how routing data may be created. Due to the fact that the creation of a suitable network topology as well as the definition of routing data, so that the above requirements are fulfilled, is not an easy task it is of interest to have appropriate algorithms available for the network design [45]. In Sect. 11.3.2 we describe how routing data can be derived algorithmically within a suitable network topology so that the above criteria are fulfilled.

11.1 The Physical Network

An SS 7 network is composed of a number of switching and processing nodes, e.g., exchanges, service control points or signalling transfer points. To communicate using SS 7, each of these nodes has implemented the necessary within-node features of SS 7, making that node a signalling point. These signalling points are interconnected by signalling link sets which contain 1–16 signalling links. The combination of these signalling points and their interconnecting link sets form the physical network. Different structures of the physical network are possible, which we call the topology of the SS 7 network. A lot of European networks are hierarchical, i.e., the signalling points are grouped into different levels, whilst in the US, networks are nonhierarchical. As an example, Fig. 11.1 shows a simple hierarchical network.

The nodes T1, T2, and T3, interconnected by link sets, form the highest level 0 and serve as central transfer nodes for the remaining nodes of the network. In

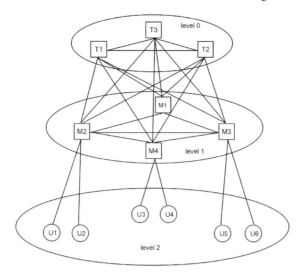

Fig. 11.1. Hierarchical network topology transfer function

addition to the transfer function they may have user functions. The nodes M1, M2, M3, and M4 form the level 1 and are interconnected as shown in Fig. 11.1. They all have user functions and the transfer function. The remaining nodes with only user functions form the lowest level 2. They are interconnected with one node each at level 1.

11.2 The Logical Network

Signalling information is conveyed by MSUs from an originating node to the destination node, where the MTP is responsible for reliable transport and delivery of the MSUs, also in the case of failures of single links and/or signalling points, i.e., signalling routes. With this objective normal and alternative routes are defined between any two nodes in the network based on the underlying topology. The set of all routes is called the logical network. These routes are defined globally and are stored locally within the nodes of the network as so-called routing data. Note that, in principle, the routes from node A to node B may be designed independently from the routes from B to A.

11.2.1 Node-Disjoint Routes and Bidirectionality

In order to achieve SS 7 network reliability the objective should be to have sufficient node-disjoint routes between any two nodes in the network, bidirectionality and loop-freeness of the routing data, in normal and in failure situations. In this respect, two routes are called node-disjoint if they have no signalling points in common, except

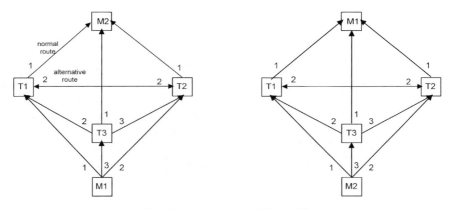

Fig. 11.2. Routing plan $M1 \leftrightarrow M2$

the originating node and the destination node. Furthermore, bidirectionality of routing data means that, whenever node A can reach another node B within the SS 7 network, then node B must also be able to reach node A, which must hold in the normal case as well as in the case of route failures.

For example, let us consider the routing plan $M1 \leftrightarrow M2$ as shown in Fig. 11.2.

For M1 the normal route to M2 is (M1,T1,M2) and the second choice is the route (M1,T2,M2), which are node disjoint. Another alternative route is defined via T3. Note, that besides of the normal route (T1,M2) from T1 to M2 there is one alternative route (T1,T2,M2) defined via T2 but not via T3 in order to avoid the signalling loop (T1,T2,T3). How to create loop-free, node-disjoint and bidirectional routing plans is shown in Sect. 11.3.2.

11.2.2 Local and Global Routes

We distinguish between local and global routes. A global route from signalling point A to destination node Z is a predetermined path, consisting of a succession of signalling transfer points and interconnecting link sets, that a message takes through the SS 7 network from A to Z. The set of all routes of the signalling relation between A and Z is called a route set. A network operator has such a global view of a signalling route. However, a signalling point belonging to a particular route only has a local view of that route, i.e., it only knows the section towards one of its adjacent nodes along that global route.

Thus, a local route from a signalling point X to the destination point Z is a link set from X to an adjacent node, along which Z can be reached. In general, such a local route of a signalling point is part of several different global routes towards Z (see Fig. 11.3).

As an example, signalling point A in Fig. 11.3 has two local routes (A,X1) and (A,X2) whilst signalling point X1 has three local routes (X1,Y1), (X1,Y2), and (X1,X2) towards Z, which are part of several global routes from A to Z, e.g., (A,X1,Y1,Z), (A,X1,Y2,Z) or (A,X1,Y1,Y2,Z).

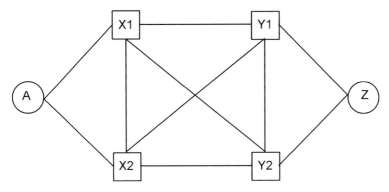

Fig. 11.3. Local and global routes transfer function

11.3 Routing and Topology

A network designer has to choose a network topology that meets specific technical and performance requirements. Based on this underlying topology signalling routes are defined between any two signalling points of the network. Thus, the underlying topology is the basis of the logical network. In the following, we first describe a suitable network topology. Then, we describe how routing data can be algorithmically created within this topology so that loop-freeness and bidirectionality are assured and that node-disjoint routes can be realized between most nodes in the network. Finally, we describe how the network can be changed without violating these general requirements.

11.3.1 The Network Topology

When designing an SS 7 network the technical restrictions of an exchange, like the limited number of signalling links and signalling link sets connected to an exchange, have to be considered. Furthermore, the overall message transfer time, which depends on handling times at the signalling points, queuing delays including retransmission delays as well as signalling data link propagation times, should not be exceeded [43]. As a consequence, there is a maximum number of transfer points between any two nodes of the network.

In order to fulfill the availability requirement for signalling route sets and to avoid (at least partial) network outages it should be the objective to realize $q \in \mathcal{N}$ node-disjoint routes between any two nodes of the network. Finally, economical factors have to be taken into account.

An SS 7 network can be represented by a unidirectional graph. Trees are special graphs, which are of interest because of their clear structure and the easy way to handle them algorithmically. However, the main disadvantage of trees is that no alternative routes are possible. Thus, the topology described in the following combines the tree structure with the realization of node-disjoint routes between the nodes of the network. It should be noted that hierarchical as well as nonhierarchical networks are covered by that topology (see Sect. 13.2.1).

The fundamental parameters of the topology are:

- The maximum number t of transfer points of the longest route
- The number q of node-disjoint routes between two nodes of the network
- The number p of link sets connected to a node
- The total number n of nodes of the network

It is not possible to vary these parameters independently. This fact can be noticed by considering the following examples. If, from an arbitrarily selected node, we would like to reach directly any other node of the network without traversing a transfer node we end up with a meshed network. This means, however, that every node in the network must be able to manage $p = n - 1$ link sets. If there are only $p = 2$ link sets connected to the nodes of the network the resulting topology is a ring and only two node-disjoint routes are possible.

The number p of link sets that can be connected to a node is an implementation-dependent matter. It depends on the total number of links that can be connected to an exchange as well as the selected number of links within a link set. The following relation holds between the parameters q and p:

$$p = m \cdot q \tag{11.1}$$

wherein m is an integer being greater than or equal to 2.

The topology consists of $l + 1$ different levels numbered by $i = 0, 1, \ldots, l$ (see Fig. 11.4). All nodes at levels $i = 0, \ldots, l - 1$ have the transfer function and may have end point functionality whilst the nodes at the lowest level $i = l$ are signalling end points having no transfer functions. The highest level $i = 0$ consists of exactly q nodes.

All nodes at levels $i = 1, \ldots, l$ are structured into

$$r_i = \left(\frac{p - q}{q} \right)^{i-1} \cdot \frac{p}{q} = (m - 1)^{i-1} \cdot m, \quad i = 1, \ldots, l \tag{11.2}$$

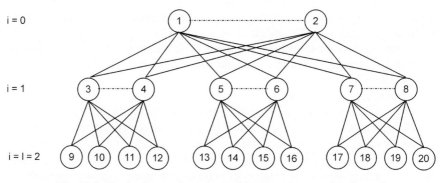

Fig. 11.4. The fundamental topology with parameters $q = 2$ and $p = 6$

groups of nodes, where every group contains exactly q nodes. The number of nodes n_i at level i is then given by:

$$n_i = \begin{cases} q, & i = 0 \\ \left(\frac{p-q}{q}\right)^{i-1} \cdot p, & i = 1, \ldots, l \end{cases} \qquad (11.3)$$

Every node at level i $(i > 0)$ uses exactly q edges to different nodes at the next higher level $i - 1$. All nodes within levels $i \neq l$ have p edges whilst the nodes at the lowest level $i = l$ have exactly q edges. We call this topology of Fig. 11.4 without the dashed lines reduced topology. If $q = 1$, i.e., level 0 contains exactly one node and every node at level i $(i > 0)$ is connected to level $(i - 1)$ once, the result is the well-known tree. Thus, the tree is a special case of our topology.

The described topology has the properties that at least $2 \cdot q$ edges (link sets) must be connected to an exchange and that q node-disjoint routes

$$W_j = (X, N_{j1}, N_{j2}, \ldots, N_{jr}, Y), \quad 1 \leq j \leq q, \quad N_{jk} \neq N_{j'k'} \text{ for } (jk) \neq (j'k')$$

exist between two arbitrary nodes X and Y, wherein $N_{j1}, \ldots, N_{jr}$ denote the transfer nodes along the route from X to Y.

Furthermore, we enhance the reduced topology of Fig. 11.4 by adding the dashed lines in order to have connections between the nodes within the groups at levels $i = 0, \ldots, l - 1$ and to allow more alternative routes. With respect to loop-freeness and bidirectionality of the routing data this interconnection must be done in such a way that only one physical path exists between any two nodes of a group. This means that, within a group, a linear structure or a star structure where all nodes of a group are interconnected via a central node (see Fig. 11.5), is possible.

Finally, since the nodes at level l have no transfer function, these may be fully meshed, which is not shown in Fig. 11.5.

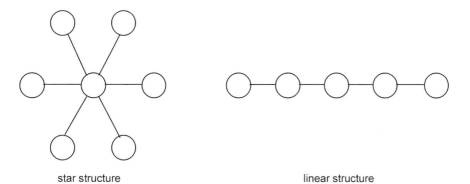

star structure   linear structure

Fig. 11.5. The connection of nodes within a group

11.3.2 The Creation of Routing Data

In the following we show how, based on the described topology, routes can be defined which are designed globally and are stored locally within the individual nodes as routing data. The general requirements are that the routes are loop-free and that bidirectionality between any two nodes in the network is assured, also in the case of failures within the network. The definition of routes within our topology and the creation of the corresponding routing data are done in parallel. The following algorithm is based on the exchange of identifications (e.g., signalling point codes), which are uniquely assigned to every node. This exchange of identifications is done on a level basis, i.e., first the identifications of all nodes at level $i = l$ are distributed in the network, then for the nodes of level $i = l - 1$ up to level $i = 0$.

Rules for the Distribution of Identifications:

(1) The identification is exchanged within the topology step by step. When a node X receives an identification from an adjacent node Y for node Z, X notes that it may reach Z via Y.

(2) If Z lies within level $i \neq l$, it sends its identification to all adjacent nodes within its group of nodes. If a node X within this group receives this identification, it passes on the identification to an adjacent node within the group which is different from the one from which the identification has been received. When all nodes within the considered group have received the identification for Z they send the corresponding identification to their adjacent nodes within the levels $i - 1$ and $i + 1$.

(3) If Z lies within the lowest level $i = l$, it sends its identification to all adjacent nodes within level $i - 1$ as well as all possible adjacent nodes at level $i = l$.

(4) If node X within level $i \neq l$ receives the identification of Z from a node at the lower level $i + 1$, it passes on the identification to its adjacent nodes within its group of nodes. After the identification of Z is exchanged between the nodes of the considered group, the nodes of that group send the identification to all adjacent nodes at levels $i - 1$ and $i + 1$ except those from which the considered identification for Z has already been received.

(5) If a node X at level i receives the identification of Z from a node at the higher level $i-1$ it passes on the identification of Z to its adjacent nodes within its group of nodes. After the identification of Z has been exchanged within the considered group the nodes of that group send the identification of Z to all adjacent nodes at the lower level $i + 1$.

Remarks:

(1) If there exists no direct connection between two nodes at level l the normal route between these nodes consists of $m \leq l$ upward links and $m \leq l$ downward links. Alternative routes, however, might have horizontal links.

(2) Identifications are passed upwards from level $i > 0$ to level $i - 1$ if and only if these are received at level i from the lower level $i + 1$.

(3) According to the rules above elementary routing loops between two nodes can only occur within the routing graph if they are adjacent and within the same group of nodes. These elementary routing loops are avoided by the MTP transfer prohibited procedure [4].

◇

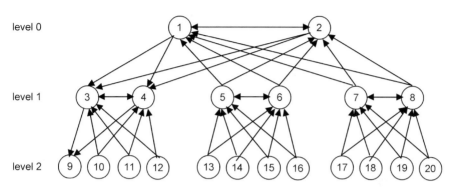

Fig. 11.6. Loop-free routing graph for destination node 9 and $p = 6$

As an example, the loop-free routing graph for destination node $Z = 9$ is shown in Fig. 11.6. In order to create the related routing data, node 9 sends, in a first step, its identification to the adjacent nodes 3 and 4 at level 1. In a second step, nodes 3 and 4 exchange the identification for node 9. These nodes then send the identification to nodes 1 and 2 at level 0 as well as to nodes 10, 11, and 12 at level 2. After this step, nodes 1, 2, 10, 11, and 12 have exactly $q = 2$ node-disjoint routes towards destination node 9 via nodes 3 and 4, and so on. From node 18, as a final example, two node-disjoint routes exist towards destination node 9, namely:

$$W1 = (18, 8, 1, 3, 9) \quad \text{and} \quad W2 = (18, 7, 2, 4, 9).$$

At the end of the procedure every node has the complete routing data for any other node of the topology for the normal as well as alternative routes. The list of routes, as created automatically by the algorithm, starts with the shortest and ends with the longest route so that this sequence can be used to assign a priority to the routes. A network operator, however, is free to assign any other priority to the derived routes and, especially, to define combined link sets.

11.3.3 Loop-Freeness, Bidirectionality, and Node-Disjoint Routes

As has been mentioned earlier a major interest of a network operator is the design of routing plans which assure q node-disjoint routes between any two nodes in the network as well as loop-freeness and bidirectionality of the routing data, also under failure situations. These requirements strongly depend on the underlying topology and the definition of the routing data. It is well known that there exists no topology which allows defining routing data such that all of these three requirements are fulfilled [44].

With this respect it is important to note that the algorithm based on the network topology, as described in Sects. 11.3.1 and 11.3.2, creates routing data which are loop-free and bidirectional and yield q node-disjoint routes between any two nodes of the network, except when both nodes are located within the same group of nodes, between which only one node-disjoint route is possible.

11.3.4 Network Changes

Another important issue is that the network can be easily changed by adding or removing nodes without violating the general requirements. On the one hand, the topology can be enhanced by adding a new level $l + 1$. In this case, however, all nodes within level l must be assigned the transfer function. On the other hand, nodes can be added at any level $i = 1, \ldots, l$ by increasing the number p of link sets connected to each node. In any case, the general structure must be kept. In the same way nodes can be removed.

The advantage is that the routing data for already/still existing nodes remain unchanged. We only have to add the routing data for the new nodes or to remove the data for those nodes that have been taken away.

Finally, a complete migration to an overall ATM or IP-based SS 7 network can be easily performed by first replacing the SS 7 links by ATM or IP-based links and then removing the hierarchical network structure ending with a fully meshed network, as described in Sect. 13.2.2. Alternatively, we may start creating the IP domain with IP signalling points, which are interconnected to the traditional PSTN switches via signalling gateways (see Sect. 4.1 and Chap. 14). Removing traditional switches decreases the PSTN domain whilst the introduction of the new IP signalling points increases the IP domain. In the end, the IP domain remains. The same holds for a transition to an ATM-based network.

11.4 Network Interconnection

In this section, we describe how the SS 7 network interconnection to other networks, the access to IN services, and the PSTN and IP network convergence should be performed to cover SS 7 network reliability issues.

11.4.1 Intermediate Networks

The worldwide SS 7 network is structured into two functionally independent levels: the international (I) and national (N) levels [46]. This structure provides a clear division of responsibility for signalling network management and allows numbering plans of signalling points of the international network and the different national

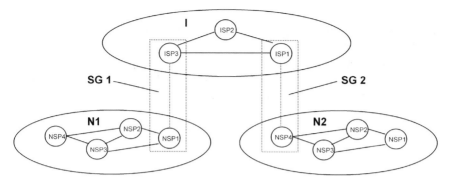

Fig. 11.7. Network interconnection and $p = 6$

networks to be independent of each other. In the same way, the networks of different national network operators may be interconnected via a national intermediate network (I). In Fig. 11.7 the fundamental concept of SS 7 network interconnection using an intermediate network is shown, where network I may be the international network of a national intermediate network. This structure allows a clear separation of the different national networks.

Special signalling points are required to interconnect the different networks and these are called signalling gateways (SG). An SG is part of different networks and, thus, assigned multiple signalling point codes (SPC), one for each network. For example, SG 1 of Fig. 11.7 is assigned the national SPC NSP1 and the intermediate or international SPC ISP3.

At a signalling gateway, the network indicator (NI) is used to distinguish the different networks to which it belongs and to determine the relevant numbering scheme and possibly the label structure. The network indicator is made up of the bits C and D of the subservice field contained in the service information octet (SIO), as shown in Fig. 11.8.

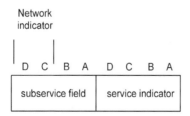

Fig. 11.8. Service information octet

The network indicator, together with the standard 14-bit signalling point code, allows for four signalling networks, each with up to 16,384 point codes. The bits '00' are allocated to the international network whilst the bits '01' are spare for international use. The bit pattern '10' is allocated to a national network and '11' is for national use, i.e., may be allocated to a national intermediate network.

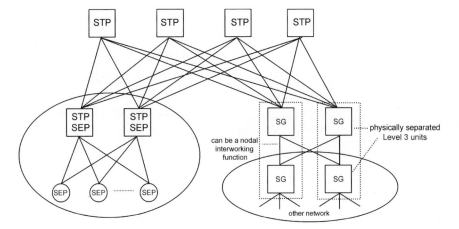

Fig. 11.9. Network interconnection via SGs

11.4.2 Network Interconnection via Signalling Gateways

Due to network security reasons, the interconnection of nonlicensed operator's networks (having no right to access the own SS 7 network) should be performed via a national intermediate network or the international network, as shown in Fig. 11.7. The signalling gateways should be stand-alone STPs where it is recommended not to use the central STPs of the proposed new network structure (see Chap. 13) but instead to access these SGs via the central nodes as shown in Fig. 11.9.

Note, however, that it must be avoided that problems spread from one network to the other via a SG (see Sect. 12.8) or that network isolation occurs. Thus, the SGs should be made up of physically separated Level-3 units, one for each network, and interconnected via a nodal interworking function or the SCCP layer. In addition, SG redundancy must be provided. Finally, in order to avoid bottlenecks in the case of high-throughput traffic, it is recommendable to realize the links between the central STPs and the SGs as IP-based high-speed links.

An advantage of performing the network interconnection in the described way is that foreign throughput traffic from one nonlicensed operator to another via the signalling gateways keeps that traffic away from the home SS 7 network so that related problems cannot spread into it.

In the same way, the PSTN and IP network convergence can be realized by accessing special SGs via the central STPs, as shown in Fig. 11.9, where now the SGs transfer the signalling information between a PSTN node and a MGC or an IPSP, e.g., an IP-resident database. In this way, the access to the Internet and the migration towards an ATM- or IP-based SS 7 network or the overall IP-based multimedia network can be performed (see Chap. 14).

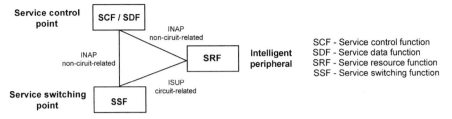

Fig. 11.10. IN architecture and signalling

11.4.3 Access to IN Services

Intelligent network (IN) services require non-circuit-related signalling, which is based on the Intelligent Network Application Part (INAP) protocol (see Fig. 11.10).

Normally, intelligent network services are realized by different IN platforms and should be accessed via the central network STPs, as shown in Fig. 11.11.

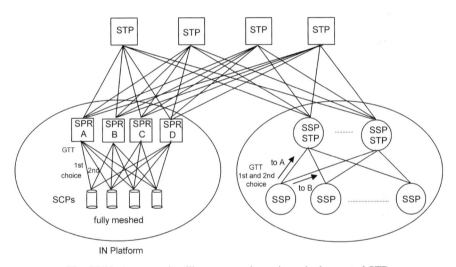

Fig. 11.11. Access to intelligent network services via the central STPs

All nodes of the SS 7 network can offer the access to IN services so that all nodes operate as service switching points (SSP). Every SSP should be able to communicate to every service control point (SCP). In Fig. 11.11 four node-disjoint routes are realized by using four signalling points with SCCP relay functions (SPR), which are connected to the SCPs. All SCPs are fully meshed with the four SPRs and every SSP is connected to the four SPRs via four central STPs. Note that bidirectionality must be assured for incomplete transactions under failure situations.

For resilience first- and second-choice SCCP destinations should be defined. At a service trigger the global title translation yields a first- and second-choice SPR whilst the global title translation at the SPR yields the first- and second-choice SCP. Different services generate different global titles. Load sharing is achieved by defining different first and second choices for different services. Note that in order not to burden the central STPs with the specific IN tasks the considered relay function is not used at these STPs. If, for example, the first-choice SPR A fails the central STPs send corresponding TFPs so that signalling traffic can be diverted to the second-choice SPR B using MTP forced rerouting or SCCP rerouting, respectively. If an SCP fails, the SPR can perform a changeover to the second choice SCP.

The realization of IN services involves a large amount of signalling traffic. In order to avoid congestion problems non-circuit-related signalling networks have to be carefully dimensioned, complete separation of circuit-related and non-circuit-related signalling traffic should be realized, and it has to be assured that congestion control works correctly. Thus, in order to avoid bottlenecks, it is recommendable to realize the access to IN services via IP-based high-speed links to possibly IP-based SCPs and intelligent peripherals. If this is done, complete separation of circuit-related and non-circuit-related signalling traffic can be achieved by using different IP links, one carrying the circuit-related signalling traffic and the other the non-circuit-related signalling traffic.

12

Potential Problems in Real SS 7 Networks

In Chap. 3 we discussed problems with the MTP procedures as well as their solutions and, in Chap. 8, we dealt with the question how SS 7 network outages may occur. We discuss now in more detail the origin of the problems in real SS 7 networks. The cause of existing problems are not faulty MTP procedures, but problems with MTP procedures can be caused in real SS 7 networks by awkward implementations, network structures, and network planning as well as the application of the MTP, especially in large SS 7 networks. These problems will occur in real SS 7 networks if the fundamental assumptions on which the MTP and SS 7 are based are violated. As described in Chap. 2 these assumptions are:

- The SS 7 network is bidirectional and loop-free,
- A signalling point only needs a local view of the SS 7 network,
- The MTP procedures are independent of the signalling network structure,
- All User Part traffic streams are of about the same characteristic,
- The MSUs from different User Parts are of about the same length,
- In the case of congestion the DPC uniquely identifies the traffic streams to be reduced.

In the following, we show in some detail how a violation of these assumptions in conjunction with improper network planning may lead to the fact that the MTP procedures do not work properly so that local problems may spread within the SS 7 network, causing the problems described in Chap. 8. In more detail, we discuss in this chapter potential problems with the SS 7 network size, the flow control, restart, and user flow control procedures as well as signalling loops and we describe the consequences of a loss of bidirectionality at the MTP level. Finally, we discuss potential problems with the network interconnection as far as MTP procedures are involved.

12.1 On the Application of the MTP

In the following we summarize those applications of the MTP in real SS 7 networks which are relevant to SS 7 network security and reliability.

Global View of the Network

New services like ISDN supplementary services or IN services require connection-oriented end-to-end signalling which, in most networks, is realized using the MTP. Thus, differing from the original philosophy, a node needs a global view of the SS 7 network.

Load Sharing of Non-Link-Related Level 3 Messages

At present, in most SS 7 networks, non-link-related Level 3 messages are sent via one link (see Sect. 3.6).

MTP Restart

In most real SS 7 networks the restart procedure is currently not applied.

Signalling Traffic Flow Control

In a large number of SS 7 networks the route-set-method (RSM) is used, i.e., the TFC rates and the congestion indication primitive rates, respectively, are created for all links of a congested route set (see Sect. 3.1 and Chap. 9).

Signalling Point Congestion

Normally no specific actions are taken in real SS 7 networks in the case of signalling point or Level 3 congestion.

User Part Availability

In most SS 7 networks the User Part availability procedure is not used (see Sect. 3.2).

Preventive TFPs via Routes with Highest Priority

When traffic towards a destination node Z is started via the normal route, preventive TFPs are sent via the route with highest priority before user traffic is started (see Sect. 12.7.3).

To Summarize:

If no specific care is taken the basic assumptions are violated so that potential problems are present in real SS7 networks, which are described in the following.

12.2 Problems with the Network Size

When the fundamentals of the MTP procedures were specified, one of the assumptions was that a signalling point only needs a local view of the SS 7 network as described in Sect. 2.1.2, i.e., it only needs routing data for adjacent nodes to which circuits are established. At that time, the size of an SS 7 network was not important regarding the function of the MTP procedures and the management of routing data and signalling point status were not considered to cause problems. However, new services like ISDN supplementary services require end-to-end signalling, which means that each node may reach any other destination node within the network, so that the network size now plays an important role. If an SS 7 network is too large, then the following problems will arise.

12.2.1 Routing Problems

End-to-end signalling requires that all necessary routing data must be stored within the nodes of a network. In large SS 7 networks this full reachability between any two nodes in the network results in extensive routing tables. On the one hand, the maintenance of these routing data is very difficult and might cause dangerous routing data errors, and on the other hand, the routing of MSUs will be delayed, which in conjunction with a high signalling traffic load and the finite performance of an exchange, may cause Level 3 congestion.

12.2.2 Mass Problems with SRM Messages

According to the original philosophy, it was considered to be sufficient to send signalling route management (SRM) messages, i.e., transfer prohibited (TFP), transfer allowed (TRA), signalling route set test (RST), and transfer controlled (TFC) messages on the basis of a single point code and not related to a point code region[1]. However, the full reachability within large SS 7 networks means that a large number of signalling relations to destination points in a wide network area are established via single link sets, as shown in Fig. 12.1.

If, due to an outage of a link set, a large number of destination nodes $Z_1, \ldots, Z_n$ becomes inaccessible for STP X, it has to broadcast a TFP message for each of these destination nodes to all concerned adjacent nodes $Y_1, \ldots, Y_m$. The number of TFP messages to be sent by X is $n \cdot m$ which, depending on the network size, can be a large number. When an adjacent node has alternative routes to these destinations, the related traffic streams are diverted. However, if an adjacent node has no alternative routes, it will also broadcast related TFP messages to concerned adjacent nodes. Thus, depending on the network structure, the full reachability within the SS 7 network can cause floods of TFPs until all concerned nodes behind STP X are informed about the inaccessibility of the destination nodes $Z_1, \ldots, Z_n$.

In addition, each concerned node has to perform a routing data update for the inaccessible destination points $Z_1, \ldots, Z_n$, which may cause the problems described in Sect. 12.2.1, and starts the related signalling route set tests. This means that all

---

[1] The possibility that SRM messages refer to more general destinations than a single point, e.g., a signalling region, was foreseen, but required further studies that have never been performed in ITU-T.

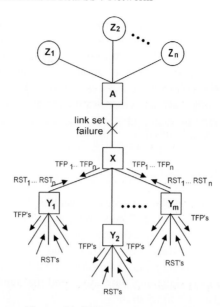

Fig. 12.1. Mass problems with SRM messages caused by network isolations

these nodes in the network area behind STP X will send, every 30–60 s (Level 3 timer T10), a RST message to the concerned adjacent nodes for each of the inaccessible destination points. These route set tests are performed until the destination nodes $Z_1, \ldots, Z_n$ are accessible again, which is indicated by a broadcast of related TFA messages. As with the TFP broadcast, floods of TFAs are sent starting from STP X until all concerned nodes within the network area behind X are informed correspondingly.

Furthermore, depending on the network structure, a similar mass problem can occur in the case of a route set or signalling point congestion due to the sending of TFC messages (see Fig. 12.2). If at least one link in the link set (X,A) from X to A is congested, all route sets via that link set to the destination nodes $Z_1, \ldots, Z_n$ are marked as congested. According to the signalling traffic flow control procedure, STP A then sends, for every eight messages received for a congested route set, a TFC message to the concerned originating nodes (see Sect. 9.1). If the number of affected destination nodes $Z_1, \ldots, Z_n$ is large, the floods of TFC messages sent by X may cause additional route set congestions in the network area behind X or a Level 3 congestion at X, leading to reduced signalling performance and the spread of congestion situations into the SS 7 network as described in Sect. 8.2.

12.2.3 Problems with the MRVT

Finally, the MTP routing verification test (MRVT) [8] may also lead to problems in large SS 7 networks. The objective of the MRVT is to determine whether the data in the MTP routing tables of the SS 7 network are consistent. It is based on a decen-

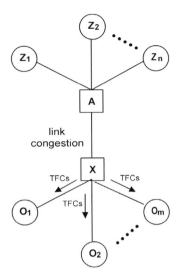

Fig. 12.2. Mass problems with TFC messages

tralized test procedure using test messages. In particular, the routing data are investigated regarding to routing loops, excessive length routes, unknown destinations as well as the bidirectionality of the considered signalling relation. The investigation of the routing data is performed for single signalling relations. Starting from any MRVT test initiating signalling point, all routes (normal as well as alternative) towards any of its destination points, contained in its routing table, are checked.

On the Function of the MRVT

According to the MRVT procedure, a signalling point A initiating the test sends an MTP routing verification test (MRVT) message for each of its local routes (see Sect. 11.2.2) to all adjacent nodes towards destination node Z. When a signalling point belonging to a global route receives an MRVT message for destination point Z and if no problems are present, then it adds its SPC to the MRVT signalling point list contained in the MRVT message. In addition, it sends for each of its local routes to all adjacent nodes such an MRVT message towards Z. At the destination point Z, each of the MRVT messages received then contains a signalling point list that corresponds to a global route of the tested signalling relation. In this way, all routes (normal as well as alternative) are checked.

An MRVT message sent by a signalling point to an adjacent node is acknowledged by an MTP routing verification acknowledgement (MRVA) message. When a signalling point X has received all expected MRVA messages from its adjacent nodes, related to all MRVT messages previously sent on receipt of an MRVT message from an adjacent node Y, it returns a corresponding MRVA message to Y and stops the test locally. This MRVA message contains the test result according to the specific knowledge of X.

When the destination point Z receives an MRVT message indicating that a trace is requested, i.e., the sequence of the STPs crossed towards Z, which corresponds to the tested global route, then Z returns to the initiating node A a corresponding MTP routing verification result (MRVR) message. If the test cannot run due to local conditions, the concerned node sends a related MRVR message to the initiating point A and stops the test locally. To summarize, an MRVT test is only completed, if

- All signalling points belonging to a global route from A to Z know the initiating signalling point A and the destination point Z,
- No routing loops are present,
- No excessive length route is detected,
- Each signalling point of the routes can perform the test.

Note: The MRVT will check all routes to a single destination point. It is not applicable in the case of a more general destination, e.g., a set of destination points or routing areas.

◇

Problems with the MRVT

Problems with the MRVT procedure will only occur if a large number of MRVT, MRVA, and MRVR messages are created, causing a route set or signalling point congestion. Considering,

- That the MRVT only checks single signalling relations and
- That the number of messages related to an MRVT is rather small (about 100)

no problems are foreseen when the MRVT test is initiated. However, problems could occur, if from a large number of initiating nodes the signalling relations to the same destination point are tested at nearly the same time. This may happen, because the MRVT can be started automatically in the SS 7 network. If the OMAP at a signalling point receives a message from the local MTP indicating that an MSU is received for an unknown destination point Z, a related MRVR message is returned to the originating node of the concerned message. On receipt of this unexpected MRVR message at that originating node, a related MRVT test is started to test the signalling relation to the considered unknown destination point Z. Thus, if in a large SS 7 network, a signalling point X receives signalling messages for an unknown destination point Z, then the MRVT procedure is started for Z in all nodes originating signalling traffic for Z at nearly the same time. These tests can cause congestion problems and related problems within the SS 7 network (see Sects. 12.3 and 8.2).

12.3 Problems with the Flow Control

The objective of SS 7 flow control is to reduce the signalling traffic at its source until the problems are removed and the congestion situation ceases, so that normal traffic may be resumed. As discussed in Sect. 8.2 a correlated and/or uncorrelated spread of congestion situations into the network is the source of network outages. Thus, in order to assure SS 7 network security and reliability it is required that the SS 7 flow control works well (for a detailed discussion of the function of the SS 7 flow control see Sect. 9.4). In real SS 7 networks flow control actions are taken by the MTP and by user and application parts, e.g., ISUP or SCCP. However, the SS 7 flow control does not work properly in real SS 7 networks for the following reasons.

Missing Adaptation of User Load Reduction and TFC Rates

In the case of a route set congestion TFC rates are created by the MTP, which are addressed to the originating nodes of the concerned signalling traffic. For the relevant User Parts, they contain the information of how much they should reduce their traffic towards the concerned destination point. The ISUP and SCCP congestion control consists of a stepwise reduction of the signalling traffic, controlled by the received congestion indication (CI) primitive rate (see Sects. 9.1.2 and 9.1.3). However, the number of steps and their size are not fixed. The reason for this is that these parameters are, in fact, network dependent. As a consequence, it is not generally fixed how fast the load reduction and enhancement has to be performed.

A Loss of Bidirectionality Destroys the Function of the Flow Control

In real SS 7 networks, bidirectionality of routing data is normally not assured. Thus, a loss of bidirectionality may destroy the function of the SS 7 flow control.

Insufficient Measures in the Case of Level 3 Congestion

As discussed in Chap. 8 a Level 3 or signalling point congestion is crucial with respect to SS 7 network outages. In real SS 7 networks, however, no specific measures are taken to handle signalling point congestion.

Loss of Messages During Congestion

If the SS 7 flow control does not work message loss will occur in real SS 7 networks. A loss of TFPs leads to elementary routing loops whilst a loss of TFAs means that available alternative routes are not used in time, so that congestion situations may occur in other network areas. Finally, a significant loss of TFCs means that the flow control does not work properly so that, again, in other parts of the network congestion situations may arise.

Problems with Growing SS 7 Networks

In the case of a growing SS 7 network, problems with the network size and the described mass problems with TFCs may occur, if no specific actions are taken. Finally, in real SS 7 networks, non-link-related Level 3 messages are normally assigned the SLC 0000. Thus, depending on the network structure and network size, congestion problems may occur with the sending of those non-link-related Level 3 messages via one link (see Sect. 3.6).

To Summarize:

If, in a real SS 7 network, the signalling traffic load is low so that no congestion situations occur and if bidirectionality and loop-freeness of the routing data are assured by network planning and if sufficient links and routes are available to handle local failures, then local problems and congestion situations may not spread within the network to cause an SS 7 network outage. However, in the case of a high signalling traffic load, a nonfunctioning flow control and restart procedure, floods of signalling route management messages as well as a loss or delay of network management messages will lead to a spread of local problems within the network, which may cause SS 7 network outages. Thus, in the case of a high signalling traffic load, network security and reliability is, normally, not assured.

◇

Regarding the function of the flow control in real networks the following questions arise:

- For the function of the flow control the number of signalling relations via a congested route set is important (see Fig. 12.3).
  A lot of originating User Parts may send traffic towards a lot of destination points $Z_1, \ldots, Z_n$ via the same route set, which may cause a congestion situation although the MSU rates to a specific destination point is rather low. Due to the fact that TFC messages as well as the user load reduction are based on single point codes the created TFC rates are, in fact, network dependent. For a specific destination node the created TFC rate may be too low so that no appropriate load reduction is performed. So, what is the actual impact of the network structure on the flow control?
- Various applications in real networks lead to different traffic streams and characteristics with MSU lengths in the range of 15 up to 4096 bytes. Concerning the

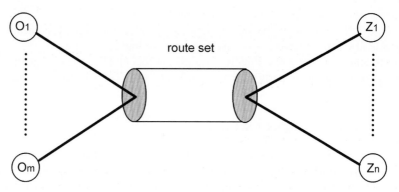

Fig. 12.3. Network structure and flow control

implemented flow control, the User Part information about their actual contribution to a route set congestion is performed based on the number of MSUs sent via the congested route set (with respect to the CLM and OM methods see Chap. 9). The MSU length, however, is not considered. Is there an influence of the MSU length, i.e., different applications, on the function of the flow control?

- As specified for the international network ISUP load reduction is performed according to a stepwise reduction of new call attempts. Existing calls, however, are not affected. In national networks with congestion priorities the sending of MSUs with priorities less than the current route set congestion status is stopped (see Sect. 9.2). Is there an influence of signalling scenarios on the function of the flow control?
- In the case of call rejection a subscriber will reattempt to set up the call with a given probability. This leads to so-called repeated call attempts (RCA). What is the influence of subscriber behavior on the function of the flow control?

In the following we treat these question in more detail. The results are obtained using transient simulation and hybrid iterative analysis methods [47]. The traffic flow control specified for the international network as well as the national option with congestion priorities are compared.

Regarding the international network we assume that the User Parts perform their load reduction within ten steps with a load reduction of 10% of the original traffic each. The timer values of the user congestion control are T29 = 300 ms and T30 = 5.1 s. The congestion thresholds of the Level 2 buffers are chosen to be $A = 11, O = 15$, and $D = 128$ (used as the maximum buffer length). In the case of the national option with congestion priorities the sending of MSUs with congestion priorities less than the current route set congestion status is stopped. The timers are set to T15 = 2 s and T16 = 1.4 s whilst the congestion and discard thresholds are set to $A1 = 11, O1 = 15, D1 = 30, A2 = 31, O2 = 35, D2 = 50, A3 = 51, O3 = 55$, and $D3 = 128$. The length of the signalling route set congestion test (RCT) messages is 13 bytes, including Level 2 overhead.

We consider the network structure shown in Sect. 9.1.1, Fig. 9.1 with only one destination node Z. The route set from STP A to destination point Z contains two equally loaded links with a transmission rate of 64 kbit/s and no transmission errors. According to the load sharing mechanism the user traffic load is equally distributed between both links so that, regarding the creation of TFC rates, there is no difference between the RSM and CLM methods. During normal operation the route set traffic load is 60%. Congestion is created by doubling the traffic after $t_a = 10s$, so that Level 2 congestion is caused at both links, i.e., route set congestion to the affected destination node Z.

12.3.1 The Influence of Different Applications

In the following we consider the influence of different applications, which create different traffic streams and characteristics, for the international network as well as the national option with congestion priorities.

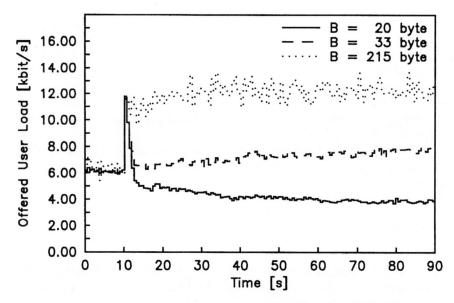

Fig. 12.4a. The influence of different applications (international network)

We consider ten User Parts in Fig. 12.4, where four User Parts send MSUs of 20 byte length, three are sending MSUs of 33 byte length, and there are three User Parts sending MSUs with 215 byte length. The MSU rates are such that all User Parts create the same traffic load of about 6 kbit/s (including Level 2 overhead). All MSUs are sent independent from each other, i.e., in this section we do not consider signalling scenarios like, for example, ISUP connection establishment. In the case of the national option with congestion priorities every User Part is sending MSUs in the same way as for the international network with the congestion priorities being distributed over 1/4 of the messages each. All ten User Parts receive a CI primitive rate and start to reduce their load contribution. In Fig. 12.4a the user load reduction is shown for the international network and in Fig. 12.4b for the national option with congestion priorities.

As is shown by these figures the MSU length has a crucial influence on the function of the flow control. According to the signalling traffic flow control, those User Parts sending short messages receive a higher TFC rate and reduce their traffic load much more than those User Parts sending long messages. If we compare the two figures, we see that the behavior of the User Parts in the case of the national option with congestion priorities is similar to the international network. However, for the national option there is no great difference between the User Parts sending 20 byte and 33 byte messages, and the overall load reduction by these User Parts is not as great as in the case of the international network. Note that for both the international and national method the User Parts sending messages with 215 byte length receive such a low CI primitive rate that they effectively do not perform a load reduction.

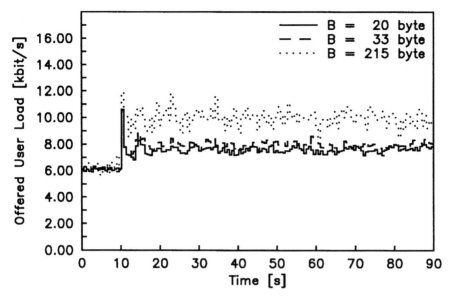

Fig. 12.4b. The influence of different applications (national option)

To Summarize:

If different User Parts which create different traffic streams with different MSU
lengths contribute to route set congestion then there will be a substantial traffic load
reduction only by those User Parts sending short messages. This means a reduction
of performance for those User Parts. Finally, the overall load reduction may be too
low so that the flow control does not work at all.

◇

12.3.2 Network Dependence of the Flow Control

In the following we consider the network dependence of the flow control. We assume
that 10, 100, and 1000 originating User Parts send the same signalling traffic load of
38.4 kbit/s (which is 60% of the total link transmission rate of 64 kbit/s) towards
one destination point. All users are sending MSUs with the same length of 32 bytes.
Congestion is created by doubling the traffic after $t_a = 10s$ so that the traffic streams
to be transmitted exceed the route set capacity. Without flow control, message loss
will occur.

    For the international network, the network dependence of the flow control is
shown in Fig. 12.5a. We see that the load reduction is slowed down, i.e., $\Delta t = t_b - t_a$
is increasing (see Sect. 9.4, Fig. 9.8) and that the stationary route set loading is growing with an increasing number of originating User Parts. Note, that in the case of
1000 User Parts no sufficient load reduction is performed. Furthermore, the situation
is getting worse with increasing number of destination nodes. If n destination points
may be reached by m originating nodes, i.e., $n \cdot m$ signalling relations exist via the

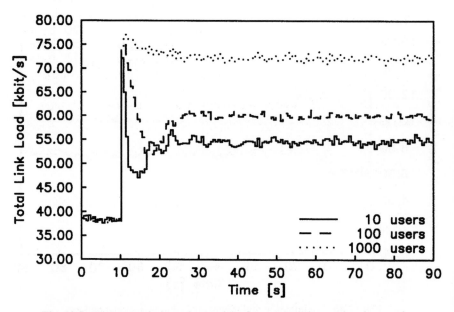

Fig. 12.5a. The network dependence of the flow control (international network)

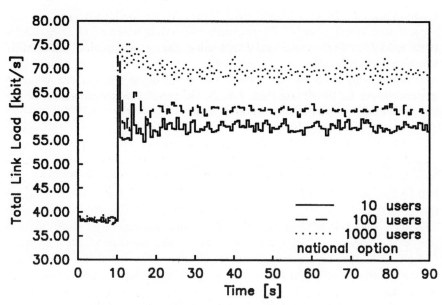

Fig. 12.5b. The network dependence of the flow control (national option)

congested route set, then the CI primitive rate for User i is reduced by a factor $1/n$ with other load conditions being equal.

The corresponding results for the national option with congestion priorities are shown in Fig. 12.5b. The shape of the curves is similar to the case of the interna-

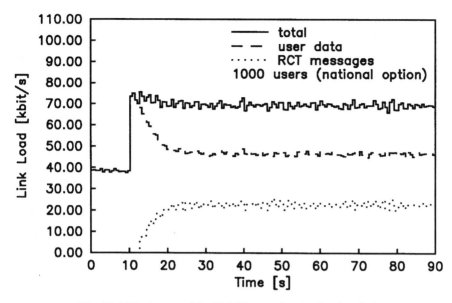

Fig. 12.6. The impact of the SRSCT procedure (national option)

tional network. However, an important difference is that the load reduction is performed faster. Short bursts of TFC messages lead to an immediate load reduction by stopping MSUs with priority 0 until the signalling route set congestion test (SRSCT) procedure is completed.

Nevertheless, also in the case of the national option, the flow control does not work in the case of 1000 User Parts. A detailed investigation of the transmission buffers shows that, in this case, according to the chosen discard threshold $D_1 = 30$ MSU, nearly all MSUs with priority 0 are discarded (see Sect. 12.3.5).

In Fig. 12.6 the total link load is subdivided into the user data portion and the RCT portion. For 1000 User Parts nearly 35% of the link load is caused by the RCT messages. With an RCT message length of 12 bytes this means that more than 50% of the transferred messages via the considered link are RCT messages. As a consequence, for the national option, the effective throughput of user data is less than in the case of the international network.

To Summarize:

We see that the function of the flow control critically depends on the network structure. In the case of too many signalling relations (about 100 User Parts to 100 destination nodes) via a congested route set, no appropriate load reduction is performed.

◇

12.3.3 The Influence of Signalling Scenarios

In the following we consider for every User Part signalling scenarios which consist of five messages of 32 bytes length, e.g., IAM, SAM, ... , REL messages, where

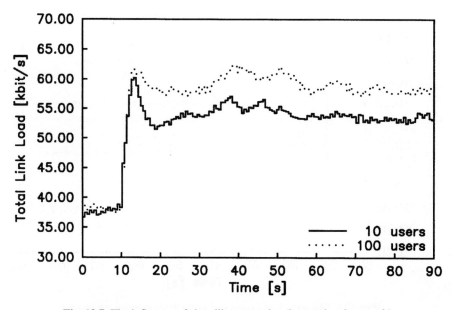

Fig. 12.7. The influence of signalling scenarios (international network)

we assume a uniformly distributed time delay between the individual messages: for the second, third, and fifth message 0.5–1.5 s and for the fourth message 20–40 s, respectively. The original link load is the same as in Fig. 12.5. Again, congestion is obtained by doubling the traffic load. In Fig. 12.7 the load reduction is shown, taking into account the signalling scenarios.

If we compare Figs. 12.5a and 12.7 we see that the increase of the link load is slowed down and the peak load of the link is damped. The reason is that, due to the time delay between the sending of the messages belonging to the individual scenarios, the flow control already works during the load increase and new call attempts are rejected.

To Summarize:

Signalling scenarios, e.g., as specified for the ISUP, which are not influenced for existing calls by the User Part congestion control during a congestion situation, do not lead to an impact on the function of the flow control.

◇

12.3.4 The Influence of Repeated Call Attempts

In the following we discuss the influence of repeated call attempts (RCA). In the case of a rejected call we assume for every subscriber a reattempt probability of 0.8, a maximum number of successive call attempts of five, and that the time between

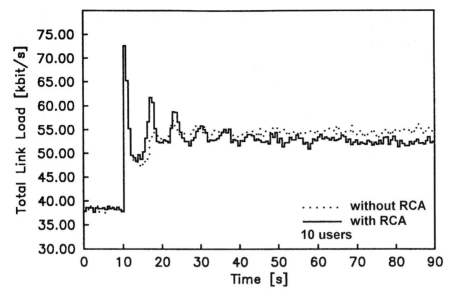

Fig. 12.8a. On the influence of repeated call attempts (international network)

two successive call attempts is uniformly distributed within the interval 4–6 s. In Fig. 12.8a the total link load is shown for ten users with and without repeated call attempts and for the international network.

The shape of both curves is nearly the same. At the beginning of the congestion the link load is more oscillatory, caused by the reattempts due to the rejected calls. The minima–maxima structure of the link load is the result of a superposition of two influences: the timer $T30 = 5.1s$ and the time delay of 4–6 s of the repeated call attempts. Compared to Fig. 12.5a, we see more clearly marked maxima with a slightly larger slope of the graph, which is a consequence of the repeated call attempts alone. However, the load reduction occurs independent of the repeated call attempts.

The corresponding results in the case of the national option with congestion priorities for 10, 100, and 1000 User Parts are shown in Fig. 12.8b.

Compared to 12.5b we see the surprising fact that in the case of ten users the load reduction is rather high. This is caused by the superposition of two oscillatory effects: short bursts of TFC messages lead to call rejection so that messages with priority 0 are stopped within the time interval of the SRSCT procedure, resulting in delayed repeated call attempts. After the completion of the SRSCT procedure these repeated call attempts, together with new calls, lead to a very fast filling of the transmission buffer so that congestion is caused very fast, so now the congestion onset level O_2 is crossed. As a consequence, MSUs with priorities 0 and 1 are stopped, which leads to a massive reduction of the average link load and, again, related repeated call attempts are created some time later, and so on.

The strong differences for 10, 100, and 1000 User Parts result from the different RCT portions to the link congestion. Since for 1000 User Parts the RCT contribution

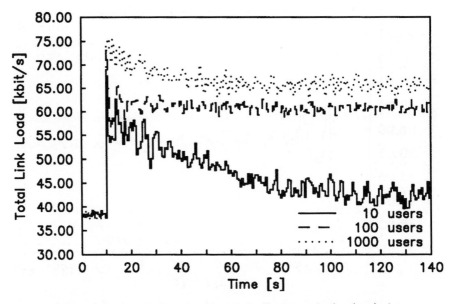

Fig. 12.8b. On the influence of repeated call attempts (national option)

to the link congestion is the highest, the reduction of the link load due to a reduction of user traffic is in this case the lowest, whilst in the case of ten users the situation is reversed.

To Summarize:

Repeated call attempts, i.e., the subscriber behavior, do not lead to an impact on the function of the flow control.

◇

12.3.5 Loss of Messages Caused by Congestion Situations

In this section we discuss in more detail the loss or delay of messages caused by congestion situations. In the case of Level 2 congestion (see Sect. 9.1.1) the load reduction and the dimensioning of the Level 2 buffers should be such that load peaks can be handled so that message loss is avoided at Level 2. However, if the load reduction is too slow and insufficient, i.e., if the flow control does not work properly, then the Level 2 buffers overflow and message discard or delay will occur.

As an example of the failure of the flow control we again consider the network dependence of the flow control. In Sect. 12.3.2 it is shown that in the case of 1000 User Parts the received TFC rate is so low that no appropriate load reduction is performed (see Figs. 12.5a and b). As a consequence, the transmission buffer of the congested link fills up and message discard occurs. In Figs. 12.9a and b the

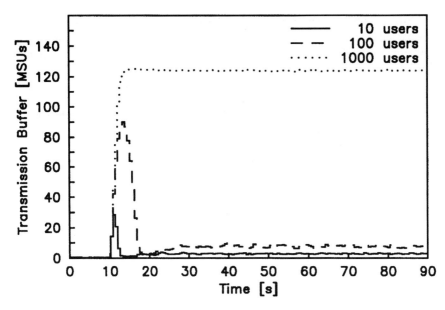

Fig. 12.9a. Transmission buffer occupation (international network)

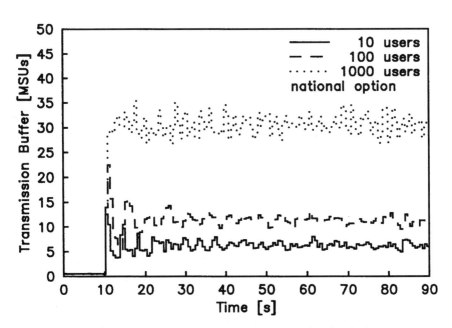

Fig. 12.9b. Transmission buffer occupation (national option)

transmission buffer occupation is shown as a function of time for the international network and the national option with congestion priorities, respectively. In the case of the international network the transmission buffer is on average completely occupied with the maximum number of 128 messages.

However, in the case of the national option with congestion priorities the transmission buffer is occupied on average with only 30 MSUs. For a congestion discard threshold $D_1 = 30$ this means that all MSUs with priority 0 are discarded, whilst more than 50% of the buffered messages are RCT messages (see Sect. 12.3.2). Thus, the effective throughput of user data is quite poor in this case.

12.3.6 Insufficient Measures in the Case of Level 3 Congestions

A Level 3 or signalling point congestion is crucial with respect to SS 7 network outages (see Chap. 8). In the ITU recommendations, however, no specific measures are specified to handle signalling point congestions because these are, in fact, network dependent. If an exchange takes any actions, it is merely required that they are compatible with those handling route set congestions.

12.4 The Network Dependence of the MTP Restart Procedure

Like the SRM procedures and the SS 7 flow control the function of the MTP restart procedure is network dependent. The White Book restart procedure works well if a node has only a local view of the network. However, if a restarting node, in conflict with the original philosophy, has a global view, i.e., if the number of destination nodes contained in the routing data is very large, then the restart procedure may not work properly for the following reasons:

- In large SS 7 networks the routing data update within the restarting node as well as the network may not be completed within the available time. As a consequence, a lot of late events (see Sect. 10.2.3) have to be treated outside the restart procedure, e.g., the indication of still inaccessible nodes by sending TFPs in response.
- The information of local User Parts on each signalling points accessibility or inaccessibility may be problematic.
- Before resuming user traffic to destination nodes a large number of preventive TFPs has to be sent.

12.4.1 Problems with the Routing Data Update

The status of an SS 7 network may change temporarily. In order that the restart procedure makes sense the network status must not change drastically during the restart procedure. As a consequence, the restart procedure should not last too long so that an overall time of the restart procedure of about 60 s has been introduced, which is reflected by the timers T20 and T21 (see Sect. 10.4). This means that the

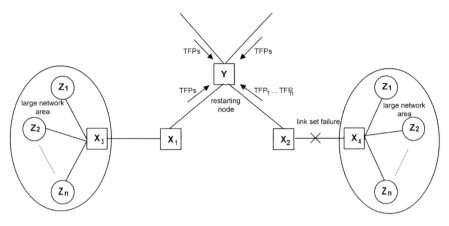

Fig. 12.10. On the network dependence of the restart procedure

overall restart time is used in an efficient way. In this respect it is preferable to make all link sets available at nearly the same time by activating first one link per link set and by applying emergency alignment for at least the first link in each link set. In this way, the routing data update can be started for all routes at the very beginning of the restart procedure. Nevertheless, the following problems occur in large SS 7 networks, where a restarting node Y has extensive routing data and is part of a very large number of signalling relations (see Fig. 12.10).

If an adjacent node X is sending a large amount of TFP messages via one link (see Sect. 3.6), Level 2 congestion may be caused. Furthermore, the number of TFP messages to be processed by the Level 3 at the restarting node Y may be huge so that a Level 3, i.e., signalling point, congestion may be caused. Note, however, that those congestion situations are not handled during the MTP restart procedure. Thus, a consequence of the Level 2/Level 3 congestion is an extensive loss of TFP messages, resulting in wrong routing data within the restarting node Y and the network as well as an outage of the concerned signalling links.

In order to avoid those congestion situations we may think about the possibility of not making available the link sets to the adjacent nodes at nearly the same time but, instead controlled by an implementation-dependent function such that the TFPs received do not cause Level 3 congestion. Activating more than one link per link set and using load sharing of TFP messages via the available links and an implementation-dependent reduction of the TFP rates sent by the adjacent nodes could avoid Level 2 congestion. All these measures mean that the routing data update is enhanced which, however, must be completed within T18. Although this timer can be adapted to the network size in a limited way, it should be noticed that the following broadcast of TFP messages must be completed within the remaining time T20–T18 so that T18 cannot be enhanced arbitrarily. The avoidance of the congestion problems during the restart procedure in large SS 7 networks therefore leads to the fact that the routing data within the restarting node and the network are faulty. This causes problems when the restart procedure is terminated and traffic to still inaccessible destination nodes is restarted. As a consequence, all of the problems without the restart procedure described in Sect. 3.4 are present.

12.4.2 Problems with Late Events

The time-delayed sending of TFPs in adjacent nodes or a delay of the link set activation at the restarting node Y may cause, in large SS 7 networks, a large number of late events. If the restarting node Y activates the direct link set to an adjacent node X at the very beginning of the restart procedure, then X has the complete time T18 available for the sending of relevant TFPs. However, due to a delayed link set activation, it may happen that adjacent nodes become available very late, a short time before T18 expires or even after T18 expired. As a consequence, the restarting node Y will receive during phase 2 a large number of TFPs, which, normally, are treated as late events outside the restart procedure, i.e., during normal operation. Those activities will then lead to problems that should in fact be solved by the restart procedure.

12.4.3 Problems with Preventive TFPs

A final problem with the MTP restart procedure is that before user traffic is restarted preventive TFPs must be sent. Depending on the network size and network structure the number of available destination nodes for the restarting node Y as well as the adjacent nodes may be rather large so that the sending and processing of these floods of preventive TFPs is problematic, which might cause the problems described in Sect. 8.2.

In order to improve this situation we have specified that the sending of these preventive TFPs may be performed within and outside the restart procedure but must be done before related user traffic is resumed.

12.4.4 Problems with the User Part Information

The MTP-PAUSE primitive used by the MTP indicates to local User Parts the total inability to provide the MTP service to the specified destination, whilst the MTP-RESUME primitive indicates that the MTP service may be used again. They both contain as a parameter the *AFFECTED DPC*, i.e., these primitives refer to single point codes. Since the Level 3 must inform all local User Parts about the availability of all relevant destination nodes the number of MTP-RESUME primitives to be broadcast by Level 3 (and possibly MTP-PAUSE primitives) after an MTP restart may be very large. The same holds for adjacent nodes when the number of destination nodes becoming accessible again via the restarted node Y is large. Because the sending of these floods of MTP-RESUME primitives may cause internal problems, this local information of the User Parts after the termination of the MTP restart is considered to be implementation dependent, i.e., the primitives may refer to signalling point regions instead of single point codes.

To summarize, we see

- That in large SS 7 networks a complete routing data update might not be completed in the available time so that faulty routing data within the restarting node and the network may cause congestion situations and a renewed failure of the restarted node, and
- That the described problems with the MTP restart procedure in large SS 7 networks cannot be solved in a satisfactory way. However, suitable network planning can avoid them (see Chap. 13).

12.5 Problems with the User Part Availability Control

If the MTP is unable to distribute a received message to a local User Part, it considers that User Part to be unavailable. When the MTP is again able to distribute received messages to a previously unavailable local User Part, the MTP considers that User Part to be available again. Note, that the terms User Part unavailability and User Part availability are implementation-dependent notions. There are implementations where the User Parts and the MTP are internally linked via central implementation-dependent connections. In those systems a User Part may become unavailable as a whole, e.g., in the case of a failure of the internal connections. In other systems, a User Part and the MTP are distributed units, so that in these systems only a partial unavailability of a User Part towards a specific direction may occur.

If in a distributed system an MSU cannot be delivered to a considered User Part, because the relevant part of that user is unavailable in the considered direction, the distribution function may be marked accordingly and a UPU message is sent to the originating node to stop that user traffic. If, after a short time, an MSU is received for the considered User Part from another direction, which might occur in the case of load sharing between link sets, that may be delivered to the User Part previously marked unavailable, the MTP now considers that User Part to be available again.

In this way, an undefined oscillation of the User Part availability status could be caused. In order to avoid this problem, it is specified within the White Book, that if the MTP detects the unavailability of a User Part, it is considered to be implementation dependent whether the distribution function is marked accordingly. In addition, the User Part availability control is not implemented in a direction-related way in those distributed systems and the problems described in Sect. 3.2, when the User Part availability control is not used, are taken into the bargain.

12.6 Consequences of a Loss of Bidirectionality

In the following we consider the simple hierarchical network structure shown in Fig. 12.11. The nodes T1, T2, and T3 of the highest level 0 are interconnected by link sets and serve as central transfer nodes for the remaining nodes of the network. In addition to the transfer function they may have user functions. The nodes M1, M2,

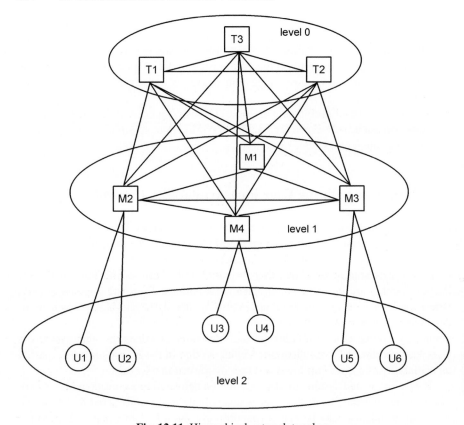

Fig. 12.11. Hierarchical network topology

M3, and M4 form the level 1 and are interconnected as shown in Fig. 12.11. They all have user functions and the transfer function. The remaining nodes having only user functions form the lowest level 2. They are interconnected with one node at level 1 each.

Normally, the loop-freeness of routing data is assured in real networks by network planning, but not bidirectionality (see Sect. 12.1). A permanent loss of bidirectionality can be caused by faulty routing data or equipment failures. A temporary loss of bidirectionality can be caused by signalling link failures as well as a loss or delay of messages due to congestion situations within the network (see Sect. 12.2). Finally, a loss of bidirectionality can be caused by interworking problems with MTP procedures, which are based on different color book versions. Let us now discuss in more detail consequences of a loss of bidirectionality.

In the following very simple routing plans, based on the physical network structure shown in Fig. 12.11, a loss of bidirectionality due to failure situations is shown.

In the routing plan T1 ↔ M3 shown in Fig. 12.12 node M3 has still one route available towards T1, but T1 has no route available towards M3 so that bidirectionality is lost due to two failure situations. This is because in the routing plan T1 ↔ M3

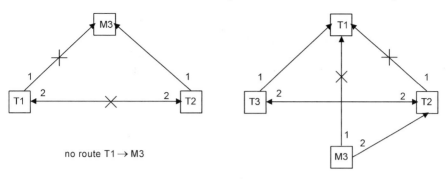

Fig. 12.12. Routing plan: T1 ↔ M3

the routes M3 ↔ T1 and T1 ↔ M3 are not defined via the same signalling points. Note that this asymmetry is forced by the fact that an alternative route via T3 is excluded in order to avoid the signalling loop (T1,T2,T3) (see Sect. 12.7).

In a similar way bidirectionality is lost in the routing plan M1 ↔ M4 shown in Fig. 12.13 due to three failure situations.

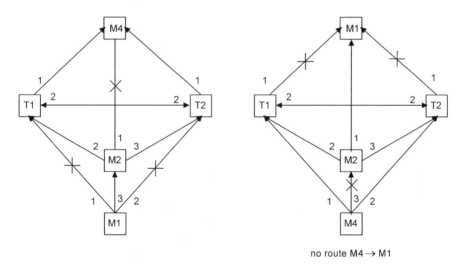

Fig. 12.13. Routing plan: M1 ↔ M4

Again, the reason is that the routes are not defined via the same nodes. For the shown failures M1 can send traffic via M2 and T1 to destination node M4 but, in order to avoid routing loops, T1 cannot send traffic via M2 to M1. Note that the described problem is symmetric in T1 and T2.

To Summarize:

A loss of bidirectionality within the SS 7 network affects the user level as well as the function of the MTP procedures. At the user level, a loss of bidirectionality is unwanted because specific emergency procedures are started and unnecessary information of the management function is performed. Regarding network reliability, however, a loss of bidirectionality within MTP is much more problematic. Note that the MTP procedures are specified based on the assumption that the SS 7 network is bidirectional. A loss of bidirectionality means that the MTP procedures do not work properly in specific situations so that the function of the MTP procedures may be affected. In situations of a high signalling traffic load, when the MTP procedures are needed to remove problems, they do not work properly so that uncorrelated congestion situations and related network outages may occur. In the following, we discuss in more detail the consequences of a loss of bidirectionality on the function of the MTP procedures.

12.6.1 Bidirectionality and Changeover

Let us consider the network configuration shown in Fig. 12.14. Signalling point M2 can reach signalling point M1 via the routes (M2,M1) and (M2,T1,M1) whilst M1 can reach M2 via the routes (M1,M2), (M1,T1,M2), and (M1,T2,M2). Due to the failures of the link sets (M1,M2) and (M2,T1) the node M1 becomes inaccessible for M2 whilst M2 is still reachable for M1 via T2.

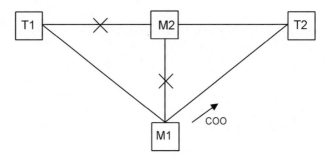

Fig. 12.14. Bidirectionality and changeover

When the last link in the direct link set (M1,M2) fails, a changeover on the alternative route via T2 is performed by Y. However, since M2 cannot acknowledge the changeover order (COO) due to the loss of bidirectionality, timer T2 (0.7–2 s) at M1 expires. In this case, M1 sends new signalling traffic via the alternative route (M1,T2,M2) where the old messages at Level 2, which could not be retrieved, are discarded. This results in an unnecessary message loss where important network management messages can get lost, leading to serious problems (see Chap. 8).

12.6.2 Bidirectionality and Changeback

The objective of the changeback procedure is to ensure that signalling traffic is diverted from the alternative signalling link(s) to the signalling link made available as quickly as possible, while avoiding message loss, duplication or missequencing.

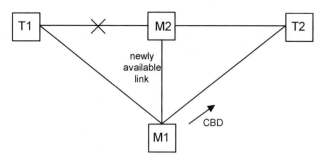

Fig. 12.15. Bidirectionality and changeback

With this objective node M1, initiating the changeback, performs the sequence control procedure. According to this procedure, node M1 stops the transmission of the concerned signalling traffic, which is stored in a changeback buffer, and sends a changeback declaration (CBD) to the adjacent node M2 at the remote end of the link made available between M1 and M2. This CBD is sent via the alternative signalling link and indicates that no more messages relating to the traffic being diverted will be sent on the alternative link (see Fig. 12.15).

On reception of the CBD the adjacent node M2 sends a changeback acknowledgement (CBA) via any available signalling route to M1. The CBA indicates that all messages relating to the concerned traffic have been received and new traffic can be routed via the link made available.

However, if due to a temporary loss of bidirectionality the CBA message is not received by M1, then timer T4 (500–1200 ms) expires. In this case, M1 resends a CBD and starts the new timer T5 (500–1200 ms). If bidirectionality is still not assured the CBA may not be received by M1 so that T5, in addition, expires. In this case, M1 sends the concerned signalling traffic on the link made available and informs the maintenance function. As a consequence, in a high signalling traffic load situation and when a large number of parallel changebacks have to be performed, this delayed traffic diversion may lead to overflow of the changeback buffer(s) and related message loss. In addition, the large number of messages sent via the newly available link at nearly the same time may cause congestion of that link.

12.6.3 Bidirectionality and MTP Restart

As a consequence of the interworking problems with the MTP restart procedure between White, Blue, and Red Book nodes a loss of bidirectionality of about 60 s occurs. For example, let us consider a restarting White Book (WB) signalling end point (SEP) Y surrounded by Red Book (RB) and Blue Book (BB) nodes (see Fig. 12.16).

When the first link to an adjacent Red Book or Blue Book node is available, these will immediately restart signalling traffic to Y and broadcast the new availability of Y to other nodes in the network using corresponding TFA messages. The White Book SEP Y, however, restarts its user traffic after the restart procedure has terminated.

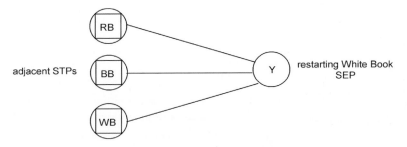

Fig. 12.16. Bidirectionality and MTP restart

If at least one adjacent node is a Red Book version, not sending a TRA message, the restart procedure in Y is normally terminated by the expiry of timer T20 (59–61 s). Besides of a loss of bidirectionality at the user level the changeback processes started by the adjacent Red Book nodes will not be completed correctly since Y does not send changeback acknowledgements during the restart procedure, causing the problems described in Sect. 12.6.2. For the considered situation an adjacent Blue Book node performs the time-controlled diversion procedure where, nevertheless, the early user traffic causes the problems described in Sect. 3.4. A similar loss of bidirectionality with the described problems occurs in the case of a restart of a White Book STP (see Sect. 10.3).

12.6.4 Bidirectionality and Flow Control

Concerning network reliability the most important problem is that a loss of bidirectionality destroys the function of the flow control. In the case of route set congestion an STP creates TFCs, which are addressed to the originating nodes of the concerned signalling traffic. However, if bidirectionality is lost, originating nodes may send traffic towards a destination node via that STP which, however, cannot send back TFCs to the originating nodes informing them about the congested route set.

As an example, let us consider the routing plans shown in Fig. 12.17. Due to the failure of the link sets (M1,T1), (M1,T2), and (M2,M4) the signalling point M1 sends traffic to destination point M4 on the available route via M2 and T1. Let us assume that the route set (T1,M4) is congested. In this case, node T1 has to inform the originating signalling point M1 about the route set congestion by sending TFC messages to M1, so that the User Parts in M1 can reduce their traffic towards M4 appropriately. However, due to the failure situations, T1 has no available route towards M1, i.e., as a consequence of the loss of bidirectionality between T1 and M1, node T1 is unable to force traffic at M1 to be reduced or stopped.

Note: A loss of bidirectionality within the MTP leads to the fact that the flow control is affected or does not work at all, which in conjunction with a high signalling traffic load, may cause correlated and uncorrelated network outages (see Chap. 8).

◇

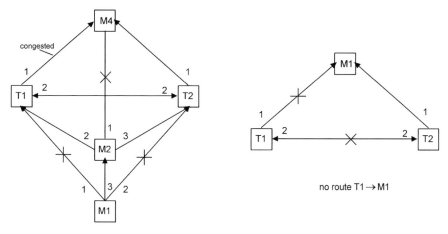

Fig. 12.17. Bidirectionality and flow control

12.6.5 Bidirectionality and User Flow Control

The objective of the User Part availability control is to stop traffic streams destined to a User Part, if the MTP in a node X is unable to distribute received MSUs to the considered User Part because that User Part is unavailable (see Sect. 3.2). In this case, the MTP sends in response a User Part unavailable (UPU) message to the originating signalling points for every MSU received for the concerned User Part.

However, if bidirectionality is lost between the considered node X and an originating node O it may happen that X receives messages from O for the unavailable User Part but X cannot send a UPU to O. As a consequence, the considered traffic stream cannot be stopped and those problems intended to be solved by the User Part availability control procedure are present.

12.6.6 Bidirectionality and Inhibiting

Finally, a loss of bidirectionality affects the function of the inhibiting procedure. For example, we consider the case that all links in the link set (M1,T1) are unavailable, i.e., blocked or failed, and one of these links shall be inhibited, requested by the management function at M1 (see Fig. 12.18).

With this objective, M1 sends a link inhibit (LIN) message to T1 via an available alternative route, e.g., STP T2. If bidirectionality between M1 and T1 is lost, i.e., if T1 has no available route to M1, then no inhibit acknowledgement (LIA) message is received and timer T14 (2–3 s) expires at M1. Since T1 is accessible for M1, it will send a LIN message for the second time which, however, will again not be acknowledged by T1. At most two consecutive attempts are made to inhibit the link, but since the destination node T1 is available for M1, management might not be informed.

Furthermore, the considered loss of bidirectionality between M1 and T1 may be caused after a link in the link set (M1,T1) has been successfully inhibited. When M1

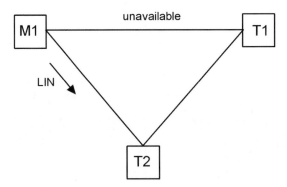

Fig. 12.18. Bidirectionality and inhibiting

is the local inhibit end of the link and if the management function at M1 decides to uninhibit the link, M1 sends a link uninhibit (LUN) message to T1. However, T1 is again not able to send an uninhibit acknowledgement (LUA) message to M1 so that timer T12 (800–1500 ms) expires at M1. Since T1 is available for M1 the procedure is restarted which, however, is again not successful. In this case, the uninhibition is abandoned and management is informed.

12.7 Problems with Signalling Loops

Correct routing data are of crucial importance regarding network reliability. On the one hand, awkward network planning may lead to bottlenecks, which may cause congestion situations as well as to a loss of bidirectionality in the case of failure situations with related problems (see Sect. 12.6). On the other hand, routing loops may be present within the network. As an example, we consider the following routing plan for the physical network structure shown in Fig. 12.19.

Normally, the signalling transfer nodes T1, T2, and T3 send their traffic to M1 via their direct link sets. If the direct link set between T1 and M1 fails, traffic is sent from T1 on the alternative route via T2. In the same way, the alternative route for T2 is via T3 and for T3 via T1. Now consider the case that all three direct link sets fail, as shown in Fig. 12.19. Then the routing loop (T1,T2,T3) is present. In the following we first discuss the consequences of signalling loops before we consider the question of how to avoid signalling loops. Within this general framework, we discuss the sending of preventive TFPs on routes with highest priority. Finally, we show that in specific network topologies bidirectionality and loop-freeness of routing data may not be achieved at the same time.

12.7.1 Consequences of Signalling Loops

When no specific measures are taken, routing loops will lead to a loss of bidirectionality and the messages continuously entering the loop together with those circulating

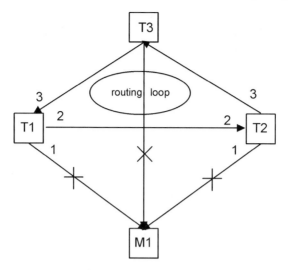

Fig. 12.19. Signalling loops

within the loop will cause link congestions and congestion situations within all nodes belonging to the signalling loop. On the one hand, if the flow control works well, all concerned traffic streams are stopped very quickly so that additional problems occur at the user level. Since the messages may circulate for a long time this unwanted situation may last for a very long time. On the other hand, if the flow control does not work well, message loss and failures of links and/or exchanges may be caused (see Sect. 8.1). However, message loss and a loss of bidirectionality mean that the MTP procedures do not work properly. Thus, regarding network reliability, it is a very important objective to avoid signalling loops in the normal case as well as in failure situations.

12.7.2 How to Avoid Signalling Loops

Elementary routing loops, i.e., signalling loops between two adjacent nodes causing a ping-pong of messages between these nodes, are avoided by the transfer prohibited procedure: the broadcast and response method as well as by the sending of preventive transfer prohibited messages.

- When an STP Y starts to route signalling traffic destined to signalling point Z via an adjacent STP X not currently used by Y for this traffic, then Y sends a corresponding preventive TFP to X before the traffic is sent via X.
- When STP Y recognizes the inaccessibility of destination point Z then Y sends to all accessible adjacent nodes a corresponding TFP message (broadcast method).
- When STP Y receives a message for destination point Z, currently inaccessible for Y, and if Y does not perform a corresponding broadcast of TFP messages, then Y sends a related TFP to the adjacent node from which the MSU was received (response method).

In other words, the reception of a TFP message related to destination point Z prevents traffic destined to Z from being transferred via the node from which the TFP was received. As a consequence, a loss of TFPs leads to elementary routing loops which are only removed by an out of service of the link, caused by congestion of that link, or by a renewed sending of the TFP message because of a renewed changeover of traffic on the considered link. Higher routing loops via three or more STPs, as shown in Fig. 12.19, are not avoided by the TFP procedure. Since no specific actions are specified within the MTP these higher rooting loops must be avoided by network planning. However, the problem is that there are network topologies where both, bidirectionality and loop-freeness of routing data may not be achieved at the same time, which is discussed in Sect. 12.7.4.

12.7.3 Preventive TFPs on Routes with Highest Priority

For a long time, the sending of preventive TFPs on normal routes, i.e., those with the highest priority, has been discussed in ITU-T and ETSI (see Sect. 3.6), but no decision has been taken up to now. The arguments are that, on the one hand, elementary routing loops are avoided by these TFPs. On the other hand, the sending of preventive TFPs on routes with the highest priority is unwanted, since every TFP message causes a route set test.

According to this test, a node that receives a TFP for a specific destination point Z sends a route set test (RST) message for every 30–60 s (Level 3 timer T10) until it receives a TFA message for Z, indicating that concerned user traffic may again be routed via the adjacent node sending the TFA message. Since this user traffic is normally sent via the normal link, this route set test does not make any sense for routes with highest priority.

The problem is that, in the normal case where no failures are present, related RST messages lead to an unnecessary fundamental loading of the SS 7 network that, when the SS 7 network is highly loaded, deteriorates the situation, especially in large SS 7 networks. Furthermore, since the sending of preventive TFPs does not exclude higher routing loops, also at the highest level, elementary as well as higher routing loops should be excluded by network planning. So, the sending of preventive TFPs on routes with highest priority is superfluous.

12.7.4 Problems with Specific Network Structures

As described in Sect. 12.6.4 the problem with the flow control, caused by a loss of bidirectionality, is based on the fact that node M1 can send user traffic via the nodes M2 and T1 but T1 has no route to M1 to send TFCs (see Fig. 12.17). Assuring bidirectionality means that T1 uses the same routes towards M1 as M1 uses to reach T1. Otherwise, bidirectionality can be lost in specific failure situations, as shown in Fig. 12.17. Thus, the problem with the loss of bidirectionality in Fig. 12.17 is that T1 does not use the route via M2 to M1. If we would like to keep three node-disjoint routes from M1 to T1, we may try to remove the loss of bidirectionality by adding node M2 in the routing plan T1 → M1 (see Fig. 12.20).

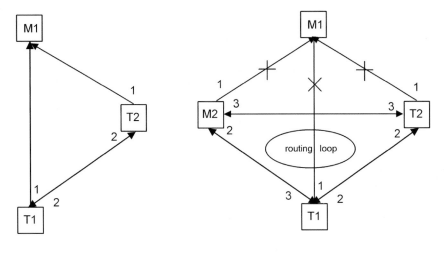

Orignal routing plan T1 → M1

Modified routing plan to assure
bidirectionality between T1 and M1

Fig. 12.20. Signalling loops and bidirectionality

Now, T1 can send messages to M1 via the direct link set (T1,M1), the alternative route (T1,T2,M1), and the third-choice route (T1,M2,M1). Since the problem is symmetric in T1 and T2, node T2 can send messages via the routes (T2,M1), the alternative route (T2,T1,M1), and (T2,M2,M1).

Finally, the routing plan M2 ↔ M1 contains the first-choice route (M2,M1) and the alternative routes (M2,T1,M1), and (M2,T2,M1). Altogether, we end up with the routing loop (T1,T2,M2), which will occur in the failure situations shown in Fig. 12.20.

This example shows that to achieve bidirectionality and loop-freeness of routing data the underlying network topology is important (see Chap. 11).

12.8 Problems with Signalling Gateways

In this section, we discuss potential problems that are related to the SS 7 network interconnection using signalling gateways. We first concentrate on potential problems with MTP procedures in signalling gateways and then discuss specific network security aspects as well as problems with signalling gateways to the IP domain.

12.8.1 Problems with MTP Procedures

If two SS 7 networks are interconnected at the MTP level via a signalling gateway, acting as an STP, without an intermediate network (see Sect. 11.4), then the signalling gateway may form a bottleneck in the case of a high signalling traffic flow between both networks. Thus, the problems described in Sect. 12.2 could be present.

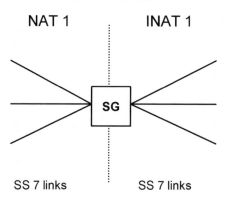

NAT 1   INAT 1

SG

SS 7 links   SS 7 links

Fig. 12.21. Potential problems with network interconnection

In order to avoid these problems, a separation of the SS 7 networks at the MTP level is required. This may be performed by creating MTP network areas which are interconnected at the SCCP level as described in Sect. 13.2.1.4, or through a network transition via a national intermediate network or the international network (see Sect. 11.4.1). At this point, it should be noted that all MTP procedures are related to one specific network, i.e., they do not operate via network boundaries.

However, there are two MTP procedures, the SS 7 flow control and the MTP restart procedure, that may cause problems with the network interconnection at the SG, since these procedures do not prevent the spread of congestion problems from one network into the other. This spread of problems from one network to the other may occur if the Level 3 layer at the SG is realized as one physical unit (see Fig. 12.21). The signalling gateway, as part of the national network NAT 1, has links to adjacent nodes in NAT 1 and may be used in that network as a transfer node. In the case of a high signalling traffic load, maybe combined with large amounts of network management activities, Level 3 congestion can be caused at the signalling gateway. If, however, the Level 3 layers at the SG are realized as one physical unit, used by both networks, this NAT 1 congestion situation will spread via Level 3 of the signalling gateway into INAT 1, causing serious problems, e.g., a network outage (see Chap. 8).

Further problems occur if, for example, all links at the signalling gateway to NAT 1 are unavailable. This means, that the signalling gateway is isolated from the network NAT 1 for some time. If one of these links becomes available again, the signalling gateway has to perform the restart procedure, which, however, is only related to NAT 1.

The objective of the restart procedure is to protect the restarting node and the surrounding network. In order to avoid the problems with early user traffic (see Sects. 3.4 and 10.1.2), the restart procedure assures that any user traffic is not restarted unless the restart procedure at the restarting node and its adjacent nodes is terminated through the exchange of the TRA messages, indicating that no problems are present anymore. However, since the restart procedure is only performed in NAT 1, the adjacent nodes in INAT 1 do not care about the signalling gateway's

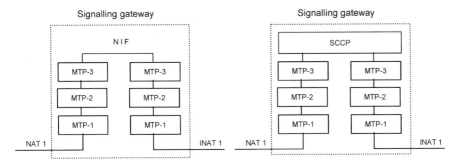

Fig. 12.22. Logical separation of Level 3 at the SG using an NIF or via SCCP

restart and may continue to use the signalling gateway as a transfer node for their user traffic. Thus, although performing the restart procedure, a signalling gateway may not be fully protected, if the network's Level 3 layers are realized as one physical unit. As a consequence, message loss and Level 3 congestion may occur, which may spread into INAT 1 and could lead to the fact that the restart procedure may not be completed within the available time, so that late events could also cause problems in NAT 1.

These problems can be avoided, if a signalling gateway is made up of physically separated Level 3 units, one for each network, interconnected via an implementation-dependent nodal interworking (NIF) function or the SCCP (see Fig. 12.22), and if the restart procedure is also enhanced to INAT 1 by taking the relevant links out of service. This action is in accordance with the recommendation where it is said that *"circumstances might cause the management entity to isolate the node, i.e. make all links unavailable, in order to facilitate recovery from a partial isolation"* (ITU-T Q.704, Sect. 9: MTP Restart). This allows one to perform the restart procedure coordinated for both networks and protects the signalling gateway whose MTPs are restarting.

12.8.2 Network Security Aspects

When interconnecting signalling networks, restrictions should be placed on the transfer traffic security, in order to prevent unauthorized use of a signalling gateway. Unauthorized signalling traffic may be STP traffic for call set up via networks other than that containing the signalling gateway, which has not been agreed bilaterally between network operators. Special procedures are needed at a signalling gateway to identify unauthorized SS 7 messages. Thus, in addition to the normal signalling message handling, it should be possible to inhibit/allow messages destined for a destination point on ones own SS 7 network based on any one or combinations of the following options:

- The combination: DPC/incoming link set
- The combination: outgoing link set/DPC
- The combination: OPC/DPC

A signalling gateway identifying unauthorized SS 7 messages must discard them and inform the management correspondingly. In addition, a violation fault report should be issued giving the unauthorized message content [48].

12.8.3 Problems with PSTN and IP Network Convergence

In the following, we discuss potential problems with PSTN and IP network convergence caused by signalling gateways to the IP domain, the different possibilities for PSTN and IP network interconnection, and the migration towards the IP-based multimedia network. As in the case of intelligent and mobile networks the increasing amount of traffic between the PSTN and IP networks (e.g., Internet traffic) can lead to a bottleneck via the SG with related problems (see Sect. 11.4).

From the SS 7 network security and reliability point of view it must be avoided that local problems at the SG spread into the SS 7 network creating global problems within the nodes of the SS 7 network at nearly the same time which may lead to an outage of the nodes and thus the whole SS 7 network.

12.8.3.1 Large Amounts of SRM Messages

Such a spread of problems into the SS 7 network can occur in the case of an isolation of the IP domain, e.g., through a failure of SCTP associations or MGC/IPSPs, through a large number of SRM messages flooding the SS 7 network (see Sect. 12.2). Finally, depending on the network structure, a similar mass problem can occur in the case of a route set or Level 3 congestion due to the sending of TFC messages. If a congestion situation occurs on the SCTP association to a MGC/IPSP and/or a signalling point congestion at the SG then the SG has to send a large number of TFC messages to the corresponding originating nodes of the signalling traffic in the SS 7 network (see Fig. 12.23).

Caused by these masses of signalling route management messages there may be congestion situations in a large number of nodes within the SS 7 network at nearly the same time. Nevertheless, if these events do not cause a congestion situation within SS 7 nodes on their own, they will lead to a correlated spread of congestion situations within the SS 7 network in conjunction with a high signalling traffic load. Those mass problems with SRM messages can be avoided by proper network planning, i.e., by avoiding bottlenecks due to signalling gateway redundancy and appropriate load sharing.

12.8.3.2 Signalling Gateway Restart

Due to faulty internal processes, a SG may run into an undefined state which may be ended merely by an out of service, followed by a restart. Such a restart of a SG is a very complicated process. Related to the restart of a SG there are two different sources of troubles: extensive MTP Level 3 activities related to the network synchronization as well as early user traffic. When the SG is isolated from the network for

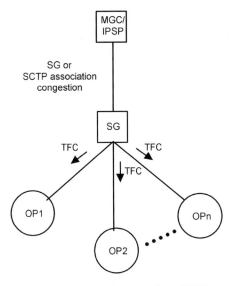

Fig. 12.23. Problems with a large number of TFC messages

some time, it cannot be sure whether its routing data are still valid. As a consequence problems could be present, when the sending of user traffic is resumed, due to wrong routing data as well as due to many parallel Level 3 activities which have to be performed within the node whose MTP is restarting. In particular, if no specific actions are taken in a restarting SG then problems can occur with SS 7 link activation, a large number of parallel changeover and changebacks, the routing data update, the sending, reception, and processing of SRM messages, local link congestions as well as an extensive message loss, which may result in a renewed failure of the SG as well as a spread of correlated and uncorrelated congestion situations within the SS 7 network (see Chap. 8).

In order to avoid these problems the MTP restart procedure must be performed at the relevant nodes. In the case of a restart of the SG with M2UA the SS 7 node and the MGC/IPSP perform the restart procedure for adjacent nodes to cover the failure of the interconnecting link set. For all other protocol structures, where the SG acts as an STP, i.e., when ASs are addressed by their own SPC, the restart procedure at the restarting SG consists of two phases.

An SS 7 network isolation is indicated by the SG to all concerned available ASPs, i.e., ASPs in the active or inactive state, using a DUNA message. When the M3UA at an MGC/IPSP receives a DUNA message indicating an SS 7 network isolation at the SG, it stops any affected traffic and clears any unavailability state of SS 7 destinations via this SG. During the first phase, SS 7 links are activated and SCTP associations are established if not already initialized. The ASP state change is conveyed by the ASP maintenance function at the MGC/IPSP to the SG. An ASP-UP message is acknowledged by the SG through an ASP-UP ACK message. However, if an ASP-

ACTIVE message is received during the restart procedure the SG delays the sending of the ASP-ACTIVE ACK message until the end of the restart procedure.

Furthermore, the routing tables within the restarting SG are updated according to the TFP and TFA messages received from adjacent SS 7 nodes. All SPMC with point codes different from that of the SG with at least one ASP that is active or that has sent an ASP-ACTIVE message to the SG during the first phase of the restart procedure are considered as available. In addition, the SG takes into account any traffic restart allowed (TRA) messages received from adjacent SS 7 nodes, where the number of received TRAs is a measure for the completeness of the received routing data.

During the second phase a major task to be performed by the SG is a broadcast of nonpreventive TFP messages regarding inaccessible destinations taking into account information about local link sets and ASs which are not available and any TFP and TFA messages received during phase 1. When the M3UA at an MGC/IPSP subsequently receives any DUNA messages from the SG it marks the effected SS 7 destinations as inaccessible via that SG. When this broadcast is finished the second phase is terminated. If the SG acts as an SEP, i.e., the ASs are addressed by the SPC of the SG, phase 2 is not present. The SG then stops the restart procedure, sends a TRA message to all adjacent SS 7 nodes via corresponding available direct link sets, and an ASP-ACTIVE ACK messages is sent to all ASPs in the active state. Finally, an indication of the end of the MTP restart is sent to all local User Parts at the SS 7 nodes showing each signalling point's accessibility or inaccessibility. When the M3UA at the MGC/IPSP receives an ASP-ACTIVE ACK message this indicates that it can resume traffic to available SS 7 destinations via this SG provided that the ASP is in the active state towards this SG.

12.8.3.3 Signalling Gateway Congestion

On the one hand, signalling route set congestion situations can occur at an SG and the surrounding network due to bottlenecks towards a specific destination. Those bottlenecks occur, if the amount of signalling traffic towards a considered destination cannot be transferred via the available routes. This can be caused by outages of local links and/or exchanges and, thus, signalling routes towards SS 7 destinations or due to the congestion of SCTP associations. Note, that since data traffic and signalling traffic are transferred via the same IP network, the transfer of signalling traffic may be affected by the transfer of bulk data traffic, leading to SCTP congestion situations.

On the other hand, digital exchanges have a finite processor speed and capacity. Thus, if the amount of user signalling messages to be handled and the network management activities to be performed by the signalling gateway are increasing or if there are node internal software or hardware problems or problems with the node internal interworking function, then Level 3 or signalling point congestion can be caused at a SG.

Congestion of a SG means that the internal buffers fill up, leading to message loss and failure situations causing further serious problems:

- A loss of message signal units (MSUs) may cause problems with the SS 7 User Parts whilst a loss of network management messages means that the MTP procedures do not work properly leading to problems within the SS 7 network.
- Due to the load sharing mechanism there is a high probability that in a high signalling traffic load situation not only one but many, if not all, links within a route set are congested. Due to the fact that both directions of a route are nearly equally loaded, a lot of links of the signalling gateway may be concerned. Note that Level 3 congestion may lead to a congestion of all links of the exchange. Related link failures lead to the fact that, in a high signalling traffic load situation, the status of the signalling gateway gets worse, so that more and more links are taken out of service. Thus, at some stage, the signalling gateway is completely isolated or performs a restart because of *too many* failed links.
- If a congestion situation at the receiving end of a SS 7 link does not terminate within 3–6 s, then the Level 2 timer T6 expires which leads to an *out of service* of the concerned link.
- Due to the nature of SS 7, local congestion situations will spread within the whole SS 7 network if no specific actions are taken to remove the congestion situation.

In order to avoid these problems bottlenecks via an SG must be avoided, i.e., SG redundancy should be provided and it is recommendable to realize a SG as a high-performance stand-alone STP. Furthermore, before severe SCTP congestion occurs, it is more likely that the SS 7 links from the adjacent SS 7 node to the SG form the bottleneck. In the case of high-throughput traffic these SS 7 links should be replaced by, e.g., IP-based high-speed links.

Finally, the function of the SS 7 flow control must be assured in the SS 7 over IP environment, i.e., the specific SCTP flow control actions (see Sect. 9.5.2) must be realized, the adaptation layers must create the congestion indication primitive rate as expected by SS 7 User Parts and the MTP network management functions must be provided in the SS 7 over IP environment. In particular, it must be avoided that due to the collection of affected DPCs in the SCON message the TFC rate is distorted, which destroys the function of the SS 7 flow control.

12.8.3.4 SPMC Inaccessibility and User Part Unavailability in the IP Domain

Finally, problems with SPMC inaccessibility and SS 7 User Part unavailability occur when MGCs or IPSPs are realized as distributed systems in the IP domain. An application server provides partial User Part functionality so that an SS 7 User Part is represented in the IP domain by all related application servers uniquely identified by a routing key, e.g., DPC, SI, and CIC values, SSNs or TCAP transaction IDs (see Sect. 6.1).

For MTP network management purposes application servers can be grouped together. Such a set of application servers represented by the SG to the SS 7 network by the same SPC is called a signalling point management cluster (SPMC) (see Sect. 6.1.2). For example, a centralized PSTN switch, having several MTP-3 User Parts, may be distributed in the IP domain represented by corresponding application servers, which may be grouped together to form one SPMC, i.e., they are all addressed using one SPC, so that from the SS 7 network they appear as one traditional switch.

However, when does such an SPMC become inaccessible, accessible or congested so that the SG can send corresponding TFP, TFA or TFC messages to relevant nodes in the SS 7 network? Equally, when does an SS 7 User Part become unavailable in the IP domain?

One problem with traditional SS 7 exchanges concerns the User Part unavailability (see Sect. 3.2). In the case of the failure of a User Part, detected by the MTP-3 when it cannot transfer messages to that User Part, problems are present if the concerned messages are simply discarded. In order to avoid related problems, the User Part unavailability procedure has been specified so that the MTP-3 can stop the sending of related messages to that User Part by sending UPU messages to the originating nodes of these messages. Note that a UPU message indicates the failure of the whole SS 7 User Part. As discussed in Sect. 12.5, the problem is that in most implementations an SS 7 User Part is distributed over the exchange where parts of the User Part may become unavailable but where the failure of the User Part as a whole is rather unlikely. Since the sending of UPUs would declare the whole User Part unavailable the UPU procedure is normally not used in most SS 7 networks.

The same problem occurs with distributed MGCs/IPSPs where an application server of a SPMC becomes unavailable, which means a partial failure of a User Part. Should the SG send a UPU in this case or not? As in SS 7 networks the preference would be not to send UPU so that a loss of user messages is taken into the bargain, although unwanted.

A similar problem occurs in the IP domain where MGCs/IPSPs are realized as distributed systems with SPMC inaccessibility and accessibility. Note that a TFP sent for a destination point indicates that the concerned signalling point is inaccessible as a whole, due to a failure of that node or the interconnecting route set. Equally, TFA and TFCs refer to a destination node as a whole. Now, if a SG determines that the transport of SS 7 messages to an application server of a particular SPMC is interrupted, i.e., when partial inaccessibility of that SPMC occurs, then the related messages are lost if the concerned traffic is not stopped or diverted. One possibility to avoid that message loss is to make all other application servers of the SPMC inaccessible so that the SG can send a corresponding TFP message. However, the price is that traffic to all other still available application servers of the SPMC will be unnecessarily stopped or diverted. Thus, the same philosophy as with SS 7 User Part unavailability is applied to SPMC inaccessibility, i.e., partial inaccessibility is ignored and an SPMC is only considered to be inaccessible if the transport of SS 7 messages to all ASPs in the SPMC is interrupted. In a similar way, an inaccessible SPMC is considered to be accessible again when the SG determines that the transport of SS 7 messages to at least one ASP in that SPMC can be resumed.

How to Avoid SS 7 Network Outages

If in a real SS 7 network the signalling traffic load is low and bidirectionality and loop freeness of the routing data is assured by network planning and if sufficient links and routes are available to handle local failures, then local problems and congestion situations cannot spread within the network causing an SS 7 network outage. However, a high signalling traffic load, a nonfunctioning flow control and restart procedure, floods of signalling route management messages as well as a loss or delay of network management messages will lead to a spread of local problems within the network which may cause SS 7 network outages. Thus, in the case of high signalling traffic load, network reliability is normally not assured in real SS 7 networks.

When we are trying to solve the described problems we will find that the cause of the problems is not faulty MTP procedures, but the causes may be sought within implementations, the network structure and network planning as well as the application of the MTP, especially in large SS 7 networks, as discussed in the Chap. 12. Since the MTP is considered to be stable, the MTP procedures cannot be changed. Thus, the problems cannot be solved, but they can be avoided by a suitable network structure, proper network planning, and by realizing specific measures which are summarized in the following. Finally, specific SS 7 over IP applications offer new approaches to improve the situation.

13.1 Specific Measures to Avoid SS 7 Network Outages

We first describe in this section specific measures to avoid correlated and uncorrelated network outages and discuss the possibility of realizing the described measures.

13.1.1 General Discussion

Network outages are based on the very fast correlated or uncorrelated spread of local problems into the network before links and exchanges fail (see Chap. 8). Regarding such a spread of local problems into the network the Level 2 timer T6, the SS 7 flow control and restart procedure, the sending of masses of SRM messages as well as a high signalling traffic load have a crucial influence.

The Influence of a High Signalling Traffic Load

The higher the traffic load, the faster the internal buffers fill up, and the faster the spread of congestion situations within the network. Thus, in the case of the unavailability of a route towards a specific destination point, the concerned signalling traffic should be diverted to alternative routes or stopped very quickly in order to avoid the filling of internal buffers. In particular, bottlenecks should be avoided by realizing sufficient node-disjoint routes in order to avoid a correlated spread of congestion situations into the network.

The Influence of Extensive Network Management Activities

As described in Sect. 8.2 the reception, processing and sending of large amounts of SRM messages may cause congestion situations in a large number of nodes within the network at nearly the same time. Note that these congestion situations are not removed by the SS 7 flow control since TFC messages are not sent for network management messages.

If these events do not cause a congestion situation within an exchange on their own, they will lead to a correlated spread of congestion situations within the network in conjunction with a high signalling traffic load. Those mass problems with SRM messages are avoided by realizing small MTP networks, which may be achieved by network planning (see Sect. 13.2) and by the introduction of new high-performance switches allowing a reduction of the number of nodes in the network. In addition, since a restart of a failed exchange is related to a large number of network management activities, the restart procedure should be introduced within the nodes of the network in order to avoid sources of correlated and uncorrelated network outages. Finally, in gateway nodes, screening concerning MSUs for unknown destination points should be performed (see Sect. 12.8.2) in order to avoid problems with SRM messages.

The Influence of Nonfunctioning MTP Procedures

As discussed in Sect. 8.1 uncorrelated congestion situations may be caused within different nodes somewhere in the network due to a loss or delay of network management messages. In order to avoid uncorrelated network outages, routing loops and the loss of bidirectionality should be avoided by proper network planning, in the normal case as well as under failure situations, in order to assure that the MTP procedures work well and no congestion situations occur.

The Influence of Flow Control

In order to avoid SS 7 network outages a functioning flow control is of crucial importance. Thus, in the case of route set or signalling point congestion, signalling traffic streams should be reduced appropriately in order to avoid correlated and uncorrelated spread of congestion situations within the network and message loss. Furthermore, the availability of routes should be indicated very quickly in order to terminate or avoid congestion situations somewhere in the network and routing loops must be avoided. In addition, it is of advantage not to sent preventive TFPs on routes with the highest priority (see Sect. 12.7.3) in order to avoid an unnecessary fundamental loading of the SS 7 network with RST messages, which is crucial in the case of a high signalling traffic load to avoid congestion situations.

On the Influence of the Level 2 Timer T6

Finally, regarding a correlated spread of congestion situations, the value of the Level 2 timer T6 is important. If T6 is too large then local congestion situations will spread throughout the network before links and related exchanges are taken *out of service*. In this respect, the objective could be to choose the value of T6 rather small so that T6 expires before the congestion situation spreads into the network, assuring that related changeover and rerouting procedures could be started in time.

However, lowering the value of T6 does not solve the problem. This is because, normally, a link set contains more than one link and in the case of a link failure, the concerned traffic is diverted to alternative links within the same link set (combined link set). However, the concerned traffic is handled by the same node, so that other links will become congested and fail. Through this sequence of link failures within a link set (combined link set) the concerned traffic is stored within the node so that, despite a small T6 value, congestion situations may spread within the network before links are taken *out of service*. In addition, other route sets are affected so that the local congestion situation will spread to other areas.

One might argue that the problems are avoided if there is only one link in the link set so that, due to the immediate link failure, a spread of the congestion situation is avoided. However, through the link failure the actual problem, i.e., the high amount of signalling traffic, is not solved because due to rerouting of the concerned high signalling traffic load to alternative routes an outage of a large amount of links and routes can be caused within the network and, in this way, the problems may spread.

To summarize, regarding the changeover and rerouting timer values (1–2 s) the value of T6 should not be chosen less than 3 s whilst regarding the correlated spread of congestion situations it should not be larger than 6 s, i.e., the T6 timer value (3–6 s) should be kept. However, it is recommendable to have the same timer value within all nodes of the network.

13.1.2 On the Possibility of Realizing the Described Measures

In order to avoid SS 7 network outages we have seen in the previous chapters that a loss of network management messages, mass problems with SRM messages as well as bottlenecks within the SS 7 network should not occur, that the SS 7 flow control and restart procedure are essential, and that the network should be bidirectional and loop-free. Are these measures necessary and can they be realized?

The realization of ISDN supplementary services or the introduction of IN services requires connection-oriented end-to-end signalling. The source of the problems with the network size, as described in Sect. 12.2, is the realization of this end-to-end signalling using the MTP, which is done in most existing real networks. As long as the networks are small, i.e., the number of nodes is less than or equal to 200, the described problems will not occur and related measures to avoid the problems are not necessary. However, if an SS 7 network is growing, then the problems will occur at some stage and the described measures to avoid them are required.

Independent of the network size it is important to realize loop-freeness and bidirectionality of routing data and to provide sufficient node-disjoint routes. Since this is not assured in most networks a sufficient network security and reliability cannot be reached without changing the network (see Chap. 11 and Sect. 13.2).

One of the key issues to improve SS 7 network security and reliability is to separate different traffic streams in order to prevent problems with one stream from being transferred to other traffic streams, causing in that way a spread of problems within the network. This may be achieved by network planning or by the introduction of ATM or IP network technology, which is discussed in the following.

13.2 New Network Concepts

In the following we discuss some examples of network topologies, which all are different realizations of the general network structure as described in Sect. 11.3, so that they automatically assure bidirectionality and loop-freeness of routing data. Furthermore, we show how, as a short-term solution, the creation of routing areas can avoid the problems with the MTP in large SS 7 networks and how ATM- and IP-based networks can be designed in order to replace older transport technology. Finally, we discuss the role of stand-alone STPs with respect to network security and reliability.

13.2.1 Examples of Network Topologies

13.2.1.1 Hierarchical Network with Two Node-Disjoint Routes

In Fig. 13.1 a hierarchical network topology is shown where $q = 2$ node-disjoint routes are realized. In order to increase the accessibility between two nodes of the same group within level 1, one possibility is to realize the same number of links within the direct link set between them as in the other route sets with two node-disjoint routes. Another possibility is to realize two parallel link sets (corresponding to two routes) between the considered nodes of a group, as shown in Fig. 13.1. Furthermore, IP-based high-speed links (see Sect. 5.1) can be used to connect the nodes of a group. In any case, the links should be physically independent, so that a failure of the physical path for one link does not cause a failure of the alternative link. Finally, the nodes of the lowest level can be interconnected directly so that three node-disjoint routes can be realized between these nodes.

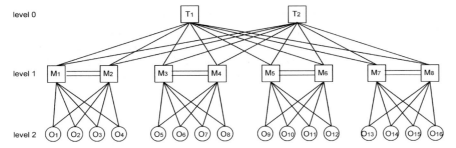

Fig. 13.1. A hierarchical network with two node-disjoint routes

13.2.1.2 Hierarchical Network with Three Node-Disjoint Routes

In order to increase SS 7 network security and reliability three node-disjoint routes can be realized between other nodes in the network than those at the lowest level. For this, the network can be changed as shown in Fig. 13.2. Only between the nodes at the right and left end of a group like, for example, M1 and M3 there exists only one node-disjoint route.

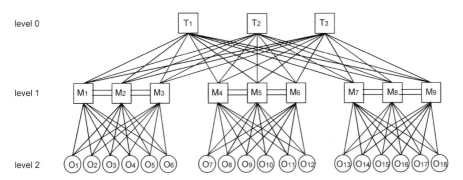

Fig. 13.2. A hierarchical network with three node-disjoint routes

Notes:

(1) If the intermediate node within a group of nodes fails, the signalling relation between the two neighboring nodes is interrupted. For the signalling relations of the intermediate node to its adjacent nodes in a group this disadvantage does not exist since these signalling relations will only fail if the destination nodes fail (and, in this case, the number of node-disjoint routes for the considered relation is not relevant) or the direct link sets fail. However, as in Fig. 13.1, the accessibility can be increased by a suitable selected number of links within the interconnecting link set, by parallel link sets between the nodes or the introduction of, e.g., IP-based high-speed links between the nodes of a group.

(2) If the central nodes of the highest level 0 are interconnected as indicated in Fig. 11.4 then, depending on the network size, problems with the restart pro-

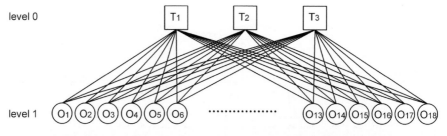

Fig. 13.3. A nonhierarchical network with three node-disjoint routes

cedure can occur (see Sect. 12.4). Thus, in large SS 7 networks, direct interconnection of these nodes is not recommendable in terms of network security and
reliability.

◇

13.2.1.3 Nonhierarchical Network with Three Node-Disjoint Routes

If we want to remove the disadvantage that no q node disjoint-routes can be realized
between all nodes of a group only two levels should be used within the topology:
the highest level where the central nodes should not have end point functionality,
i.e., which are stand-alone STPs, and the lowest level with signalling end points,
having no transfer functions (see Fig. 13.3). Note that, besides of loop-freeness and
bidirectionality, three node-disjoint routes are realized in this topology between all
nodes at the lowest level having end point functions. Finally, the nodes at the lowest
level can be interconnected directly so that four node-disjoint routes can be realized
between them.

The described networks can be enhanced up to 200 switches without causing
problems. However, if during the network evolution it is necessary to introduce more
than 200 switches it is recommendable in terms of network security and reliability
to structure the overall network into different network areas or clusters, which is described in the following section. Note that the network change can be evolutionary,
i.e., it is possible to first assure loop-freeness and bidirectionality by realizing the network structure of Fig. 13.1 and then evolve the network towards one of the network
structures shown in Figs. 13.2 or 13.3, i.e., changing the number of node-disjoint
routes or the number of levels.

13.2.1.4 Creating Network Areas

If connection-oriented end-to-end signalling is realized using the MTP, it is not possible to solve the potential problems in large SS 7 networks (with more than 200
switches) but to avoid them. This is done by going back to the original philosophy of SS 7 and to use the MTP in the original sense. One possibility is to reduce
the number of switches within the network below 200 through the introduction of
new high-performance switches, e.g., based on ATM technology. As a short-term
solution, another possibility is to introduce different network areas or clusters as described in the following.

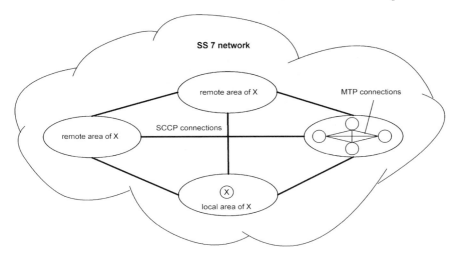

Fig. 13.4. The creation of MTP areas

The basic idea is that the end-to-end signalling is realized using the SCCP, which allows global structuring of the SS 7 network into smaller and independent MTP areas or clusters. This means that every signalling point of the SS 7 network is uniquely assigned to one and only one MTP area (see Fig. 13.4).

The number of these MTP areas depends on the total number of nodes in the SS 7 network as well as the maximum size of an area, which is fixed by the requirement that within such an MTP area the MTP procedures work well. This can be assured up to a size of 200 nodes. The MTP area to which a node X is assigned is called the local area of X. The other MTP areas are called remote areas of X. All nodes within the local area of X are reachable through MTP addressing. Such a structuring of large MTP networks is often used but the problem with these networks is that the MTP areas are interconnected at the MTP level. In order to avoid the problems with large SS 7 networks the MTP areas should be exclusively connected using SCCP connections. Through this measure a separation of the individual MTP areas is achieved at the SCCP level.

The MTP areas have to be designed such that the routing data are bidirectional and loop-free and that q ($q = 2, 3, 4, \ldots$) node-disjoint routes exist between most nodes in the MTP areas, as described in Sect. 11.3. The same holds for the SCCP connections between the individual MTP areas.

Advantages

(1) The separation of the SS 7 network into different and independent MTP areas assures that the routing data within an exchange can be kept small and that the routing of messages is simple and thus fast. Within an MTP area a simplified structured routing of MSUs can be used, however only really existing switches should be contained within the routing data of an MTP area. Thus, routing problems as present in large SS 7 networks do not occur (see Sect. 12.2.1).

(2) If a new switch is introduced into an MTP area the routing data related to that switch need only be adapted within this MTP area and not in the nodes of the whole SS 7 network.

(3) The separation of the SS 7 network into smaller and independent MTP areas simplifies MTP network management. In particular, mass problems with SRM messages are avoided (see Sect. 12.2.2).

(4) The sending of preventive TFPs is no longer a problem. Through suitable network planning the sending of preventive TFPs via routes with the highest priority is superfluous, which avoids the unnecessary fundamental loading of the SS 7 network with RST messages during normal operation (see Sect. 12.7.3).

(5) Within an MTP area the function of the SS 7 flow control can be assured. The adaptation of the user load reduction to the received TFC rate can be performed depending on the size of the MTP areas, which need not be modified if other MTP areas are enhanced or introduced (see Sect. 12.3.2).

(6) In small MTP areas signalling point congestion is no longer a problem since the measures to be taken can be adapted to those handling route set congestions, being integrated in this way into the overall SS 7 flow control (see Sect. 12.3.6).

(7) Although, if no adaptation of the flow control is performed, selective discarding of user messages at the SCCP layer, in the case of a high signalling traffic load, can avoid congestion situations at the MTP and related loss of important MTP network management messages without the need to introduce priorities within the MTP (see Sect. 12.3).

(8) Problems with the restart procedure do not occur in the smaller MTP areas, so that a coordinated restart of a failed exchange can be performed without causing problems within the network (see Sect. 12.4).

(9) Mass problems with SRM messages within the overall SS 7 network, which would occur in the case of an outage of an MTP area, can be avoided at the SCCP layer by sending one transfer prohibited message for the whole MTP area at the SCCP.

(10) In analogy, mass problems with TFC messages can be avoided by suitable measures within the SCCP flow control (see Sect. 12.3).

(11) The network concept assures that the MTP need not be modified, which is one of the overall requirements.

Disadvantages

(1) Although the MTP need not be changed, some modifications to SCCP procedures are necessary, e.g., enhancing the SCCP management regarding the management of MTP areas or necessary changes to the SCCP flow control.

(2) Changes within ISUP are necessary regarding the use of the SCCP and the network change as well as adaptation of the SS 7 flow control.

To summarize, the described network concept offers the possibility to avoid the problems in large SS7 networks while assuring full reachability between any two nodes of the SS 7 network. This concept is thought to be an intermediate solution to improve SS 7 network security and reliability with current switch and transmission technologies.

13.2.2 ATM- and IP-Based SS 7 Networks

The most elementary signalling network consists of originating and destination points directly interconnected by one signalling link set, which may contain up to 16 links. If, for all signalling relations, the originating and destination nodes are directly connected in this way then the network operates in the associated mode of signalling and we call such a network fully meshed. However, for technical and economic reasons the simple associated network has not been considered to be suitable and a quasi-associated network is usually implemented, in which messages relating to a particular signalling relation are conveyed over two or more link sets in tandem passing through one or more signalling transfer points and where the path taken by the message through the signalling network is predetermined and, at a given point in time, fixed. However, in large SS 7 networks, the quasi-associated network structure causes a lot of problems with the MTP procedures under high signalling traffic load (see Chap. 12).

A network operator may wish to migrate to an IP-based SS 7 network in order to replace the older transport technology by the IP network technology, which would yield operational cost and performance advantages. An IP-based SS 7 network uses the services of the underlying reliable common signalling transport protocol, called stream control transmission protocol (SCTP) (see Sect. 7.2). The SCTP is a connection-oriented, reliable application-level datagram transport protocol, which provides in-sequence delivery of user data within streams, but in a more general sense than other transport protocols [18]. For an IP-based SS 7 network different protocol structures are possible (see Chap. 5). An overall IP-based SS 7 network allows the removal of the described shortcomings with current SS 7 networks since the SCTP allows the realization of thousands of associations, i.e., IP based links, connected to one IP signalling point and, thus, the implementation of a fully meshed associated network at reasonable costs (see Fig. 13.5), which is much simpler than a hierarchical network.

However, it should be noted that the IP datagram delivery service is unreliable in nature and that IP relies on the upper layer protocols to provide reliability (see Sect. 7.1). Within an IP network, there is always the possibility that a routing loop exists or that a datagram may not be deliverable due to, for example, an unavailable IP route to a destination host. In order to provide sufficient reliability, the *time-to-live* field has to be carefully fixed by the network operator; it is used as a hop counter where its value indicates the number of router hops that a datagram is allowed to take before it is removed from the network. Furthermore, the multi-homing feature of IP must be used in order to realise q node-disjoint IP routes.

Similarly, an ATM-based SS 7 network offers the same features. ATM supports connections of different bit rates up to several Mbit/s with fine granularity and it allows the integration of bursty traffic and continuous bit streams in one network. Separate ATM virtual channel connections (VCC) can be established between any two nodes in the network and provided with bandwidth on demand, thus avoiding impact on real-time critical applications. Furthermore, extremely reliable self-healing ATM networks are possible, which restore a failed virtual path connection very quickly

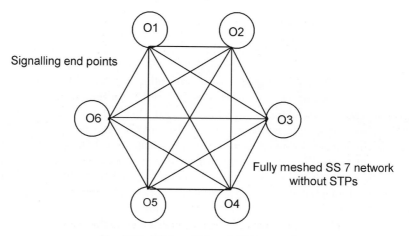

Signalling end points

Fully meshed SS 7 network
without STPs

Fig. 13.5. ATM- or IP-based SS 7 networks

without loss or duplication of messages. An ATM-based link is made up of the physical layer, the ATM layer, and the signalling ATM adaptation layer (S-AAL) [13]. The SAAL consists of the segmentation and reassembly sublayer (SAR), which segments the protocol data units into the cells of the ATM layer, the service-specific connection-oriented protocol (SSCOP) providing the assured data delivery between SSCOP users and the service-specific coordination function (SSCF), which provides the final adaptation to the needs of the MTP-3 (see Sect. 2.3.3).

13.2.3 Increasing Reliability by Changing the Network Structure

Based on the discussions of the previous sections the major change to further develop a real SS 7 network towards one of the secure network structures, as described in section 13.1, is to introduce a suitable number of central high-performance stand-alone STPs including the SCCP functionality, which form the highest level (see Fig. 13.6).

Via these stand-alone STPs network interconnection to other national and international networks as well as the intelligent network platforms, mobile and Internet access could be performed. The central STPs can serve as transfer nodes for signalling traffic within ones own SS 7 network and between ones own SS 7 network and other networks including mobile networks. Furthermore, the convergence of the own SS 7 network and the IP network domain should be performed via these STPs. In addition, the central STPs provide central access to own IN services from all other networks. Finally, it allows keeping throughput traffic between other network operators off the own SS 7 network. Thus, this network structure allows separating those traffic streams from the own signalling traffic.

This network change can be performed continuously without drastic changes of the current SS 7 network. Note, however, that depending on the traffic load, highly loaded links to the central STPs should be realized as ATM- or IP-based high-speed links in order to avoid congestion and failure situations. This is because an SS 7 link

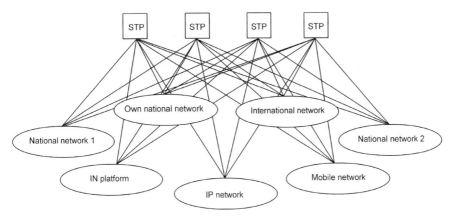

Fig. 13.6. Stand-alone STPs as central nodes of the network

set or combined link set may contain up to 16 SS 7 links with a 64 kbit/s transmission rate and running at 0.2 Erl. This limits the overall transmission rate of a link set to approximately 0.2–0.6 Mbit/s, which may be the cause of bottlenecks within the SS 7 network. However, if IP-based high-speed links are used, this solves the limitation of 16 links per link set and, thus, the corresponding upper limit of the transmission rate of a link set.

13.2.4 On the Need for Standalone STPs

In Figs. 13.1, 13.2, and 13.3 network structures are shown that assure bidirectionality and loop-freeness so that in this respect the introduction of stand-alone STPs would not be required. However, there are other strong arguments from network security and reliability as well as the need for the further development of an SS 7 network regarding the realization of IN services, mobile or geographic number portability, fixed-mobile network integration, network interconnection or the PSTN and IP network convergence, to realize the central nodes of the highest level as stand-alone STPs including SCCP functionality (see Fig. 13.6).

Traditional centralized switches, having transfer and endpoint functionality, offer a low performance regarding message throughput (typically 3000–5000 MSU/s) and SS 7 network management. However, especially the central nodes in the network have to provide important functions, e.g., the transfer of large amounts of signalling traffic, the network management for large network areas or SCCP global title translations. If the amount of signalling traffic to be handled is low those traditional switches may perform all of these tasks. However, for growing networks, there is an increasing amount of signalling traffic and network management activities, which may lead to congestion of these nodes. If they are not removed very quickly, network outages could be caused (see Chap. 8). A first and important step to improve the situation is to remove the endpoint functionality from these central nodes, thus ending with stand-alone STPs which stand alone without User functionality. High-performance stand-alone STPs, specialized to transfer and SCCP relay functionality, can help to avoid those congestion situations and thus improve network reliability.

Another aspect to be considered is that intelligent, mobile, and other applications lead to traffic streams and characteristics with MSU lengths of up to 4096 bytes, which significantly differ from those created by ISUP or TUP (see Sect. 2.3). The SCCP segmenting mechanism causes the sending of those long messages via one link, in order to assure in-sequence delivery, which can result in link congestions.

A uniform distribution of those traffic streams via different and independent routes is of crucial importance. Intelligent network and mobile services require transfer nodes to route related messages to service control points and databases. Since all nodes of the network can be service switching points the central nodes of the network should serve as those transfer nodes so that it is recommendable to realize these transfer nodes, where all these traffic streams concentrate, as stand-alone STPs.

Furthermore, the proposed network structures assure a nearly uniform distribution of these traffic streams over the SS 7 network. The same arguments hold for network interconnection and PSTN and IP network convergence where the transition between networks is performed at special signalling gateways (see Sect. 11.4.2). Again, if these SGs are accessed via the central nodes of the network, this assures a uniform distribution of the related traffic streams.

Finally, the presented network concepts require that up to 800 links (200 nodes · 4 links) or 200 link sets or more can be connected to a central node of the network, which is normally not offered by traditional centralized switches.

13.3 SS 7 over IP Applications

As already discussed several applications of SS 7 over IP are foreseen, e.g.,

- The realization of IP-based high-speed links that could help to avoid congestion problems in SS 7 networks, e.g., between SCPs/HLRs and the intermediate transfer nodes, caused by the increasing INAP traffic to SCPs or MAP traffic to HLRs, or Internet traffic via SGs, or network interconnection, respectively.
- To provide the SS 7 network functions adapted to the specific needs in a simplified point-to-point relationship.
- To perform PSTN and IP network convergence in order to improve the Internet and PSTN network transition to allow SCN signalling points access to databases and other devices in the IP domain that do not employ SS 7 links and, likewise, to provide IP telephony applications access to SS 7 services as well as to realize the migration of PSTN and mobile networks towards an IP-based multimedia network.

When these applications are realized, SS 7 network security and reliability issues should be considered and a spread of problems from the IP domain into the SS 7 network via the signalling gateways, e.g., through congestion situations or mass problems with network management messages, should be avoided. In particular, the function of the SS 7 flow control must be provided within the SS 7 over IP environment and it must be avoided that one traffic stream can affect other traffic streams.

In the following we summarize necessary measures to assure the function of the SS 7 flow control in the SS 7 over IP environment, describe how M3UA and M2PA, i.e., IP-based high-speed links, could be used to separate different traffic streams to increase SS 7 network reliability, how the PSTN and IP network convergence can be performed taking care of SS 7 network security and reliability, and how the simplified point-to-point relationship in the SS 7 over IP environment can be used to avoid the potential problems mentioned in Chap. 12.

13.3.1 Increasing Reliability with IP-Based High-Speed Links

M2PA is used to realize IP-based high-speed links in order to provide communication of traditional SS 7 signalling points over an IP network where the full MTP-3 functionality is available. Besides avoiding bottlenecks within the SS 7 network, due to the high transmission rate of IP-based links, there are other possibilities to increase SS 7 network reliability within the SS 7 over IP environment.

IP-Based Links and the Congested Link Method

Together with the described SCTP flow control measures, as described in Sect. 9.5.2, the link-based flow control can be realized. For this M2PA should buffer MSUs on a per-link basis. Whenever SCTP congestion occurs, indicated by a corresponding congestion indication primitive from SCTP, M2PA stops sending messages to the concerned transport address, leading to a filling of the related M2PA transmission buffer. If an implementation-dependent congestion onset threshold is exceeded M2PA can trigger the SS 7 flow control on a link basis.

Separation of Different Traffic Streams by User-Specific SS 7 Links

There is the possibility to increase SS 7 network security and reliability in the new SS 7 over IP environment by the separation of different traffic streams. In more detail, it would be of advantage to introduce user-specific SS 7 links, i.e., to transfer only similar traffic streams via the same link. One link, i.e., one SCTP association, per application would be sufficient since load sharing between links within a link set or combined link set is no longer needed with IP-based high-speed links. To this end, load sharing should be changed so that, besides the SLS, the service indicator and/or the message length should be considered. For example, based on the SLS and SI, MTP-3 could select the appropriate link. This would allow the application of the SS 7 flow control to different traffic streams in an optimized way and thus improve the function of the SS 7 flow control.

IP Links and Changeover

If M2PA receives a primitive from SCTP indicating the peer's inaccessibility, M2PA sends a link out of service primitive to its local MTP-3, which starts a changeover to an alternative link. Note that, in this respect, an SCTP endpoint failure should be detected in time, i.e., the SCTP timer and counter values must be set appropriately. If an SCTP endpoint failure is not detected fast enough a changeover cannot be performed in time, which leads to a delay and loss of SS 7 messages as well as congestion situations, which may spread within the SS 7 network. However, it must be assured by network planning that no changeover of bulk data traffic onto normal SS 7 links occurs in order to avoid link congestions and failures.

13.3.2 Separation of Different Traffic Streams

As discussed in Sect. 9.5.2 no separation of traffic streams sent via different SCTP streams can be guaranteed in the case of SCTP congestion since we do not have a stream-based flow control. This, however, could be easily realized at the SCTP upper layer by introducing IP-based links, which use the M2PA protocol (see Sect. 7.3), or by using the MTP-3 user adaptation layer (M3UA) (see Sect. 7.5) as an alternative to M2PA.

13.3.2.1 M2PA-Based IP Networks

M2PA uses two streams in each direction, where stream '0' is used for link status messages and stream '1' for user data. Together with the described SCTP flow control measures link-based flow control can be realized. For this M2PA should buffer MSUs on a per-link basis. Since the M2PA is not the source of the user traffic the purpose of the M2PA flow control is to inform MTP-3 about an SCTP and/or M2PA congestion, so that it can trigger the SS 7 flow control and decide whether the association should be aborted if an SCTP congestion lasts too long. An SCTP congestion situation can occur at the receiving and sending endpoint as well as the interconnecting IP path. In these situations the SCTP receive and transmit buffers fill up.

Receive Congestion

M2PA assumes that it will be informed about an SCTP receive congestion. If M2PA receives a corresponding notification from its lower layer SCTP, M2PA sends the link status *Busy* to its peer on that association. When the peer M2PA receives a link status *Busy* it starts the remote congestion timer T6 (recommended value 1–6 s). If T6 expires M2PA should abort the association and inform the MTP-3 about the *out of service* of the link. The peer M2PA should continue transmitting messages to SCTP while its timer T6 is running. Because of the remote receive congestion these messages will be stored at the sending SCTP side so that, if an implementation-dependent congestion onset threshold is passed, an SCTP transmit congestion is caused, triggering the SS 7 flow control. If M2PA receives a notification from its lower layer SCTP that the receive congestion ceases, M2PA should send a link status *Busy ended* to its peer on that association. On receipt of the link status *Busy ended* the peer M2PA should stop timer T6.

Transmit Congestion

In the same way M2PA assumes that it will be informed about an SCTP transmit congestion. If M2PA receives such a notification from its lower layer SCTP it stops sending messages to the concerned transport address, leading to a filling of the related M2PA transmission buffer. If an implementation-dependent congestion onset threshold is exceeded, M2PA sends a corresponding congestion indication primitive to its MTP-3. Equally, congestion primitives are sent indicating that specific congestion discard and abatement thresholds are crossed as specified by the SS 7 signalling traffic flow control (see Sect. 9.1).

Improvements of the SS 7 Flow Control

In Sect. 12.3 we described the shortcomings of the SS 7 flow control. When a local MTP-3 detects a local or remote route set congestion it has to notify its local User Parts. However, since the MTP-3 has no means to detect which of his local User Parts is/are responsible for the congestion all local User Parts are informed with the same congestion indication primitive rate, independent of their actual sending rate. This works well if all user traffic streams are equal, which was one of the basic assumptions of the SS 7 flow control (see Sect. 3.1). However, we now have user and application parts with different traffic characteristics. We saw that traffic streams with different message length have an influence on the function of the flow control or may destroy it. As an example, network management or maintenance activities could affect the basic telephony service, which is, in fact, unwanted.

The simplest way to avoid these problems is separation of the different traffic streams. In more detail, in order to improve the function of the SS 7 flow control, it would be of advantage to transfer only similar traffic streams via the same link or links, i.e., to introduce user-specific SS 7 links (see Fig. 13.7).

Note that M2PA does not rely on SCTP multi-homing and failover procedures so that, for security reasons, two IP links for each User Part seams to be sufficient. In addition, load sharing should be changed which, however, is considered to be implementation dependent so that, besides the SLS, the service indicator and/or the

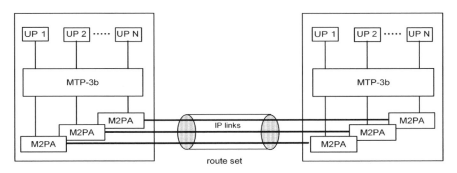

Fig. 13.7. Separation of traffic streams with user-specific IP links

message length should be considered. For example, based on the SLS and SI, M2PA selects the appropriate IP link. In addition the CLM should be used so that a separation of different traffic streams is achieved. Thus, in the case of IP link congestion, the correct User Part is forced to reduce its traffic, as indicated by the received CI primitive rate.

Furthermore, besides of the influence of different applications, the network size may affect the function of the SS 7 flow control. In Sect. 12.3.2 we saw that in the case of too many signalling relations via a congested route set no appropriate load reduction is performed. Again, in an overall IP-based network, this problem is avoided by realizing a fully meshed network. This means that the number of signalling relations existing via the considered congested route set corresponds to the number of User Parts exchanging traffic between the peer endpoints and which is much lower than 1000. The only problem which still exists concerns Level 3 or signalling point congestion. As discussed in Sect. 12.3.6 it is only specified in the ITU recommendation that *"any resulting action taken, and messages and primitives sent, should align with those procedures, messages and primitives specified for signalling route set congestion"* (see Q.704, Sect. 11.2.6: Signalling point/signalling transfer point congestion). This means that a node is allowed to send TFC messages for every eight received MSUs to the originating nodes of the traffic received, even if they are adjacent. Nevertheless, this problem is also ameliorated, because in an IP-based network the number of nodes would be much smaller because of the new transmission and switching technology.

Finally, because of the simple network structure, the SS 7 user load reduction can be easily adapted to the received CI primitive rate so that we are able to assure the function of the SS 7 flow control.

13.3.2.2 M3UA-Based IP Networks

The M3UA protocol is designed to transport MTP-3 user (ISUP, SCCP, TUP, etc) messages over IP using the services of SCTP and to enable seamless operation of MTP-3 User Parts in the SS 7 and IP domains. This protocol may apply between two IP signalling points, where the M3UA does not itself provide the full MTP-3 functions and services. However, because of the fully meshed network and since M3UA relies on the SCTP multi-homing and failover procedures the MTP-3 changeover, changeback, forced, and controlled rerouting procedures are no longer needed.

All services and primitives between MTP-3 and MTP-3 User Parts are provided by the M3UA upper layer interface. In particular, if M3UA is informed about local SCTP/IP congestion by receiving a corresponding notification from its lower layer SCTP, M3UA should send an MTP-STATUS primitive with cause *CONGESTION* to the concerned local User Part for the first and every eight messages received from that User Part. The CI primitives are used to indicate the partial inability of providing the MTP-3 services, because of SS 7 network congestion towards the affected destination. In the case of signalling point congestion, the SS 7 network congestion (SCON) message may be sent from the M3UA of the ASP to an M3UA peer, indicating that the M3UA or the ASP is congested. Note that the SCON message may

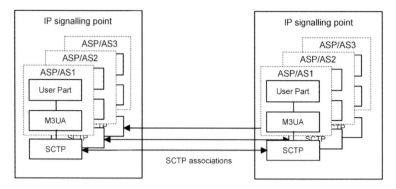

Fig. 13.8. Separation of traffic streams using M3UA

contain the optional congestion level parameter, used for the national option with congestion priorities.

In an overall IP-based SS 7 network an SCTP association is established between two application server processes (ASP) (see Fig. 13.8). An ASP provides (partial) SS 7 user functionality in the IP domain. In order to avoid a single point of failure, at least two ASPs, resident in different hosts, should be available to handle the considered user traffic. The logical collection of all ASPs that provide this partial User Part functionality of a considered logical IP signalling point is called an application server (AS) (see Sect. 6.1).

Furthermore, an ASP may be configured to process signalling traffic related to more than one AS over a single SCTP association. At an ASP the routing context parameter is used to uniquely identify the range of signalling traffic associated with each AS. In order to avoid mixing of different traffic streams the routing context parameter should be carefully used in an IP-based SS 7 network. In particular, in order to improve SS 7 flow control, an ASP should only register in those AS offering similar traffic characteristics.

13.3.3 Simplified Point-to-Point Relationship

In a real SS 7 network simplified point-to-point relationships may be present, e.g., the interconnection of two paired databases within the IN or mobile network, whilst in an IP-based SS 7 network the signalling points would be fully meshed, so that the full SS 7 network functionality is not needed in these cases.

Suitable Protocol Structures

In those situations the adaptation layer protocols are used end-to-end, where the protocol structures shown in Figs. 5.1, 5.6, and 5.8 may be used depending on whether we would like to rely on SCTP multi-homing or not and whether the MTP-3 and/or the SCCP are present or not. When the SCCP layer is present it should be adapted to the SCTP using M3UA, which, however, does not itself provide the full MTP-3 functions and services. Nevertheless, in the case of SCTP congestion, it must provide the congestion indication primitive rate to its local User Part. Since the M3UA uses the SCTP streams as normal SS 7 links, identified by the stream identifier S, it should buffer the user messages on a stream basis. In order to improve SS 7 network security and reliability different SCTP streams could be used to transfer different traffic streams. Again, as for M2PA, the load sharing mechanism should be changed using, besides the SLS value, the service indicator and/or the message length. This allows in the case of a congestion situation to perform the flow control actions on a stream basis if the SCTP flow control measures as described in Sect. 9.5.2 are realized.

When extra flexibility in developing IP-based networks is desired, especially when interaction between legacy signalling (e.g., ISUP or TUP) is not needed, SUA can be used. However, in the case of SCTP congestion, the SUA must invoke the sending of N-PCSTATE indication primitives with the restricted importance level value to its local users, which is used by the SCCP user to decide not to send any primitives of importance numerically below the level indicated that will result in messages towards the remote endpoint, thus leading to a traffic reduction.

Simplification of MTP Network Management

An overall IP-based network would be realized with the easiest network structure, i.e., all nodes of the network would be fully meshed (see Sect. 13.2.2) so that the network operates in the associated mode of signalling. This means that, from an SS 7 point of view, any two nodes of the network are adjacent, i.e., interconnected by one link set, which acts as a route set in this simplified point-to-point relationship. The advantages of new IP-based networks[1] are

- That the complexity of the SS 7 protocols is reduced,
- That the network structure is simpler than that of hierarchical networks (see Sect. 13.2.4) so that it is easier to manage and faults are avoided,
- That the number of high-performance IP signalling points can be smaller and
- That message transfer and queuing delays are reduced compared to current SS 7 routes, especially for longer messages.

For example, the transfer prohibited and transfer allowed procedures, the forced and controlled rerouting procedures as well as the signalling route set test are not needed. Furthermore, if route set congestion is detected, no TFC messages are sent because only local User Parts need to be informed. This simplifies the signalling traffic flow control. Finally, if the M3UA protocol structure is used in an IP-based SS 7 network, i.e., if we rely on SCTP multi-homing, the MTP changeover and changeback procedures would be superfluous.

As a consequence, the problems with the sending of large amounts of SRM messages, as described in Sect. 12.2.2 are avoided. In addition, the described problem with the sending of preventive TFPs on routes with highest priority does not occur (see Sect. 12.7.3). Since the number of high-performance IP signalling points may

---

[1] The same advantages exist for ATM-based networks [49]

be much smaller than in existing SS 7 networks and since in an IP-based SS 7 network no signalling transfer nodes are present, TFC messages will only be sent in the case of signalling point or Level 3 congestion, so that the problems with the network dependence of the SS 7 flow control are avoided (see Sect. 12.3.2).

Finally, the problems with the restart procedure are avoided since the restart procedure would only be performed for adjacent signalling end points. This means that the problems with the routing data update, the problems with late events and the sending of large amounts of preventive TFPs, as well as the information of local User Parts on each signalling points accessibility or inaccessibility is no longer a problem (see Sect. 10.2).

Note that the problems are transferred to the IP network layer. Within the IP network there is always the possibility that a routing loop exists, that a datagram may not be deliverable or that bidirectionality is violated (see Sect. 7.1). However, the advantage of an IP-based network is the high transmission rate and that, when using the type of service concept of IP, signalling traffic can be given priority over data traffic.

13.3.4 How to Avoid Problems with Network Convergence

The problems with PSTN and IP network convergence, described in Sect. 12.8.3, can be avoided in the same way as for the IN access or the network interconnection by using high-speed links and high-performance switches (see Sect. 13.3.1). In the following we discuss how to avoid the described problems with SPMC inaccessibility and User Part unavailability in the IP domain.

The problem with SPMC inaccessibility and accessibility can be avoided by realizing an MGC or IPSP as a traditional centralized switch, where the UPU problem is ignored as in most SS 7 networks. However, the use of distributed systems offers the possibility to solve the problems and to improve the situation. Since M3UA places no restrictions on the SS 7 point code representation, every application server can be assigned an individual SPC.

If an application server becomes unavailable, this allows sending TFP messages in the case of a partial SPMC failure and to stop or divert the relevant traffic stream appropriately. In addition, the application server unavailability means a partial User Part unavailability where now a UPU message can be sent for a part of an SS 7 user, which is now, because of the DPC, from the SS 7 network considered as a whole User Part. This is especially of interest if an ASP is configured to process signalling messages related to more than one application server over a single SCTP association. At an ASP the routing context parameter is used to uniquely identify the range of signalling traffic associated with each application server that the ASP is configured to receive. Note that the adaptation layers provide the corresponding management of application servers.

Finally, the distribution of the User Part functionality together with the above-described assignment of individual SPC to the related application servers offers the possibility to improve the SS 7 network security and reliability in the SS 7 over IP environment by the separation of different traffic streams. Since SCTP associations

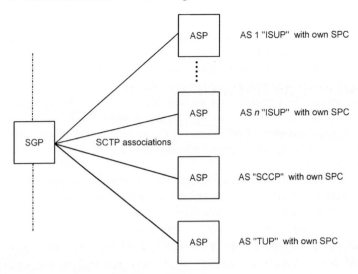

Fig. 13.9. Separation of different traffic streams through distributed systems

are established between SGPs and ASPs this allows different user-specific traffic streams to be sent via different SCTP associations so that M3UA is able to treat these traffic streams in an optimized way, e.g., can trigger the SS 7 flow control for the concerned traffic streams (see Fig. 13.9).

Note that M3UA should use different SCTP streams for different traffic streams in order to provide separation of these traffic streams (see Sect. 13.3.2). In this way, the function of the SS 7 flow control can be improved. To summarize, distributed MGC/IPSP architectures offer important advantages over traditional centralized switches.

14

Migration to an IP-Based Network

In the following, we discuss how the PSTN and IP network convergence can be performed. In this respect the different adaptation layers and protocol structures as described in Chap. 5 can be used. However, the question is which of them should be selected? Furthermore, regarding MGCs and IPSPs, should they be traditional centralized switches or distributed systems within the IP domain? The answer to these questions depends on the specific application envisaged, up to which degree the SS 7 network reliability and performance requirements should be provided as well as which degree of flexibility a network operator would like to have.

14.1 General Discussion on PSTN and IP Network Convergence

In order to meet the stringent SS 7 signalling reliability and performance requirements a network operator should ensure that no single point of failure is present in the end-to-end network architecture between an SS 7 node and an IP-based application. This can be achieved by distributed architectures and redundant network structures.

Application server redundancy is a key element to provide the stringent SS 7 reliability and performance requirements and which is provided by at least two ASPs being part of an AS and which are resident in different hosts and, thus, available over different SCTP associations. M2UA and M3UA are designed to be flexible enough to allow their operation and management in a variety of physical configurations, enabling network operators to meet their performance and reliability requirements. In order to select the appropriate adaptation layer and protocol structure for the PSTN and IP network interconnection several questions have to be answered.

Is Signalling Gateway Redundancy Needed or Not?

The first question to be answered is whether a network operator would like to have, in addition, signalling gateway redundancy or not and how it can be provided? On the one hand, an MGC/IPSP can be accessed from the SS 7 network via one signalling

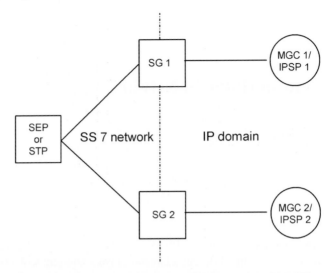

Fig. 14.1. Network interconnection via SGs acting as SS 7 SEPs

gateway. For this network interconnection all of the adaptation layers can be used, i.e.,

- M2PA with the protocol structure shown in Fig. 5.2
- M2UA with the protocol structure shown in Fig. 5.3
- M3UA with the protocol structures shown in Figs. 5.4 and 5.5
- SUA with the protocol structure shown in Fig. 5.7

Note that, when M2UA is used, the SS 7 node and the IP node are adjacent from the SS 7 point of view, interconnected via one link set.

As a consequence, if the signalling gateway (link set) fails, the MGC/IPSP is inaccessible from the SS 7 network. However, in order to avoid bottlenecks between the SG and MGCs/IPSPs as well as an isolation of the SS 7 and IP network signalling gateway redundancy must be provided. To this end, further (SG,MGC) or (SG,IPSP) pairs should be provided by the network operator (see Fig. 14.1). If M2UA and the related protocol structure is used, SG1 and SG 2 shown in Fig. 14.1 are considered as two physically separated units of one signalling gateway SG. The same holds for the other adaptation layers if the MGC/IPSP is addressed by the SPC of the SG so that, from an SS 7 point of view, the SG is considered to be an SEP hosting the peer User Parts actually located in the IP domain.

However, this solution seams not to be very flexible and, especially with respect to SS 7 network security and reliability, the use of signalling gateways as STPs seems to be a better approach. Thus, in order to avoid the unavailability of an AS within the IP domain due to the failure of the SG or the SS 7 link set between the SS 7 node and the SG, more than one SG, each with its own SPC, should be used to transfer signalling messages between the SS 7 and IP networks (see Sect. 6.4.2). As a consequence, the concerned ASs in the IP domain must be addressed by an SPC

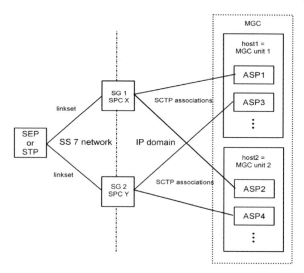

Fig. 14.2. Network interconnection via SGs acting as SS 7 STPs

different from those of the SGs. This means that the SGs act as SS 7 STPs, which requires that the MTP-3 is present at the SG so that the protocol structure shown in Fig. 5.3 using M2UA is excluded. To summarize: signalling gateway redundancy and application server redundancy together with the most flexible network architecture, as shown in Fig. 14.2, is provided by the following adaptation layers:

- M2PA with the protocol structure shown in Fig. 5.2
- M3UA with the protocol structures shown in Figs. 5.4 and 5.5
- SUA with the protocol structure shown in Fig. 5.7

Is the SCCP Functionality Needed or Not?

If a network operator would like to offer OMAP services and access to IN services from IP-based applications the SCCP services are needed. Again, most flexibility is reached if the SCCP functionality is available at the SG. If non-circuit-related signalling transfer and thus SCCP is needed the appropriate adaptation layers and protocol structures are

- M2PA with the protocol structure shown in Fig. 5.2
- M3UA with the protocol structures shown in Fig. 5.5

Is the Availability and Performance of MTP-3 Needed?

The main difference between M2PA and M3UA and the related protocol structures is that M3UA relies on SCTP multi-homing and failover procedures in the case of IP path failures and ASP failover in the case of a failure of the SCTP association whilst

M2PA supports a corresponding changeover at MTP Level 3. It is up to a network operator to decide up to which degree the SS 7 network reliability and performance requirements should be provided.

In this respect it is important whether direct or indirect IP routing applies, i.e., whether the SGP at the SG and the ASP at the MGC/IPSP reside on the same IP network or subnetwork or whether they are interconnected via several IP networks and routers (see Sect. 7.1.2). If indirect routing applies it is more likely that delays occur during the transmission of messages so that the SCTP cannot guarantee the quality of service along the complete IP path. In this case, it would be more secure to use M2PA and the availability and performance provided by MTP Level 3. However, IP incorporates the concept of type of service, which allows applications to request that particular routes are chosen such to meet specific requirements on reliability and delay, which can be used. Together with the realization of static routes (see Sect. 7.1.2) between the SGP and ASPs sufficient availability and performance could be achieved when using M3UA.

To summarize, the selection of the adaptation layer and protocol structure depends on the preferred network design and is the responsibility of a network operator.

14.2 Protocol Structures for an IP-Based SS 7 Network

On the one hand, a network operator may wish to migrate completely to an IP-based SS 7 network in order to replace the older transport technology by the IP network technology, which would yield operational cost and performance advantages. This means that the SS 7 User Parts are kept so that the SS 7 network functionality must be provided. If, besides other SS 7 applications, ISUP is present using MTP and SCCP services, M2PA would be the most suitable adaptation layer. In addition, in order to remove the message length restriction of the MTP-3 and since data retrieval from an unavailable IP-based link requires the use of the ECO and ECA messages anyway (see Sect. 7.3.4), the broadband MTP-3b [14] should be used. The protocol structure for an IP-based SS 7 network that does not rely on SCTP multi-homing and which can be realized with existing protocols is shown in Fig. 14.3.

In order to fulfil the stringent SS 7 time-dependent transport and availability requirements as described in Sect. 4.2 the M2PA does not rely on SCTP multi-homing and failover to alternative destination transport addresses. As described in Sect. 7.2.6 the endpoint and path failure detection are based on the retransmission timer T3-rtx expiry. According to the recommended timer values the SCTP retransmission timer may vary between 1 and 60 s with an initial value of 3 s. However, SS 7 messages are considered to be old at Level 2 and, thus, are discarded in order to avoid message missequencing if they are not transferred to the peer node within about 2 s.

Although the SCTP timer and counter values may be adapted to the specific SS 7 needs it remains a fact that the SCTP cannot by itself provide the availability and performance of the MTP-3, since the SCTP cannot guarantee the quality of service along the complete IP path taken by an SCTP message. The SCTP can only try to

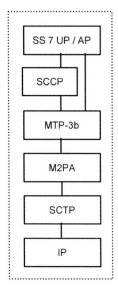

Fig. 14.3. Protocol structure for an IP-based SS 7 network using MTP-3b

increase the availability of the underlying IP network using multi-homing. Regarding the realization of IP-based links it is considered to be more secure not to rely on SCTP multi-homing and failover procedures but, instead, to perform a changeover to an alternative link, i.e., transport address, at MTP Level 3. Therefore, the SLC of the IP link is uniquely mapped onto one transport address, i.e., IP address combined with a port number. As a consequence, only one user data stream (stream 1) can be realized in the underlying SCTP association as described in Sect. 7.3.1. In order to allow for multiple links between two adjacent nodes, different port numbers, one for each link, are used.

Alternatively, based on the underlying IP network design, a network operator may decide to rely on SCTP multi-homing and failover procedures. In this case, M3UA could be used as part of the protocol structure shown in Fig. 14.4.

On the other hand, because of the emerging demand for broadband services, the need for high-speed transmission, switching, and signal processing technologies, the need to integrate both interactive and distributed services, and the need to integrate both circuit and packet transfer modes into one universal network, a network operator may prefer to migrate completely to an IP-based multimedia network to support a wide range of data, voice, audio, video, and multimedia applications in the same network. Regarding this overall IP-based multimedia network a new application layer signalling protocol called session initiation protocol (SIP) [50] is currently specified within IETF for creating, modifying, and terminating multimedia sessions or calls with one or more participants. These multimedia sessions include multimedia conferences, distance learning, telephone calls, and multimedia distribution. SIP can invite parties to both unicast and multicast sessions where media and participants can be added to an existing session.

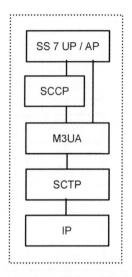

Fig. 14.4. Protocol structure for an IP-based SS 7 network using M3UA

Furthermore, SIP transparently supports name mapping and redirection services, allowing the implementation of ISDN and IN services as well as personal and terminal mobility. Via signalling and media gateways PSTN parties are connected to the multimedia network and can also use SIP to set up calls between them. In addition, SIP can be used in conjunction with other call set up and signalling protocols. In that mode an end system uses SIP exchanges to determine the appropriate end system address and protocol from a given address that is protocol independent. For example, SIP might be used to determine that the called party (callee) is reachable via a PSTN and indicate the phone number to be called, possibly suggesting an IP to PSTN gateway to be used.

SIP is designed as part of the overall IETF multimedia data and control architecture currently incorporating protocols such as resource reservation protocol (RSVP) for reserving network resources, the real-time transport protocol (RTP) for transporting real-time data and providing QOS feedback, the real-time streaming protocol (RTSP) for controlling delivery of streaming media, the session announcement protocol (SAP) for advertising multimedia sessions via multicast, and the session description protocol (SDP) for describing multimedia sessions. However, the functionality and operation of SIP is not tied to any particular conference control protocol.

Finally, SIP is independent of the lower layer transport protocol and could use the transport facilities of TCP or UDP. However, there are advantages to using SCTP compared to UDP and TCP [51]. The reasons are that

- SCTP requires no additional headers or syntax,
- SCTP can quickly determine the loss of a packet as a result of its usage of SACK and a mechanism which sends SACK messages faster than normal when losses are detected,

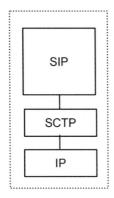

Fig. 14.5. Protocol structure for the control of multimedia sessions using SIP over SCTP

- SCTP maintains congestion control over the entire association,
- SCTP provides transport layer fragmentation, and
- SCTP supports multi-homing.

The protocol structure for SIP using SCTP is shown in Fig. 14.5.

However, the detailed description of the SIP protocol and the multimedia network is outside the scope of this book and the reader is referred to the corresponding IETF drafts and RFCs.

Appendix A

Timer Values

A.1 MTP Level 2 Timer Values

The following timer values are taken from ITU-T Q.703, Sect. 12.3: Timers.

T1 (64 kbit/s)	= 40–50 s	Timer "aligned ready"
T1 (4.8 kbit/s)	= 500–600 s	Timer "aligned ready"
T2	= 5–150 s	Timer "not aligned"
T3	= 1–2 s	Timer "aligned"
T4n (64 kbit/s)	= 7.5–9.5 s	Normal proving period timer
T4n (4.8 kbit/s)	= 100–120 s	Normal proving period timer
T4e (64 kbit/s)	= 400–600 ms	Emergency proving period timer
T4e (4.8 kbit/s)	= 6–8 s	Emergency proving period timer
T5	= 80–120 ms	Timer "sendig SIB"
T6 (64 kbit/s)	= 3–6 s	Timer "remote congestion"
T6 (4.8 kbit/s)	= 8–12 s	Timer "remote congestion"
T7 (64 kbit/s)	= 0.5–2 s	Timer "excessive delay of acknowledgement"
T7 (4.8 kbit/s)	= 4–6 s	Timer "excessive delay of acknowledgement"

A.2 MTP Level 3 Timer Values

The following timer values are taken from ITU-T Q.704, Sect. 16.8: Timers and timer values.

T1 = 500–1200 ms	Delay to avoid missequencing on changeover
T2 = 700–2000 ms	Waiting for changeover acknowledgement
T3 = 500–1200 ms	Time-controlled diversion delay to avoid missequencing on changeback
T4 = 500–1200 ms	Waiting for changeback acknowledgement (first attempt)
T5 = 500–1200 ms	Waiting for changeback acknowledgement (second attempt)

T6 = 500–1200 ms	Delay to avoid message missequencing on controlled rerouting
T7 = 1–2 s	Waiting for signalling data link connection acknowledgement
T8 = 800–1200 ms	Transfer prohibited inhibition timer (transient solution)
T9	Not used
T10 = 30–60 s	Waiting to repeat signalling route set test message[1]
T11 = 30–90 s	Transfer restricted timer
T12 = 800–1500 ms	Waiting for uninhibit acknowledgement
T13 = 800–1500 ms	Waiting for force uninhibit
T14 = 2–3 s	Waiting for inhibition acknowledgement
T15 = 2–3 s	Waiting to start signalling route set congestion test
T16 = 1.4–2 s	Waiting for route set congestion status update
T17 = 800–1500 ms	Delay to avoid oscillation of initial alignment failure and link restart
T18	Timer within a signalling point whose MTP restarts, for supervising link and linkset activation as well as the receipt of routing information. The value is implementation and network dependent
T19 = 67–69 s	Supervision timer during MTP restart to avoid possible poin-pong of TFP, TFR, and TRA messages
T20 = 59–61 s	Overall MTP restart timer at the signalling point whose MTP restarts
T21 = 63–65 s	Overall MTP restart timer at a signalling point adjacent to one whose MTP restarts
T22 = 3–6 min	Local inhibit test timer (provisional value)
T23 = 3–6 min	Remote inhibit test timer (provisional value)
T24 = 500 ms	Stabilizing timer after removal of local processor outage, used in LPO latching to RPO (national option)

Note: The values of the MTP restart timers (T18–T21) defined above are for use during normal operation. It might be advantageous for the network operator to define an alternative value for each timer, for use in potential network failures. Such an emergency might be recognized by an abnormally large number of outages, and it would be at the descretion of the operator to use the emergency set of timer values within the network. Thus, the selection of the appropriate timer set is the responsibility of the network operator.

◇

---

[1] The maximum value may be extended at the discretion of the management function in certain situations, e.g., many signalling points being unavailable or signalling points of known long-term unavailability.

A.3 SCTP Timers and Protocol Parameter Values

SCTP Timers:

T1-init	Association initialization timer
T1-cookie	Cookie timer
T2-shutdown	Association shutdown timer
T3-rtx	Retransmission timer

For the rules to determine the proper timer values we refer to RFC 2960, Stream Control Transmission Protocol, Sect. 6.3: Management of Retransmission Timer.
Recommended protocol parameters:

RTO.Initial	$= 3$ s
RTO.Min	$= 1$ s
RTO.Max	$= 60$ s
RTO.Alpha	$= 1/8$
RTO.Beta	$= 1/4$
Valid.Cookie.Life	$= 60$ s
Association.Max.Retrans	$= 10$ attempts
Path.Max.Retrans	$= 5$ attempts (per destination address)
Max.Init.Retransmits	$= 8$ attempts
HB.interval	$= 30$ s

These values are taken from RFC 2960, Stream Control Transmission Protocol, Sect. 14: Suggested SCTP Protocol Parameter Values.

A.4 M2UA and M3UA Timer Values

The following default values are recommended:

T(r)	$= 2$ s	Recovery timer "AS pending"
T(ack)	$= 2$ s	Acknowledgement timer
T(beat)	$= 30$ s	Heartbeat timer

These values are taken from RFC 3331, Signalling System 7 (SS7) Message Transfer Part 2 (MTP2) - User Adaptation Layer, Sect. 6: Timer Values.

A.5 SUA Timer Values

The following timer values are taken from RFC 3868, Signalling Connection Control Part User Adaptation Layer (SUA), Sect. 8: Timer Values.

T(r)	$= 2$ s	Recovery timer "AS pending"
T(ack)	$= 2$ s	Acknowledgement timer
T(beat)	$= 30$ s	Heartbeat timer
T(ias)	$= 7$ min	Inactivity send timer
T(iar)	$= 15$ min	Inactivity receive timer

Appendix B

Abbreviations

AE	Application entity
AMF	Network address translation and mapping function
AP	Application process
ARP	Address resolution protocol
AS	Application server
ASE	Application service elements
ASP	Application server process
ASPSM	ASP state maintenance
ASPTM	ASP traffic maintenance
ATM	Asynchronous transfer mode
B-ISDN	Broadband ISDN
BEAT	Heartbeat
BSN	Backward sequence number
CBA	Changeback acknowledgement
CBD	Changeback declaration
CC	Connection confirm
CI	Congestion indication
CIC	Circuit identification code
CLDR	Connectionless data response
CLDT	Connectionless data transfer
CLM	Congested link method
COAK	Connection acknowledge
CODA	Connection-oriented data acknowledgement
CODT	Connection-oriented data transfer
COERR	Connection-oriented error
COO	Changeover order
CORE	Connection request
CR	Connection request
CP	Common part
CR	Circuit related

CS	Capability set
DAUD	Destination state audit
DAVA	Destination available
DPC	Destination point code
DUP	Data User Part
DRST	Destination restricted
DUNA	Destination unavailable
DUPU	Destination User Part unavailable
ECA	Extended changeover acknowledgement
ECO	Extended changeover order
FISU	Fill-in signal unit
FSN	Forward sequence number
FSNC	Forward sequence number of the last message accepted by the remote endpoint
GT	Global title
GTT	Global title translation
HLR	Home location register
IAM	Initial address message
ICMP	Internet control message protocol
IETF	Internet Engineering Task Force
IN	Intelligent network
INAP	Intelligent Network Application Part
IP	Internet protocol
IPS7	Internet protocol Signalling System No. 7
IPSP	IP signalling point
ISDN	Integrated services digital network
ISSP	Inter-soft switch communications protocol
ISUP	ISDN User Part
ITU	International Telecommunication Union
IUA	Q.921 User adaptation layer
LAN	Local area network
LIA	Inhibit acknowledgement
LIN	Link inhibit
LSSU	Link status signal unit
LUDT	Long unitdata
LUDTS	Long unit data service
M2PA	SS 7 MTP-2 user peer-to-peer adaptation layer
M2UA	SS 7 MTP-2 user adaptation layer
M3UA	SS 7 MTP-3 user adaptation layer
MAC	Media access control
MAC	Message authentication code
MAP	Mobile Application Part
MG	Media gateway
MGC	Media gateway controler
MGCP	Media gateway control protocol

MGCU	Media gateway control unit
MGMT	Management
MIS	Number of inbound streams
MRVA	MTP routing verification acknowledgement
MRVR	MTP routing verification result
MRVT	MTP routing verification test
MSU	Message signal unit
MTP	Message Transfer Part
MTU	Maximum transmission unit
NI	Network indicator
NIF	Nodal interworking function
NTFY	Notify message
OM	Octet method
OMAP	Operations, Maintenance, and Administration Part
OPC	Originating point code
OS	Number of outband streams
OSI	Open Systems Interconnection
PDU	Protocol data units
PLMN	Public land mobile network
PSTN	Public switched telephone network
RCT	Signalling route set congestion test
RELCO	Release complete
RELRE	Release request
RESCO	Reset confirm
RESRE	Reset request
RIL	Restricted importance level
RKM	Routing key management
RL	Restriction level
RLC	Release complete
RLSD	Connection released
RSC	Reset confirmation
RSL	Restriction sublevel
RSM	Route set method
RSR	Reset request
RST	Signalling route set test
RTO	Retransmission time-out
RTT	Round-trip time
SAAL	Signalling ATM adaptation layer
SCCP	Signalling Connection Control Part
SCMG	SCCP management
SCN	Switched circuit network
SCON	SS 7 network congestion
SCP	Service control point
SCRC	SCCP routing control
SCTP	Stream control transmission protocol

SDU	Service data units
SEP	Signalling end point
SG	Signalling gateway
SGP	Signalling gateway process
SGU	Signalling gateway unit
SI	Service indicator
SIG	Signalling transport
SIGTRAN	Signalling transport working group (IETF)
SIO	Service information octet
SIOS	Status indication *out of service*
SIP	Session initiation protocol
SLC	Signalling link code
SLS	Signalling link selection
SMS	Short message service
SPC	Signalling point code
SPMC	Signalling point management cluster
SRM	Signalling route management
SRSCT	Signalling route set congestion test
SRTT	Smooth round trip time
SS 7	Signalling System No. 7
SSA	Subsystem allowed
SSC	Subsystem congested
SSCF	Service-specific coordination function
SSCOP	Service-specific connection-oriented protocol
SSCOPMCE	Service-specific connection-oriented protocol in a multi-link and connectionless environment
SSCS	Service-specific convergence sublayer
SSN	Subsystem number
SSN	Stream sequence number
SSNM	SS7 signalling network management
SSP	Service switching point
SSP	Subsystem prohibited
SST	Subsystem status test
STP	Signalling transfer point
SUA	SCCP user adaptation layer
TCB	Transmission control block
TCP	Transmission control protocol
TFA	Transfer allowed
TFC	Transfer controlled
TFP	Transfer prohibited
TFR	Transfer restricted
TMN	Telecommunications management network
TRA	Traffic restart allowed
TSN	Transmission sequence number
TUP	Telephone User Part

UDP	User datagram protocol
UDT	Unitdata
UDTS	Unitdata service
UPU	User Part unavailability
VCC	Virtual channel connections
VoIP	Voice over IP
XUDT	Extended unitdata
XUDTS	Extended unitdata service

References

1. ITU-T Recommendation Q.700, *Introduction to CCITT Signalling System No. 7*
2. ITU-T Recommendations Q.720–Q.729, *Telephone User Part (TUP)*
3. ITU-T Recommendations Q.740–Q.749, *Data User Part (DUP)*
4. CCITT Blue Book, Volume VI, Fascicle VI.7, *Specifications of Signalling System No. 7, Recs. Q.701–Q.704, Q.706, Q.707, Message Transfer Part (MTP)*
   ITU-T Recommendations Q.701–Q.709, *Message Transfer Part*
5. CCITT Blue Book, Volume VI, Fascicle VI.8, *Specifications of Signalling System No. 7, Recs. Q.721–Q.766, Q.766, ISDN User Part (ISUP)*
   ITU-T Recommendations Q.760–Q.769, *ISDN User Part*
   ITU-T Recommendations Q.730–Q.739, *ISDN Supplementary Services*
6. CCITT Blue Book, Volume VI, Fascicle VI.8, *Specifications of Signalling System No. 7, Recs. Q.711–Q.714, Q.716, Signalling Connection Control Part (SCCP)*
   ITU-T Recommendations Q.711–Q.719 *Signalling Connection Control Part (07/96)*
7. ITU-T Recommendation X.200, *Information Processing Systems—Open Systems Interconnection, Basic Reference Model*
8. ITU-T Recommendations Q.750–Q.759, *Signalling System No. 7 Management (OMAP)*
9. ITU-T Recommendations Q.1000–Q.1099, *Public Land Mobile Networks (PLMN)*
10. ITU-T Recommendations Q.1200–Q.1999, *Intelligent Network*
11. ITU-T Recommendations Q.770–Q.779, *Transaction Capabilities Application Part (TC)*
12. ITU-T Recommendations Q.2000–Q.2999, *Broadband ISDN*
13. ITU-T Recommendations Q.2100 *B-ISDN Signalling ATM Adaptation Layer (SAAL)*
    ITU-T Recommendation Q.2110, *B-ISDN Signalling ATM Adaptation Layer (SAAL)—Service Specific Connection Oriented Protocol (SSCOP)*
    ITU-T Recommendation Q.2130, *B-ISDN Signalling ATM Adaptation Layer (SAAL)—Service Specific Coordination Function for Signalling at the Network Node Interface (SSCF at NNI)*
14. ITU-T Recommendation Q.2210, *B-ISDN MTP*
15. R. Swale, *Voice over IP: Systems and Solutions, BTexact Technologies Series 3*, The Institution of Electrical Engineers, London, 2001
16. L. Ong, I. Rytina, M. Garcia, et al., *Framework Architecture for Signalling Transport*, IETF RFC 2719, October 1999
17. J. Postel, *Internet Protocol*, IETF RFC 791, January 1981
    P. Miller, *TCP/IP Explained*, Digital Press, 1997

D. E. Comer, *Internetworking with TCP/IP, Protocols and Architecture*, Prentice Hall International, 1991

S. Feit, *TCP/IP Architecture, Protocols and Implementation*, McGraw-Hill, 1993

18. R. Stewart, et al., *Stream Control Transmission Protocol*, IETF RFC 2960, October 2000

    R. Stewart, et al., *Stream Control Transmission Protocol (SCTP) Specification Errata and Issues*, IETF RFC 4460, April 2006

    L. Ong, et al., *An Introduction to the Stream Control Transmission Protocol (SCTP)*, IETF RFC 3286, May 2002

    R. Stewart, et al., *Stream Control Transmission Protocol (SCTP) Partial Reliability Extension*, IETF RFC 3758, May 2004

    M. Tuexen, et al., *Padding Chunk and Parameter for the Stream Control Transmission Protocol (SCTP)*, IETF RFC 4820, March 2007

19. T. George, et al., *Signalling System 7 (SS 7) Message Transfer Part 2 (MTP-2)—User Peer-to-Peer Adaptation Layer (M2PA)*, IETF RFC 4165, September 2005

    K. Morneault, et al., *Signalling System 7 (SS 7) Message Transfer Part 2 (MTP-2)—User Adaptation Layer (M2UA)*, IETF RFC 3331, September 2002

    K. Morneault, et al., *Signalling System 7 (SS 7) Message Transfer Part 3 (MTP-3)—User Adaptation Layer (M3UA)*, IETF RFC 4666, September 2006

    J. Loughney, et al., *Signalling Connection Control Part User Adaptation Layer (SUA)*, IETF RFC 3868, October 2004

20. ITU-T Recommendation Q.2111, *Service Specific Connection Oriented Protocol in a Multi-Link and Connectionless Environment (SSCOPMCE)*

21. Delayed Contribution D.61/XI, *Effects from Asymmetric Load Distributions on the MTP Flow Control*, CCITT Study Group XI, Working Party XI/2, Geneva, March 1989

    Delayed Contribution D.253/XI, *Additional Investigations to the MTP Flow Control*, CCITT Study Group XI, Working Party XI/2, Geneva, October 1989

    CCITT White Book, Volume VI, Fascicle VI.7, *Specifications of Signalling System No. 7, Rec. Q.704, Message Transfer Part (MTP), Sect. 11.2.3*

22. J. Postel, *Transmission Control Protocol*, IETF RFC 793, September 1981

23. P. Ziemann, *Signalisierungsinformationen in IP-Netzen*, Funkschau 17/99, pp. 78–80

    L. Ong, I. Rytina, M.Garcia, et al., *Framework Architecture for Signalling Transport*, IETF RFC 2719, October 1999

24. F. Andreasen, B. Foster, *Media Gateway Control Protocol*, IETF RFC 3435, January 2003

25. T. George, et al., *Signalling System 7 (SS 7) Message Transfer Part 2 (MTP-2)—User Peer-to-Peer Adaptation Layer (M2PA)*, IETF RFC 4165, September 2005

26. K. Morneault, et al., *Signalling System 7 (SS 7) Message Transfer Part 2 (MTP-2)—User Adaptation Layer (M2UA)*, IETF RFC 3331, September 2002

27. K. Morneault, et al., *Signalling System 7 (SS 7) Message Transfer Part 3 (MTP-3)—User Adaptation Layer (M3UA)*, IETF RFC 4666, September 2006

28. J. Loughney, et al., *Signalling Connection Control Part User Adaptation Layer (SUA)*, IETF RFC 3868, October 2004

29. D. Plummer, *Ethernet Address Resolution Protocol*, IETF RFC 826, January 1982

30. J. Postol, *Internet Control Message Protocol*, IETF RFC 792, January 1981

31. R. Stewart, et al., *SCTP Checksum Change*, IETF RFC 3309, September 2002

32. CCITT White Book, Volume VI, Fascicle VI.7, *Specifications of Signalling System No. 7, Rec. Q.703, Signalling Link, Sect. 9*

33. R. Stewart, et al., *SCTP Extensions for Dynamic Reconfiguration of IP Addresses and Enforcement of Flow and Message Limits*, Internet draft, work in progress, draft-ietf-tsvwg-addip-sctp-01.txt, June 2001

34. A. Jungmaier, M. Tüxen, G. Rufa, *Fair Treatment of Multiple SCTP Streams*, (to be published)

35. CCITT Blue Book, Volume VI, Fascicle VI.7, *Specification of Signalling System No. 7*, Rec. Q.704, Message Transfer Part, Sect. 9

36. Delayed Contribution D.251/XI, *Problems on the Signalling Point Restart Procedure*, CCITT Study Group XI, Working Party XI/2, Cologne, October 1989

37. Delayed Contribution D.607/XI, *Open Problems with the Signalling Point Restart Procedure*, CCITT Study Group XI, Working Party XI/2, Geneva, March 1990

38. Delayed Contribution D.910/XI, *Further Problems with the Signalling Point Restart Procedure*, CCITT Study Group XI, Working Party XI/2, Geneva, 1–12 October, 1990

39. Delayed Contribution D.909/XI, *Interworking Problems with the MTP Restart Procedure*, CCITT Study Group XI, Working Party XI/2, Geneva, 1–12 October, 1990

40. AMERICAN NATIONAL STANDARD T1.111.4, *Signalling Network Functions and Messages*, 1990

41. ITU-T Recommendation Q.704, *Message Transfer Part*, Sect. 9

42. ITU-T Recommendation Q.701, *Functional Description of the Message Transfer Part (MTP) of Signalling System No. 7*, Volume VI, Fascicle VI.7

43. ITU-T Recommendation Q.706, *Message Transfer Part Signalling Performance*, Volume VI, Fascicle VI.7

44. W. Poguntke, *Graph Problems related to Common Channel Signalling*, Proc. Twente Workshop on Graphs and Combinatorial Optimisation, 1989

45. L. Kraus, G. Rufa, *On the Design of a Hierarchical SS 7 Network: A Graph Theoretical Approach*, IEEE Journal on Selected Areas in Communications, Vol. 12, No. 3, April 1994, pp. 468–474
    W. Klein, *Routing Planning in a Large Scale Signalling Network*, Teletraffic Science for New Cost Effective Systems: Networks and Services, ITC-12, 1989

46. ITU-T Recommendation Q.705, *Signalling Network Structure*, Volume VI, Fascicle VI.7

47. J. Zepf, G. Willmann, G. Rufa, *Transient Analysis of Congestion and Flow Control Mechanism in Common Channel Signalling Networks*, Proc. ITC 13, Copenhagen, June 1991, pp. 413–419
    J. Zepf, G. Rufa, *Congestion and Flow Control in Signalling System No. 7—Impacts of Intelligent Networks and New Services*, IEEE Journal on Selected Areas in Communications, Vol. 12, No. 3, April 1994, pp. 501–509

48. ITU-T Recommendation Q.705, *Signalling Network Structure*

49. R. Franz, K.D. Gradischnig, M.N. Huber, R. Stiefel, *ATM-Based Network Topics on Reliability and Performance*, IEEE Journal on Selected Areas in Communications, Vol. 12, No. 3, April 1994, pp. 517–525

50. M. Handley, et al., *SIP: Session Initiation Protocol*, IETF RFC 2543, March 1999

51. J. Rosenberg, et al., *The Stream Control Transmission Protocol (SCTP) as a Transport for the Session Initiation Protocol (SIP)*, IETF RFC 4168, October 2005

Index

Printing: Krips bv, Meppel, The Netherlands
Binding: Stürtz, Würzburg, Germany